THE EDUCATION OF A
RELUCTANT RADICAL

Reconstruction

Other Books by Carl Marzani

BOOKS

The Education of a Reluctant Radical
  Book 1 *Roman Childhood*
  Book 2 *Growing Up American*
  Book 3 *Spain, Munich, and Dying Empires*
  Book 4 *From Pentagon to Penitentiary*
The Promise of Eurocommunism
The Wounded Earth: An Environmental Survey
Dollars & Sense of Disarmament (with Victor Perlo)
The Survivor (A Novel)
The Open Marxism of Antonio Gramsci
We Can Be Friends: Origins of the Cold War

PAMPHLETS

On Interring Communism and Exalting Capitalism
The Threat of American Neo-Fascism
The Unspeakable War
The Shelter Hoax & Foreign Policy (editor)
Cuba vs. the CIA (with Robert Light)

TRANSLATIONS

Inside the Khrushchev Era by Giuseppe Boffa

FILM DOCUMENTARIES

Dollar Patriots
The Great Swindle
Deadline for Action
Air Force Report
War Department Report

THE
EDUCATION
OF A
RELUCTANT
RADICAL
by Carl Marzani

BOOK 5

Reconstruction

Monthly Review Press
New York

Library of Congress Cataloging-in-Publication Data
(Revised for vol. 5)
Marzani, Carl.
  The education of a reluctant radical.
  Includes indexes.
  Contents: bk. 1. Roman childhood — bk. 2. Growing up American —
bk. 3. Spain, Munich and Dying Empires — bk. 4. From Pentagon to
Penitentiary — bk. 5. Reconstruction.
  1. Marzani, Carl. 2. Radicals—United States—Biography. I. Title.
HN90.R3M36   1992   303.48'4   91-43016

ISBN 1–58367–062–9 (cloth)
ISBN 1–58367–063–7 (paper)

Monthly Review Press
122 West 27th Street
New York, NY 10001

Designed and typeset by Illuminati, Grosmont
Manufactured in Canada

10 9 8 7 6 5 4 3 2 1

Contents

The editors would like to dedicate this book to the men and women who have assisted (for little or no renumeration) in the editing and production of all the volumes of *The Education of a Reluctant Radical*:

Jennifer Dent
Donald Davidson
the late Arthur Hamparian
Susan Heath
Harry Magdoff
Frank Rosengarten
Harry Schroder
John Simon

Introduction

Carl Marzani died on December 11, 1994. At the time of his death, *From Pentagon to Penitentiary*, the fourth volume of *The Education of a Reluctant Radical*, was at the printers. He knew his days were numbered: he told Charlotte he was sorry he would not live to see the bound volume. At that time he was feverishly working on Book 5—had he lived another six months we would not be writing this introduction.

The chapters Carl completed are of a piece with the first four volumes. But they only provide an outline of his life up to the 1970s. Without trying to guess what he would have written, we would like to point out two important threads in the balance of his life: writing and real estate.

Carl's adventures in house-building are referred to from time to time in the memoirs. From the Second World War, when he moved to Washington with his first wife Edith and bought a bungalow in Arlington, Virginia, until the end of his life, the only period in which he was a renter was when he had separated from Edith but had not yet married Charlotte. He was absolutely determined to use his skills as a builder to make it possible to write by not having to pay rent. He was never involved in a building project that was not intended as the living space for his family.

The house in Arlington was quite small, so when his daughter Ricky was born in 1944 and Carl needed space for his mother to stay, he built an addition. In 1947, when it became clear that Washington was not going to be a hospitable place to live or work, Carl and Edith moved back to New York with Ricky and their infant son Tony. Carl sold the house in Arlington, which gave him money for a down payment on a brownstone on the West Side on 88th Street, creating a studio apartment and a couple of rental units. These purchases and the renovations which follow-ed were done on a shoestring, with Carl undertaking most of the work.

Jail afforded Carl time to write. Prior to this he had published only a few magazine articles about the Spanish Civil War. In jail he wrote two manuscripts. His prison diary, which was confiscated by the prison authorities and only came to light in the 1980s, has remained unpublished until now; it forms the second part of this book. The other manuscript, together with an introduction by W. E. B. Du Bois, became *We Can Be Friends*, probably his best-known book.

While living on 88th Street the Marzani family visited the then rustic oceanside community of Ocean Bay Park, on Fire Island. Thinking it an ideal summer vacation spot for the children, they bought five lots with a loan from Edith's father. In 1953 Carl started building a simple wood-framed house. By the time he was done, in 1962, he had two substantial houses. The only paid labor in the entire nine years was to a bricklayer who began a fireplace and a brick wall. When the workman took off, one July 4th weekend, Carl finished the brick wall and the chimney himself (which bulges to this day). Everything else—carpentry, electricity plumb-ing, even the cesspool—was built by Carl, his friends, or his son Tony (when he became old enough).

By 1953 Edith, who had developed multiple sclerosis after Tony was born, was unable to negotiate stairs. Carl sold the house on 88th Street, and found a double brownstone in the same neighborhood, on 87th Street, where the family could all be on one level. He renovated the parlor floor of both buildings to make a large apartment for his family, creating ten rental units to help pay the mortgage. When Carl and Edith separated in 1961, she and the children stayed in the house at 87th Street and Carl rented a railroad flat in Hell's Kitchen. After they had been separated for four years, they divorced.

After joining Angus Cameron in the publishing business, Carl brought out *The Open Marxism of Antonio Gramsci*, the first translation of Gramsci in America. With the encouragement and support of Angus, Carl wrote his only novel, *The Survivor*, published by Cameron Associates in 1957. In the 1960s, as he recounts in this volume, he was involved in a wide variety of publishing projects; however, his major effort of this period, *Peaceful Co-Revolution*, was never published.

In 1966 Carl married Charlotte Pomerantz. They had been colleagues for years and shared a political affinity. Carl asked her father for his blessing on the marriage. True, there was an eighteen-year age differ-ence—she entered college the year Carl entered jail—but, he assured

Abe, if he were to die she would be a young and attractive widow. Abe agreed to the marriage. When Carl reported back, Charlotte asked: "And what if he had said no?" Carl pondered this for a few seconds and replied: "Then fuck 'em."

The house-building resumed. Carl was looking for a single brownstone to convert, but found four very dilapidated contiguous rooming houses in Chelsea on West 21st Street, owned by an over-extended developer. His account in this volume details the process of renovating the brownstones one by one. He put in punishing but exhilarating fourteen-hour days working on the project as owner, contractor, and foreman. Charlotte's contribution at the end of her working day was to have a bath ready for him in the kitchen—they were still living in her tiny Hell's Kitchen apartment—as well as a 32-ounce Pyrex measuring cup of scotch and soda. For years afterwards he spoke rapturously of arriving home, grimy and tired, to be greeted by a steaming bath and a big drink. The only other moment that evoked this feeling of luxury was when he was in isolation in jail and, late at night, a guard at the end of his shift would flip him the last drag of a cigarette.

Carl and Charlotte soon had two children: Gabrielle (Posy), born in 1967, and Daniel, born in 1969. Charlotte was a first-time mom but he was a second-time dad, at ease with newborns. Charlotte was afraid they would fall off the changing table, even when strapped down, while he would watch them for long periods, delighting in the waving and kicking of their arms and legs. In later years when the children climbed trees and he saw Charlotte watching fearfully, he would say, by way of reassurance: "What's the worst thing that could happen—they could break a leg." Many in the neighborhood remember him taking the kids out in the early morning to buy the paper. Picture a bearded man in his fifties, in a long red-hooded bathrobe, looking for all the world like an escaped monk, with a diapered tot on his shoulder. People still talk about this quaint and endearing sight.

The renovation of all four brownstones created thirty-five rental apartments, all managed by Carl. John Lewis, the building superintendent, was like a brother to Carl and a second father to Gabrielle and Daniel. He had not been the super for long when Carl discovered that John had been paying a loan on a kitchen appliance with an interest rate so high that it would never be repaid. Carl called the loan officer and arranged to expedite payment of the loan. The loan officer said, "It's none of my business, but why are you doing this for your super?" Carl replied, "Because I'm a Red."

When Charlotte's mother Phyllis died, Carl, who had been very fond of her, agreed reluctantly to adopt her cat, Whoopi. He went to work at once installing an electric cat door which would recognize and admit Whoopi but keep other cats out. In a household content with a ten-inch black-and-white television, portable typewriters, and no microwave, blender, or electric coffeepot, this high-tech feline portal was an oddity. The door had to be chiseled through a brick wall and Carl spent some ten hours on his hands and knees installing it. He spent another two weeks teaching the cat to use it. It took two more years for the cat to train Carl to allow her on the bed.

When their young son Daniel developed asthma, Carl and Charlotte searched for a way to spend winters in a warm climate. One year when they were visiting the south coast of Puerto Rico, Carl found, yes, another half-built wreck of a house. He set to work at once to make it habitable. For the next five years the Marzani family spent the winter months in Guanica.

In 1972 Carl produced *The Wounded Earth*, a book about ecology written for a student audience. He was also hard at work on a book about George Orwell, which was originally commissioned as a pamphlet on the Spanish Civil War. As Carl's attitude toward Orwell underwent many changes, so the book went through innumerable reworkings. His writing during the 1980s also includes *The Promise of Eurocommunism*, which described the complex relationships of the Catholic Church and the Communist parties in Western Europe. He also wrote articles for *Monthly Review*, *The Nation*, and *In These Times*, among others.

By the late 1980s Carl knew he needed more time to write. Managing the apartments was too time-consuming. So he arranged to sell all four buildings, with a proviso that he would get a twenty-year lease on his own apartment. It soon became obvious that the Marzanis' monthly payment was considerably less than the maintenance would be for their apartment. So Carl's spectacular real estate career was capped by an agreement that the Marzani family would buy their apartment for one dollar, and pay the normal maintenance.

There was one last instance of Marzani real-estate madness: a ski cabin in New Paltz—for a family in which no one skied. He was determined to have his young children and granddaughter Jennifer learn how to build a house (Posy was thirteen at the time; Danny and Jennifer were twelve). When Charlotte reminded him that he was sixty-eight, he protested, "I'm not going to build it, the kids are going to build it. Once they know carpentry and plumbing, they'll never want for anything."

The family bought him a director's chair, but he rarely sat in it: he worked side-by-side with the children, who indeed learned building skills.

While constructing the "ski lodge" Carl kept working on the Orwell manuscript. But by the end of the 1980s, after many submissions, he realized it was not going to find a publisher. The unpublished manuscript, together with the rest of Carl's papers, is in the Tamiment Library at New York University. The years he spent on Orwell had kept him from beginning his memoirs, which Carl had intended to write since the early 1960s. As 1990 approached he enlisted Tony to work with him twenty hours a week. Tony did research, photocopying, filing, and bill paying. Because he was unsure of how much time he had left, Carl decided on a series (six originally) of small books.

Angus Cameron often said, "Carl is one of the five people I've ever known who think all the time." Carl would fish at the end of a dock in Puerto Rico, silent for hours. When asked what he was thinking, he said he was trying to get into the mind of the fish. It seemed comical that a man with such keen insights was frustrated by his inability to outwit a fish. (He often came home fishless.) In his later years when he was too tired to write, he would sit by the pond in his New York back yard, sometimes reading, more often just staring at the fish. There were three: Abner, Crombie, and Fish. When asked what he thought about them, his answer was immediate. Crombie, the biggest, was aggressive and greedy. Abner, the middle-sized one was also aggressive but not greedy. Fish, the smallest, was a wimp. He was a wimp and would always be the smallest because he didn't fight to get his fair share.

Carl's remarks about the fish recall his comments about Miguel, a pizza-maker in Guanica. Miguel had been fired from every pizza joint he had ever worked in, for the simple reason that his pizzas were a disaster: unyielding dough, with a watery topping. To be fair, Miguel was an exceptionally honest and diligent worker. Carl tried to help him on various occasions with loans, culinary tips, and business advice—to no avail. The family expressed sadness when Miguel left, but Carl gave the final eulogy: "Miguel was born a schmuck, he lived a schmuck, he'll die a schmuck."

Miguel aside, Carl had an enormous faith in the ability of people to change. He would put the same amount of energy and passion into a speech before three hundred people as he would in talking to one bewildered plumber. For Carl the worst nightmare was to be thought irrelevant—he was determined to share what he had learned. That is why at the age of seventy-seven, in uncertain health, he decided to devote the rest of his life to writing his memoirs.

Charlotte remembers walking into Carl's study on the first morning he sat down to write. Over the years she had become accustomed to his two-finger banging on a typewriter. Now, curiously, his fingers on the computer keyboard sounded like gentle rain. What came to mind was Blake's poem about the piper: "And I made a rural pen. And I stained the water clear." She looked over his shoulder and read the first sentence: "I am seven and a half years old…" She thought, "Ah, at last he's going to tell me a story."

Charlotte Pomerantz Marzani
and Tony Marzani, 2001

PART I
Reconstruction

—1—

Subverting Federal Prisons

I entered the Danbury Correctional Instututution on March 22, 1949, to serve out a prison sentence of three years—for my political beliefs. Throughout my trial and appeals the government maintained that there was nothing political about my case: I had broken the law—I was a criminal, a plain garden-variety criminal. As the Truman–McCarthy inquisition rolled into high gear, dozens of individuals went to jail for contempt of Congress or contempt of court, prosecuted under the Taft–Hartley Act, the Smith Act, the McCarran Act, and so on. Yet the inquisitors maintained that these people were not political prisoners— which were after all prohibited by the Constitution.

The prison authorities at the Danbury Correctional Institution kept up this fiction even as their actions proved the contrary. The most glaring example was the punishment I received when I tried to smuggle a manuscript out of the prison in September 1950. (I was writing two books in jail, one on my trial and my life in jail, with the working title *Prison Days*,* and one on the Cold War, which would be published by Liberty Book Club in 1952, under the title *We Can Be Friends: The Origins of the Cold War*.) In 1950 the Korean War looked very dangerous and, in personal terms, ominous. I feared I would be kept in jail, or my manuscript on the Cold War confiscated. Hence the attempt to smuggle out *Prison Days*. It was to be a rehearsal; its failure would cost me extra months, served in isolation.

I think, however, that the unplanned chain of events that followed may have saved *We Can Be Friends*. When the smuggled manuscript was

---

* This manuscript is published for the first time as Part II of this volume under the title *Prison Notebooks*.

discovered and the guards were on the way to get me, I received five minutes' warning through the prison grapevine. Under stress, I came up with a way to conceal the content of the Cold War book. I had been writing it in a loose-leaf notebook; as I found pertinent material, I would quote it, footnote its provenance, and stick it in place as "Insert X." When there was a modification, it would be marked "Insert Y" to the X. After a while, there were inserts X, Y, Z, throughout. What I did was to shuffle the unpaginated sheets; magically, it now resembled not a book manuscript but just notes. Since the seized *Prison Days* had been typed, it got all the attention; the handwritten 'notes' received only a cursory look. The shuffled manuscript of *We Can Be Friends* were sent to my home (it subsequently took me two weeks to put in order).

The penalty for my smuggling attempt was the cancellation of 166 days of "good time" (time earned for good behavior)—which, in effect, added five and a half months to my stay in prison. When measured by penalties meted out for gross misbehavior, such as smuggling drugs or weapons into the jail (considered the most serious infractions), this was an enormous penalty. On the day I was penalized 166 days an inmate was caught smuggling in a switchblade. His penalty was *three days* of good time. This wild disparity in punishments—mine fifty-five times longer—was wholly political. The Federal Bureau of Prisons feared a charge of softness toward Communists.

Following the seizure of my manuscript, the head of the Federal Bureau of Prisons, James V. Bennett, came to Danbury to investigate. During our interview he talked to me alone, and I raised the issue of the inequity of the two penalties. I had never really quite believed that the pen was mightier than the switchblade, but he convinced me. He wanted to know how I got the book out. I said I wouldn't tell him. "I'll make you," he said. I replied that we both knew he couldn't—he wasn't about to torture me. I assured him that no guards were involved, no bribery. He asked why I had tried to smuggle the book out. For he had read it, and there was nothing censurable; and I could have taken it with me in a few months. I hadn't trusted the prison authorities, I replied. "You don't trust me?" he exclaimed, offended. I said that while I trusted him on personal matters, he should remember that he was the representative of a government that had jailed me on a frame-up (see Volume 4 of these memoirs). "Oh, Carl," said Bennett, "you know you are guilty." Then he hedged, "I mean technically guilty." I answered, "The more technical you get, the less guilty I am." I reminded him that I was in jail on the unsupported testimony of one man, Anthony Panuch, who had lied.

This was possible because the country's legal framework had been demolished by the Court of Appeals and the Supreme Court. Bennett dropped the subject. He subsequently had me transferred to Lewisburg Penitentiary, where I spent six months in isolation. Once I was out I would see Bennett on two occasions in Washington, in a fruitless effort to hold him to the half-promise he had made to my wife Edith to return the manuscript. Twice he pledged to return it when the time was right. He never did: so much for trusting him.

The insistence that I was a plain criminal, not a political prisoner, was maintained at both Danbury and Lewisburg. At Danbury, two days after I was out of "quarantine" (a processing period of several weeks) and into the "population," the associate warden, Mr. Lattimer, called me in. He was a southerner, from Texas, with a reputation for fairness. He wanted to make it clear, he said, that he neither knew, nor cared to know, why I was in jail (untrue, of course), and that I would be treated like all other inmates. I assured him I would be a model convict. "No agitating," he said. "No agitating," I promised. My duty to my family was to get out as soon as possible.

Three weeks later, I was called in again. "You are agitating," said Mr. Lattimer. "I am not," I protested. "The guards say you are." "What do they know about agitating?" I thought I saw a flicker of a smile and went on: "All they mean is that they don't like my views. An inmate says Jews run the banks; I say, that's not true. It's an anti-Semitic prejudice. The guard half-agrees with the inmate so he tells you I'm agitating. For many guards, much of what I say is agitating. There's a solution: take me out of circulation." Mr. Lattimer pricked up his ears. "What do you mean?" "Put me to work at night. I'll sleep in the day." "You have a place in mind?" "Yes, sir. Night watchman in the refrigerating plant. In an emergency I pull the main switch and call the supervisor. Otherwise, I keep an hourly log of readings on the dials. I have time to read, take notes, work on a novel." "You've thought this thing out, haven't you?" "Yes, sir. I was intending to see you about it. Maybe it's a useful idea." "It is," said Mr. Lattimer. Two days later I was assigned to the refrigeration plant.

A month or so later, Mr. Lattimer and I crossed swords again on the unspoken issue of political prisoners. Once again, I was agitating—not the inmates within the gates but the world without. My letters were the problem. I took the *New York Times* (subscription arranged by Edith); in my letters home I commented on the current news. Excerpts were published in a monthly newsletter used to raise funds for our family. I was restrained in my phrasing: no invective, a minimum of sardonic humor, and a degree of deference to the censor's sensibilities. On the other hand, a spade was not called an implement, but a shovel. When Mr. Lattimer called me in, I saw a letter on his desk which I had written home two days previously. Winston Churchill had made a speech at MIT, praising the Truman Doctrine and damning Soviet expansionism. It was a rewrite of Churchill's speech at Fulton, Missouri, three years before. In my letter, I had taken his arguments apart and pointed out that a vaunted imperialist, thrown out of office by his own people, was telling Americans what to do.

After telling me to sit down, the associate warden said equably, "Carl, I don't think this letter should go out." I thought for a moment. The reason was obvious, but I wanted him to face it. Unless we could talk about the problem openly, we couldn't reach sensible compromises. I said quietly, with no hostility: "May I ask why?" "It would be better if it didn't go out." "Better for whom?" "Better for you." The answer was sharp and prompt. He was not going to give and the threat was unmistakable. I gave it a last try: "Does the letter break any prison regulation?" "No," he said, angry about being on the defensive. Despite my nonhostile attitude, asking questions showed bad prison manners. I was being "uppity." "Mr. Lattimer," I said placatingly. "I'm in a bind. The letter attacks Churchill politically. You can't censor political opinions legally, so you ask that I censor myself voluntarily. Leaving aside the principle involved, there's a practical question. Who decides? On what basis?" Thoroughly angry at the position he was in, he said stiffly, "All this is unnecessary." I plunged in, but spoke with great deference. "Look, Mr. Lattimer, this isn't personal. I have the greatest respect for you. You are fair and just—all the inmates say so. I've made no trouble, don't want to. You can make my life miserable."

His cloudy face had cleared. I went on in a less tense atmosphere. "Look at it from my point of view. The government maintains I'm a plain criminal, not that there were politics involved in my being jailed. But you come along and censor me on a political basis." He seemed slightly amused. "I am not a criminal; I'm a political prisoner, railroaded by the Department of Justice with complete cynicism. This isn't wild talk. The Appellate Court threw out nine of eleven counts in the indictment and the Supreme Court split four to four on the validity of the remaining two. Why should I knuckle under?"

Lattimer was listening—no fidgeting. I pressed home my argument. "Take my letter. It's a strange situation. Churchill, thrown out of office by his own people, comes here to propagandize us. In my opinion, his speech is a disgrace and his policy is harmful to American interests. As an American citizen why shouldn't I have the right to criticize him? An English reactionary can say anything he wants; the American leftist is in jail to be shut up. It doesn't seem right."

He evaded my eyes, no longer angry but embarrassed, possibly ashamed of the whole business. It was time to end the charade. "Churchill is wrong," I said, "and I feel strongly that the letter should go out." He stiffened. I pleaded: "Please don't be angry. There's nothing personal. I've said I respect you, and I mean it. The Bureau of Prisons is one of the few remnants of the New Deal. We should not be enemies. The conservatives who dislike me don't like the New Deal either."

There was a small pause. Then Lattimer said, "Okay, you may go." The letter went out. There were no reprisals inside the prison, no repercussions outside. The conversation must have remained private, because a month later the parole officer went over similar ground. In August I would have served twelve months, about half before Danbury (in and out of custody pending bail in appeals), and the parole officer was supposed to help me. With my application for parole, he would enclose his evaluation of my rehabilitation. "Your letters," he said, "make it difficult for me to say you are making progress in rehabilitation." I demurred: "But I am completely rehabilitated," I said. "I am in jail for lying to the FBI, and I'll never, never lie to the FBI again. In fact, I'll never talk to them again." "Don't play games," he said sharply. " I am trying to help you. Your letters are tendentious." "You mean I'm in jail for my ideas?" "Well, no but you don't have to be so abrasive." "Don't offend the feelings of the parole board?" "That's it," he said. I followed up: "I shouldn't be so rigid, so righteous?" "Exactly," he said eagerly— and pleased: I had caught on to what was needed. "Maybe even a hint that I might cooperate with the FBI?" He realized I'd been kidding him and he flared: "You're impossible. Get out."

It may seem silly to risk alienating a parole officer, but I knew that in my case he would have no input with the parole board, for or against. There wasn't any chance of parole: conservatives on the parole board wouldn't dream of it and liberals were fearful of being "soft on Communism." Edith and our lawyer, Allan Rosenberg, agreed completely with my judgment that I would never get parole, but thought it was politically important to go on applying in order to keep the case in the news.

Equally important, it was another activity to help in fund-aising for the family. My film *Deadline for Action* was shown at meetings, excerpts from my letters were published, delegations went to the parole board from the Arts, Sciences, and Professions division of the Progressive Citizens of America. Left demonstrations of all kinds would have signs calling for my freedom; the issue was a staple in May Day parades from 1949 to 1951. Most impressive was a petition in support of parole signed by over a thousand notables across the land. The first three signatures on the petition were those of Albert Einstein, General William J. Donovan, and Thomas Mann. Parole was denied in August. It would again be denied in October 1949, and in January, May, and August 1950, while the names on the petition grew to 1,600.

The prison authorities also treated me as a political prisoner in Lewisburg Penitentiary. My first six months were spent in isolation, in reprisal for the attempt to smuggle out *Prison Days*. ("Isolation" is not as cruel as "solitary confinement," which is known to have sent people mad. Solitary is often a concrete box underground, with no light except what filters through the peephole in the door, a thin blanket to lie on, a diet of bread and water, and a pail for slops. The usual confinement is three days, rarely more than a week. Isolation, in contrast, is a cell with a window, a bed, a sink and a toilet, and three meals a day pushed through a slot. But there is nothing to read, to do, to write; no one to talk to, no time outside the cell, no news, no smoking.) At this time the Korean War was at its height. General MacArthur had pulled off a brilliant stroke in the Inchon landing, his troops had crossed the border into North Korea, and he and President Truman had met at Wake Island.

Thereafter I received no news. Edith wrote once a week, but only family news was allowed. However, she was permitted a visit in mid-December. (Obtaining permission to visit a prisoner in isolation was rare; Edith accomplished this by perseverance and playing on the sense of decency of James V. Bennett, head of the Federal Bureau of Prisons.) We spent most of the time delighting in each other's company and talking about our children. Ricky, now seven years old, thought to accompany Edith to Washington to see the Director of Prisons. "I've got orange hair," she told her mother, "and maybe he likes orange hair." Tony was three years and three months old when Edith told me she walked into the living room and found him inside a circle of chairs. She asked what was he doing. "Playing jail," he said. "So you can't get out," she observed. "Oh, yes I can," he replied. "I'm the dubberment." (Following Edith's visit I was to have a recurring nightmare. A beefy redneck, a homegrown Nazi storm trooper, held a baby by a heel, swinging the little body through the air and smashing the head against a wall. As the skull cracked apart, I saw it was Tony. My screams woke me up.)

Edith also brought me up to date on the war. Despite many warnings from China, MacArthur had sent his troops (American and South Korean) close to the Yalu river on the Chinese border and the Chinese had attacked in massive force. Enormous casualties were inflicted on both sides as MacArthur's soldiers retreated in disorder, back across the 38th parallel. General Matthew Ridgway, who had been appointed field commander, stemmed the retreat.

The visit had brought me great pleasure but the news about the war was very disturbing. Anticommunist sentiment in the country was at a high level and would greatly increase with military reverses. I knew how vainglorious MacArthur was, how much he loathed Communism, and how he would exploit any opportunity to bring back Chiang Kai-shek. He had the support of the Republican Party and the China lobby. I didn't believe Truman could withstand that alliance and block MacArthur. At the very least, with the Chinese in, the war would go on, with the bombing of Chinese roads and bridges. At worst, the Soviet Union might get involved. The consequences were unthinkable.

To be "soft on Communism" or to "coddle Communists" became dreaded charges during those years. The miasma of fear lay heavy on the land, its harmful impact apparent in every sector of society. Federal prisons were the clearest example of the damage done by redbaiting. The Bureau of Prisons was in the domain of the Department of Justice, headed by the attorney general of the United States, and so is the Federal Bureau of Investigation. But whereas the FBI had remained immune from New Deal reforms (sheltered by J. Edgar Hoover's blackmailing capabilities), the Bureau of Prisons was a prime example of democratic rejuvenation. The federal prison system was taken out of the realm of political patronage and placed firmly in the sphere of professional competence. Its personnel and regulations were aligned with the guidelines of modern penology. Salaries of guards were raised to attract able people, and brains took precedence over brawn.

The living conditions in federal prisons were good. The food was decent, and once a week inmates were supplied with clean clothes, clean sheets, and clean towels. Social attitudes were liberal and—years before the Supreme Court decision forbidding segregation in schools—the bureau was oriented to eliminate segregation in prisons. Education within prisons was invigorated. Classes were held by qualified inmates in conformity with the curriculum of local high schools, which conducted final exams and issued certificates of graduation. Inmates were encouraged to think and express themselves; urged to write, read, and take correspondence courses. On the whole these humane policies worked. Incidents of violence were rare; no riots occurred.

Into this functioning system was thrown the monkey wrench of the Truman–McCarthy repression. New Deal prisons were not geared to handle political prisoners. Buildings and procedures were designed to prevent escape, curtail the smuggling of drugs and weapons, and minimize potential violence. None of these problems applied to political prisoners. Obversely, policies designed to rehabilitate criminals backfired with politicals. Self-expression became agitation; writing became propaganda. Another example was teaching. The prison had many courses and there was always a shortage of inmate teachers. I had degrees in economics, history, and literature, but no one dared use me. Once, though, at Lewisburg, when an inmate teacher was suddenly taken ill, the deputy warden asked me to teach his two-hour class. "No red stuff," said the official. "No red stuff," I promised. "And what's the subject?" His reply: "The American Revolution."

Under cover of attacking subversives, neanderthals in Congress tried to subvert the New Deal prison policies they had always abhorred. The director of the Bureau and the various wardens and staffs had to humor them, not only to protect themselves as individuals but also for the sake of their agency. Congress held the purse strings and at budget time it could give the Bureau a hard time. (Even after I was out of jail, Senator Homer Ferguson of Michigan used me to browbeat director Bennett, accusing him of coddling me. Bennett defended himself by pointing out the harshness of my punishment.)

Ironically, one of the most reactionary congressmen became an inmate at Danbury while I was there. He was J. Parnell Thomas, chairman of the HUAC (House Committee on Un-American Activities), who was indicted for taking kickbacks from the salaries of his staff (including $1.50 a week from his secretary), convicted, and sentenced to eighteen months. To top the jest, God also had in Danbury at the same time three men jailed for contempt of HUAC—Dr. Jacob Auslander, of the Joint Anti-Fascist Refugee Committee (a group formed to help Spanish Republicans who had fought Franco), and Lester Cole and Ring Lardner, Jr., of the "Hollywood Ten." Auslander refused to give Thomas's committee the membership list of the Refugee Committee, and Cole and Lardner had declined to answer questions from Thomas and HUAC concerning membership in the Communist Party. Thomas entered

Danbury in January 1950; Auslander around May; Cole and Lardner in July. I had been there since March 1949.

I had not met Auslander previously. I knew Lardner from the Office of Strategic Services days, when we tried to get him and Ian Hunter into the Presentation Division. The FBI allowed Hunter in but not Lardner. I saw him again on fundraising tours and also met Lester Cole. Having these soulmates around made prison life much more pleasant, and I was utterly captivated by the Vienna-born doctor, Auslander, a charmer with his Old World manners and gentle humor. He was assigned to the hospital and nested in a special dormitory building of single cells for people with odd hours—bakers, myself, Parnell Thomas in charge of chickens on the farm, and so on. The cells were never locked. Auslander's cell was next to mine, and as I came off work in the morning, he'd be brushing his teeth. "Morning, Jake," I'd say. "Good morning, Carl," he'd reply and go on to tell me a Jewish joke—a different joke every day for three months. I'd go to sleep smiling, cradled in affection. (A couple of years later, in Jake's presence, I was telling friends about this little ritual and how I marveled at his huge repertoire of jokes. Auslander chuckled and said: "I had a thick book of Jewish humor and every day I'd pick something for you.")

When Thomas came to Danbury, I set myself the task of winning his confidence and learning what made him tick. At 6:30 every morning we would cross paths, he exiting and me entering, as the guard opened the door of the dorm. I would say pleasantly, "Good morning, Parnell," and at first he would brush by wordlessly. I persisted, and after a few days he grunted. Eventually he said, "Good morning." That was phase one. Phase two revolved around my *New York Times*. A friendly inmate on my floor would borrow it, and at one point asked whether he could pass it on to Thomas. I agreed. For a few days, he'd pass the paper to Thomas, who would give it back to him and he would return it. After a few days I said to my friend that this was silly; "Tell Parnell just to drop it on my bed." Thomas did, usually when I wasn't there, but once in a while I was and he'd drop the paper at the foot of the bed and silently scuttle away. He was as wary as a stag at a watering hole, and I pondered a good deal on what I should say to hold him.

The space between the bed and the door was about six feet. As he dropped the paper, I said: "You know Parnell, I don't understand your case." He had stopped at the door. "You didn't do anything other congressmen don't do." "That's right," he said eagerly. "Someone had it in for you..." "Exactly," he cut in, "just like you." I filed his remarks mentally for later exploration. At this moment nothing should wilt our sprouting rapport. We went on to inconsequential chitchat. That was phase two. Phase three was talking freely. For instance, Parnell told me that he used to meet J. Edgar Hoover in a hotel room, where Hoover would give him files against unfriendly witnesses. At the time this was illegal.

Unfortunately this third phase was abruptly truncated by Parnell's insensitivity to prison etiquette. One dinner time, as the inmates of our dorm were gathered at the entrance waiting for the door to be unlocked so we could go to the dining hall, Parnell came down the stairs from his floor, slapped me jovially on the back and said loudly: "Well, Carl, Eisler got away, but we got you, eh?" (Gerhart Eisler, a German Communist, had been on the way to Mexico from France when his ship berthed in New York at the time of Pearl Harbor. By law, Germans were taken off the ship, interrogated by the FBI, and kept in the United States. Eisler thus spent the war in New York City, where he was an air-raid warden and did translations for government agencies. At the end of the war his exit visa was approved by the FBI. About to leave, he was subpoenaed by HUAC and ended up in contempt of Congress because he refused to answer questions by chairman Thomas. He jumped bail and stowed away on the Polish liner *Batory*. When the ship made port in London, Eisler was arrested by the British at the behest of the United States and taken off the ship. A British court ruled he was not a criminal. Eisler was duly released, went on to East Germany, and became head of East German radio and television.)

Thomas thought he was being humorous, but if there is one thing you don't do in prison, it is to brag that you've put another inmate in jail. It is an affront to prison etiquette. Consequently I was expected to hit him. This put me in a quandary. Over the months I had achieved a certain standing with my fellow convicts and had made many friends. If I failed to react, I would lose their respect, which was an important factor for my safety in jail. On the other hand, I wasn't about to hit him and risk heavy punishment. But I could, and did, give him a tongue lashing. "You miserable fuck," I roared. "Bragging you put me in jail!" The words were so many blows. He recoiled, bewildered, sputtering "But... but..." He was surrounded by grinning faces, enjoying the show. "You're so stupid you don't even know that Truman put me in here, not you. But you, you stinking creep, went after Eisler for cheap publicity for your committee."

Thomas tried to rally. "Eisler was a spy! Number one Russian spy

sent here by..." My yelling overrode his voice. "Bullshit! You don't
know anything about Eisler. So I'm gonna tell you," I said and I did, to
the delectation of the other inmates. I ended by telling the group that
Thomas used to sit on two telephone books, when he was at his desk, to
look impressive for the camera. The men were laughing and Thomas
sputtering as a guard unlocked the door. Red-faced and seething, Parnell
Thomas fled. (A couple of years later, Parnell Thomas wrote an article
for *Life* magazine, in which he claimed that I had beaten him up in jail.
The editors didn't check with me or the prison authorities. But I can
well believe that this was Parnell's memory of the tongue-lashing. Lester
Cole, in his *Hollywood Red*, relates a distorted version of this incident,
based on hearsay. It took place before Lester came to Danbury.)

What struck me most about Thomas was the amorality of the man:
issuing subpoenas with an eye on the television cameras, bullying witnesses, taking kickbacks, sending people to jail—all in a day's work. The
lack of interest in the wreckage he caused and the fears he engendered
was staggering.

* * *

Occasionally, situations occurred in jail that verged on slapstick. Such
was my release from Lewisburg.

As already mentioned, I had lost 166 days of "good time" for at-
tempting to smuggle out a manuscript. Instead of being released in
January 1951, I was now due to be freed on August 1. In June, Congress
terminated the educational provisions of the GI Bill of Rights for veterans of World War II. Veterans not enrolled by July 25, 1951, would lose
the benefits—a year's tuition for every year or part of a year in service,
plus a stipend of $90 a month. I had three years coming to me, and was
counting on that stipend when out of jail. But in order to qualify I
needed to get back six days of good time. This could be granted by
administrative action on the part of the prison authorities; it was, after
all, existing policy to help released convicts return to school, and six
days out of 166 did not seem a big deal.

Warden Humphrey maintained that giving me back good time was the
prerogative of Washington; Director Bennett said it was within the
purview of the prison. The ball went back and forth a couple of times,
with different phrasing but essentially the same game. Edith and Allan
Rosenberg kept the ball in play by phone and by letter. They had to
keep me informed, as my letters to the warden and to the Bureau went
unanswered. Neither the warden nor the director spoke to the substance

of the problem, It was tacitly agreed that giving me back six days was a sensible solution. But who would do it? Who would bell the cat of HUAC & Co.? I had underestimated the climate of fear.

The days passed and the pressure grew. The Veterans Administration (VA) was brought into play, and a desiccated little man came from the regional office: I should apply to his office for an extension of the deadline of July 25. Angered, I said I would do no such thing. First, I doubted that the agency had any such power. Second, the regional office would kick the request to Washington. Third, fourth, and fifth, Washington wouldn't touch the problem with a ten-foot pole. It was not the VA's business, but that of the prison system, and was well within established policies and procedures. And time was running out.

Edith and the children were in Vermont with her parents. Her illness, multiple sclerosis, had flared up; she was in a wheelchair and in some pain, but she stuck to the telephone and got Bennett to say categorically that this was the warden's business and he would not intervene, period. Edith sent me a telegram to this effect. I insisted on an interview with Warden Humphrey. He, of course, had read the telegram. Congress's cut-off date of July 25 was a Tuesday and my interview took place the Tuesday before, July 18.

The warden's office was an oasis of elegance in the austerity of the penitentiary—a rug on the floor, paintings on the walls, indirect lighting. I was a mendicant in my prison garb. I sat on a chair at the side of his large desk and spoke quietly but firmly. I was being treated unfairly. The prison authorities were denying me three years of education and subsistence. There wasn't a prisoner in the system, no matter how heinous his crime, who, under these circumstances, would not be given back ten, twenty, thirty days' good time. Someone could have raped his grandmother and his granddaughter in the same afternoon, and he would get the six days I was requesting. And in my case those six days were from a forfeited 166 days, itself an excessive penalty.

Warden Humphrey was on the defensive. If I were already admitted to a university, things would be easier, he said. "I can't get admitted if I'm not out," I responded. "Let me out and if I don't get admitted I'll come back." "That's ridiculous," he said. "No more so," I said, "than what is taking place."

Couldn't my wife get me admitted? She was in Vermont, and ill. He said there must be someone who could go to Columbia University on my behalf. I saw he was moving my way and I said yes, perhaps Russ Nixon from the United Electrical, Radio & Machine Workers Union (UE) could try. I reached for the phone between us and the warden said sharply: "Take your hand off!" (It was a basic rule that no inmate could touch a telephone.) He then picked up the phone, I gave him the number, and he dialed. "Federal Bureau of Prisons," he said. He seemed shocked and looked at me helplessly: "They won't talk to me." "Mention my name," I said. "I'm calling for Mr. Marzani," he said (I was already "Mister"), "to speak to Mr. Nixon." He relaxed and smiled at me: "They are getting him."

It took a little time. I found out later that Nixon was in Cleveland, Ohio. The intelligent woman at the New York switchboard held the call from Lewisburg, Pennsylvania, on one line, got Nixon in Ohio on the other, and connected them. When Nixon got on the line, the warden was so pleased that he handed me the phone. We exchanged greetings and I brought Nixon up to date. "The warden says if Columbia lets me in, he'll let me out." The warden was nodding. "Don't worry," Russ said, "I am leaving immediately."

I put down the phone and thanked the warden warmly. "Whether I get in or not, you have been wonderful." He waved his hand: "It was nothing much." "Oh yes, it was," I said. "Tomorrow some congressman will say that Warden Humphrey is soft on Communists." Warden Humphrey's face turned white. The blood drained out. Incredible as it seems, he had never faced the reality of the situation, although all along he and Bennett had been acting with that threat in the back of their minds. He said, half to himself, "I'm retiring in six months." I leaned over and said to that white face: "It hurts, doesn't it? Why do you think I'm here?" He looked at me vacantly, his mind elsewhere. He shook his head, came to, and growled, not unkindly: "Get out. You could talk a leg off a donkey."

On Thursday morning came a telegram. "You are admitted to the School of General Studies. You must report to Dean Arbolino on Monday morning, July 24." On Saturday, July 22, 1951, I was out. A guard drove me to the bus station; I shook his hand and stepped onto the bus to New York City. I sat in a rear seat, watching the Pennsylvania landscape roll by; it struck me forcefully how fresh, green, aand zestful everything was. A man out of prison feels like a convalescent out of doors after a long illness. Sensations are heightened; the very air feels different. Prison air is brackish, tinged with yellow stone and black iron bars, laden with overtones of jangling key rings and arbitrary boss voices. It is a heavy ozone. The outside air stretched illimitable, scrubbed by winds from Hudson Bay and the Gulf of Mexico, from Aden, Suez, Spitzbergen, and Kamchatka, from Cape Hatteras and Luang Prabang,

Tierra del Fuego and Trinidad, Yalta, Tehran, Quemoy, Matsu—the whole glorious nomenclature of earthlings making a home of their planet.

It is a heady draught, a draught for antic moods. The tiniest event is a source of pleasure. The piece of pie freely chosen at a roadside stand, the latch of privacy in a gas-station toilet, the hiss of brakes, the crunch of gravel, the wheeling treetops around a bend, the avid, headlong rush of the bus from a two-lane highway, to four lanes, to six, to the huge complex of approaches to Manhattan, the big signs snatching at the sky: LONG ISLAND, NEW ENGLAND, NEWARK, BAYONNE, JERSEY CITY, a stirring Wolfean litany. Where do you want to go? Anywhere. What do you want to do? Anything. To savor freedom, go to jail.

—2—

Becoming a Writer

In my lifespan of eighty-odd years, I have been jack of many trades and master of none. Still, when asked my occupation I put down "writer." From the age of four, when I learned to shape the letters of the alphabet and join them, dallying with words has been, with eating, the one continuous conscious activity, surviving to this time of infirmities. At school in Rome, we started composition in the second grade—brief descriptions of places or people, little incidents, and so on—with teachers guiding and encouraging us. I enjoyed writing: words came easily, it was fun putting them together, it was pleasant to be praised. By the age of twelve when I left for America, I could write, if not with felicity, with facility.

In America I was writing good English while still struggling with my accent. Writing was my royal road to Americanization. I began school in September 1924 with a vocabulary of a few hundred words, advancing as it increased: first, second, third grade one year; fourth, fifth, sixth the following year; then seventh grade (1927) in junior high, where I won first prize in a story contest—a copy of *Pudd'nhead Wilson* by Mark Twain. Two years later, in high school, I won first prize in a one-act play competition—$15, the same as my father's weekly wages.

At Williams College, I edited the literary magazine for three years, wrote a score of short stories, had two one-act plays produced locally (one a hit, one a flop), and wrote three full-length plays, which have been interred in a drawer these past sixty years. In New York, during the intervening year before going to Oxford University, I tried reviewing books and was told by the editor, Irita Van Doren, that I would never make a writer. My reviews *were* flawed but so was her well-meant judgment. I responded by starting a novel, which grew by fits and starts over twenty years and became *The Survivor* (published in 1957).

Oxford furthered my writing apprenticeship. I had to write two essays a week in philosophy, politics or economics. Equally important, I sold three articles, one to the English *Spectator* for $27.50 and two to the American *Ken* magazine at $150 each—a stupendous sum at the time (my fellowship was $2,000 a year). Over the same time, I finished a three-act play on Spain, *An Army is Born*, which was taken by Unity Theater and put into rehearsal, but was aborted by the Munich Agreement. Unity rushed to put on a satirical musical, *Three Little Angels of Peace Are We*.

When I went to work in Washington I was confident, but kept learning—clarity and conciseness from Hu Barton, wariness about adjectives from David Zablodowsky. Our work entailed a substantial amount of writing, and the cumulative effect was noticeable. By the time I wrote *Deadline for Action* in 1946 I had been putting words together for twenty years—between half a million and a million words, about par for an apprentice wordsmith.

The script for *Deadline for Action* was a competent job. That script, the book *We Can Be Friends: The Origins of the Cold War*, and the twenty-seven monthly issues I produced of the *UE Steward* have constituted in my mind a rite of passage in my becoming a professional writer. This triad makes the UE (United Electrical, Radio and Machine Workers of America) the most important positive influence on me from 1946 to 1954, a period that shaped my life's work. And within the UE my guiding star, boss, and comrade was Julius Emspak.

* * *

Julius Emspak was born in 1904, the youngest of four children of Hungarian immigrants who had settled in Schenectady, New York, where the General Electric Company started. His father, who worked at the GE plant, died when Julius was nine, and his mother went to work scrubbing floors. The family was class-conscious, socialist-oriented though nominally Catholic, and fiercely anticlerical. At his father's interment, as the now-covered coffin was being lowered, Julius's mother noticed the cross on the lid. She stopped the proceedings until the cross was removed.

Julius's brothers were workers, and at fourteen Julius himself began a GE apprenticeship in tool- and die-making. He became a toolmaker. Though his skill was well paid, he was very conscious of the low level of wages and the lack of any union. His foreman was a member of the Socialist Labor Party;

in their long talks Julius had a vague notion of becoming a labor lawyer. At age twenty-three, he gave up his high-paying job and went back to high school. Cramming four years into four semesters while working summers at GE, he finished high school and entered Union College in Schenectady, graduating in 1931. His interest had shifted from law to philosophy and, thinking of teaching, he decided to study for a doctorate in that discipline. He borrowed from a GE welfare fund the $900 needed for room, board, and tuition, and entered Brown University in the fall of 1931.

At the university, Emspak was turned off by academia—the backbiting among faculty and the frivolous attitude of students. Feeling that the answers to workers' problems were to be found by the workers in their workplace, he returned to the bench, first at an RCA plant in Camden, New Jersey, and then, at his mother's urging, back in Schenectady where he became active in union organizing. In 1936 an international union (it included Canada) was formed from the electrical industry, radio manufacturing and machinists— the United Electrical, Radio and Machine Workers of America (UE)—and Julius Emspak was elected secretary-treasurer.

The UE flourished as CIO organizing swept the country, and became one of the big three—steel, auto, electrical—with 600,000 members at its peak. Like other left-wing unions, it was a rank-and-file union, its leaders from top to bottom were elected honestly, and a high degree of autonomy was exercised by the locals. Thus only members of the local could attend or speak at meetings without express permission of the executive board. Even UE president Albert J. Fitzgerald ("Fitzie") had to be invited. More important, the power of the purse was in the locals. They collected the union dues and transmitted an agreed share to the national office. Salaries of officials and staff wages at every level were consonant with the wages of skilled workers. These various practices nourished democracy and the muscles of the rank and file; they were unusual even within CIO unions, and scarce as hens' teeth in the American Federation of Labor.

The UE was, and probably still is, the most democratic union in the United States (I say "probably" because I have lost touch with the locals; its headquarters, once in New York City, are now in Pittsburgh. I receive the weekly UE News and it reads much as it did forty years ago.) The UE opposed the Truman Doctrine and the escalation of the Cold War by solid majority vote of freely elected delegates to its annual conventions. It came under ferocious attack by the FBI and other agencies, by Congressional committees and by rival unions. The membership went down from 600,000 in 1946 to 150,000 by the end of 1951. Attrition continued, though at a much reduced rate. By the spring of 1954 the officers were forced to cut out the UE

Steward *and its editor—me. The last issue of the magazine was June 1954. There was no monetary corruption in the UE beyond staff use of postage stamps. There were practically no perks or expense accounts. James Matles, director of organization, set the rules for expenses, and Dave Ratner, accountant, enforced them. Both were frugal men, and on this issue had fostered a remarkable* esprit de corps—*the union money was the workers' dues.*

* * *

When I left jail at the end of July 1951 I had no idea what I would do for a living. As a condition of my release, I attended Columbia University under the GI Bill of Rights, with a monthly stipend of $65. Since it was the middle of summer there were only two courses I could take: one a refresher course in contemporary European history for high-school teachers and the other a class in creative writing. The first was a bore, the second a farce. A dozen students sat around a long table and at each session they would read, in turn, a piece of their writing, which would be criticized by the others. The "professor," a book editor, contributed "good evening" at the start and "good night" at the end. The only relief were two students on either side of me, Howard Zinn and Daniel Browne. After the second session, as we were parting, Dan said to me: "Are you the Marzani who was in jail?" I said yes, and he said to Howard, "See, I told you." Whereupon Howie exploded: "What the hell are you doing here?" I explained. They were both on the left and we became good friends.

Visiting the UE, I discovered that Julius Emspak, its secretary-treasurer, with whom I had worked on *Deadline for Action,* felt a degree of responsibility for my going to jail. I didn't share that feeling, but I wasn't above making use of it, so I asked whether there might be a place for me in the union. "I've been thinking about it," Julius said. "Let me talk it over with the other officers [Albert J. Fitzgerald, president, and James Matles, director of organization]. Get back to me in a couple of weeks." I did and Julius had it all worked out. The officers had agreed to start a leadership magazine, the *UE Steward,* which I would run. The UE had 16,000 shop stewards and it also had a list of several thousand supporters—politicians, academicians, journalists, and so on—who would take the magazine. The *UE Steward* should be sophisticated, wide-ranging, ecumenical. It should be sprightly, with photos and graphics. Julius and I would work out its contents.

I had been listening with rising excitement. A new magazine designed from scratch! I had no doubt that I could do a credible job. Then Julius ruined it all. "We thought," he said, "that you'd set up a little business, a corporation, that would be independent of the UE. It would produce the *UE Steward* under contract to the union." My mind had been racing once I got the drift of his ideas and my reaction was sharp. "Julius," I said, "it won't work! I can't run an inside magazine as an outsider. I have to go into the locals, talk to their officers and their stewards and they have to feel I'm one of them. I have to be in the UE. No matter how pro-labor I am, no matter about *Deadline*, an outsider is an outsider." Julius listened. "There's the matter of pay," he said. "Our people get a hundred a week; as an independent you can pay yourself twice that." "And how will that make Tom Wright feel, or Jim Lerner [editors of the weekly *UE News*]? Isn't their paper as important as the *Steward*? You guys are worrying about redbaiting, aren't you—about putting a convicted Communist on your staff." Emspak was silent. I ripped along. "Let me tell you something, Julius Emspak: in the world out there, the UE is seen as far more red than Carl Marzani. On the staff, I'm just one more red but running a separate outfit; I'll make a nice, juicy target. I ended on a quiet note. Emspak was shaking his head: "Christ, you can talk," he said. He eyed me speculatively. "Go see Fitzie, whatever he decides is okay with me."

I went to see Fitzie and made my pitch at length. I hardly knew Fitzie, our contacts while making *Deadline* had been brief, but we had got along. Our cultural Catholicism—he, devoted; me, lapsed—put us both at ease. He was an old-type Irish politician, easygoing, affable, and very shrewd. Not highly educated, he had a clear eye for his milieu. He saw and fought corporate power; to him, *Deadline* was not propaganda but sober history. His base was in Lynn, Massachusetts, where he had become president of a GE company union which he had led into the UE.

I stressed that no matter what the UE did about me, it would be redbaited, but if I went on staff the attacks would be minor and short-lived. When the *UE Steward* appeared, without me on the masthead, no one would pay attention. But connect the two as a separate enterprise, and we'd never hear the end of it. I reserved my most powerful argument for the end: "Fitzie," I said, "if I run the magazine you expect me to be loyal to you. Well, loyalty is a two-way street; you have to be loyal to me." Fitzie hadn't spoken a word after our opening courtesies. He had listened attentively and now he said: "Okay, we'll see." I had no idea whether I had made a dent. The next day, Julius called me: "You're on the payroll. Come and get a desk."

I got my desk by taking over half a floor—my first act on the UE payroll. There was an educational department (called public relations) in a middle-sized room on the third floor, occupied by four people: Bill Kahn in charge; Jane Janis, writer and editor; Fred Wright, cartoonist and graphic artist; and Fannie Klein, secretary, file clerk, and solicitous den mother. Their desks, files, and Fred's tiny drafting board crowded the room; one more desk would freeze all motion. I suggested to Julius that he should be ashamed to allow such working conditions, and added "What about the sixth floor? Julius stared at me. "Yeaaah," he said. "Of course."

The sixth floor was empty. It had low ceilings, six foot in the front half but well over seven foot in the back, due to a stepped-up roof. It had plenty of light but was hard to get to, up a narrow iron stair—really an inside fire escape—that went up the whole building. After the making of *Deadline*, Julius had had a vague notion we could put Union Films there and had shown me the place. Apparently a more convenient staircase had been taken out, but the framing of the stairwell was still in place and stairs could be put back in a few days. The floor was no good for a movie outfit, but the front part could be used for files and the back for our office. Ten days later we moved up there, with elbow room for everybody but especially for Fred Wright. He got a four-foot drawing board, state-of-the-art, adjustable every which way, with lighting to match. He got a map file with large shallow drawers for his drawings. The top could be used to assemble layouts. Best of all, Fred got an airbrush kit—a spray gun, a tank of gas, the works. He was ecstatic: "Never dared to ask for it," he said shyly.

While our work place was being prepared, I started working on the format of the *UE Steward*. Julius and I agreed on a pocket-size (5" × 8") magazine, sixteen pages, self-cover, one color beside black. That meant color on the front and the back and, given two printing sheets, color on six inside pages as well. I had a free hand and contacted Oliver Lundquist, the designer from Presentation Division, now an architect in New York City. The design was simple. A small box in the upper left-hand corner, an inch and a quarter, carried the union logo, "UE," in block capitals on a black background. The word "steward" in black against whatever color of the cover ran across the top. Below, the entire space was taken by a photograph, sometimes with the title of an article superimposed on it. I tried not to be rigid; at the same time, I attempted to keep the same feeling from issue to issue. Sometimes the photograph might be a bit smaller, leaving room for titles on the side or below.

Fairly quickly, as the *UE Steward* caught on, we began to receive little clips, notices, ideas. At the same time, I traveled to various locals and got to know people, and in a matter of a couple of months the *UE Steward* was very much integrated into the union. We tried to keep the level of the magazine high, for I have always believed that it was better that someone not understand something than be bored. My compass of left and right was our president, Albert J. Fitzgerald. Fitzie had a gift for the pulse of the membership, in part because he lived among them; everybody deferred to Fitzie. If Fitzie said no, no it was. Since Emspak and Matles tended to agree with Fitzie's judgment, I went directly to Fitzie. For example, during the whole rampage of Senator Joseph McCarthy, who followed the repressive road opened by Truman, I was itching for the UE to take the senator on. Civil liberties, after all, are the foundation stone of trade unions, and McCarthy was getting away with murder. Fitzie said that unions had enough problems without also tackling McCarthy. In fact, he just did not want to get ahead of his membership. Then the day came when President Eisenhower's elder brother—Arthur Eisenhower—called McCarthy a fascist. I stuck the quotation into my prepared roughs and showed it to Fitzie, who grinned and said, "Well, I guess if Ike's elder brother says that McCarthy is a fascist, that's good enough for me." A whole issue of the *UE Steward* was dedicated to McCarthy, and Fred did a wonderful caricature for the cover: "When I think of McCarthy, I automatically think of Hitler." The issue proved very popular, and we were inundated with orders.

Fitzie has been enormously underestimated, in part because he was viewed as a politician—an unpopular breed. In fact, though, a good politician is an essential part of democracy, reconciling different views and interests. It is only the power of money that demeans the process and allows petty men to diminish it. I remember at one of our conventions, just before the meeting began, Fitzie was surrounded by several newspapermen, including Abe Raskin, labor editor of the *New York Times*. Raskin had the rank of lieutenant colonel during the war, working from the office of the under-secretary of war, where he was essentially an errand boy. I never saw the sense of his colonelcy except as a reflection of the power of the *New York Times*. Anyway, he stepped up to Fitzie and said, "Well, Fitzie, are you ready to go into your trained seal act?" I grabbed Ernie DeMaio's arm as he was about to slug Raskin (Ernie was vice-president), but Fitzie remained cool, just giving Raskin a look of utter contempt. Fitzie remains a hero—one of the shining figures of the UE period.

* * *

My stay at the UE was one of the seminal experiences of my life. During two and a half years I enjoyed an atmosphere of affection and brotherhood, working for a common purpose. That doesn't mean I liked everybody, and I am sure everybody didn't like me, but we all got along. I was forty years old when I first began working there, and my stay powerfully reinforced what is considered "Marzani's madness." Within the left, there are two major, contradictory, opinions of me: on the one hand, as Calvino says, I am a man of hard-headed reasoning; on the other hand, I have a deep belief in the essential love of freedom of the American people, which many people on the left believe is obsolete. To me, these are not contradictory, and if they are it's because life is contradictory. They flow from all the experiences, great and small, that I have had.

Consider this. Here are 600,000 UE members, drawn from all sections of the working class, all religions, all backgrounds, all colors and, under sensible leadership, all in agreement or all in sufficient agreement to make the UE the outstanding left-wing union against the power of the mightiest government on earth, against the power of the greatest corporate structure ever seen, against the power of an integrated media, educational, and social institutions. They're not perfect and they have holes; nevertheless it's amazing that such a union should have been built and still survives. Even after twenty years of the most ruthless attacks from the entire establishment, it has survived—smaller in numbers, but it has survived. If that is not the taproot to my belief, I don't know what is.

People do not realize the degree to which establishment propaganda goes only skin deep, and does not always succeed. I'll give an example. One of our locals in Connecticut was on strike and asked for my help in getting out some leaflets and so on, so I went up there. As I got off the train, I was met by the president of the local and a couple of companions. The president was a 60-odd-year-old Italian, who welcomed me by slapping me on the shoulder and saying: "Carl, I hear you're a Communist. If you are, we'll kill you." I turned on him in a fury. "Fuck you," I said. "I'm taking the train right back. What the hell do you care if I'm a Mohammedan. You asked for my help. I volunteer. You don't want me to help, I'll go back." The poor man didn't know what hit him. He apologized profusely; he didn't mean it, he said. Of course he meant it, but his anticommunism was not as strong as his need for help. The UE remains the most extensive example of how my faith in democracy has been maintained against fearful odds.

—3—

Books on the Barricades

This book spans a period of forty years, from my entering jail in March of 1949 to November of 1989, when the Berlin Wall came down. It touches nine presidencies—those of Truman, Eisenhower, Kennedy, Johnson, Nixon, Ford, Carter, Reagan, and Bush—all dominated by the Cold War. That long period contained some of the most traumatic events in the history of the United States: the assassinations of John F. Kennedy, Robert Kennedy, Martin Luther King, and Malcolm X, as well as the wars in Korea and Vietnam. For fifteen years (1954 to 1969) at the heart of this period, I was a publisher, the first five of them with Angus Cameron. Publishing sounds like a mild, somewhat passive occupation, but Angus and I were active on the barricades, firing books at the Establishment. Through Liberty Book Club and Prometheus Paperbacks we distributed our selections from various publishers, though many titles originated with our newly formed firm, Cameron Associates. I became a publisher by happenstance, a fugitive combination of unrelated factors. Each was a consequence of the Cold War, which affected everything, including my employment.

Following publication of the final issue of the *UE Steward*, in June 1954, I was unemployed. I spent the summer on Fire Island, building a beach house with used lumber, doors, and windows, bought from a wrecking yard. An hour's drive from New York City, Fire Island is a barrier reef thirty miles long which protects Long Island from the assaults of the Atlantic Ocean. I had begun building in 1952, and by 1954 there was one large room with a kitchen and a bath. Another bathroom, four bedrooms, and porches were added by 1962, when asbestos shingles were put on.

For ten years the place was an eyesore, continually under construction. (Edith called the house, "Gonna-be Gardens.")

In late August 1954 I received a phone call from David Freedman, a lawyer whom I had met years before when he was working with Joe Brodsky at the International Labor Defense office. David was acting as counsel for the Liberty Book Club and he invited me to lunch to discuss the possibility of my running the club. I told him that I knew nothing about publishing. "But you know about organizing" was his response. We made a date.

Liberty Book Club had been founded in 1948 by the novelist Howard Fast, with the support of the Communist Party. Financial support had come from a Christian Marxist (so self-defined) by the name of Alex Munsell, a director and majority stockholder. (The Munsell Color Chart, widely used in printing, had been invented by Alex's father, who had made millions and left some of them to his son.) The fortune had been dissipated over the years, in part by unduly generous contributions to various charities, but chiefly in three divorces. Each divorce had taken a hefty slice of Alex's diminishing assets, and by 1954 he was left with a brownstone house on West 20th Street. Marion Munsell, his fourth wife, was also a Christian Marxist, who made a scanty living for them by working at the *National Guardian*, a left-wing weekly newspaper.

At lunch, David told me that Howard Fast was still the guiding spirit of the book club. Howard, vacationing in Mexico, had heard I was out of the UE, and had sent a telegram to the directors of the book club urging that I be approached. I was not wholly unfamiliar with the club; in 1952 my book on the Cold War had been a selection. I liked the manager, Sidney Russell, a small bustling man with a trim mustache. He loved books and knew a lot about them. He had left in 1953 and formed a firm with his son, Russell & Russell, which published important books that were out of copyright. David told me that Russell had left because he thought the club no longer viable, its membership eroding in the climate of witch-hunting and redbaiting begun by the Truman administration and institutionalized by Senator Joseph McCarthy. The board of directors had chosen to replace him a Jamaica-born trade unionist, Charles Collins; he, however, had been unable to stem the erosion and had finally quit. The ship lacked a skipper.

It didn't look like a job with much of a future. I asked David why I should take on a job that had daunted Russell, who was much more knowledgeable about books. David smiled his wonderfully benign smile and he addressed the question head-on. Why? Because I was a committed radical who would rather make a modest living within the left than a good living within an exploitative establishment. I asked him about the salary. Russell and Collins had been getting $90 a week ($10 less than my UE pay) . The club was solvent, but barely. If I could stem the decline, increase membership and the rate of acceptance, I could pay myself whatever I thought proper. "But Dave," I remonstrated, "if Russell didn't think the club was viable in this political climate, it's certainly not going to get better. Eisenhower will get re-elected in 1956; Nixon follows him in 1960. Russell is no fool." "Russell is old and defeatist," said David and proceeded to demonstrate his skill as an advocate by mixing facts and flattery. I was younger than Russell, more energetic, and far better known because of my trial and speaking tours. Jail had given me a certain cachet, *We Can Be Friends* was highly regarded, and I was a good speaker. "Between you and Russell," said David, "there is no comparison." David's arguments had some validity: I did have a following and, to a degree, my name was known on the left.

I had been considering the proposal since David's phone call. I decided that I would assume the task if I had a co-worker who was familiar with books and publishing—a true professional. I asked David if the board of directors would agree to this. He asked me if I had someone in mind. I told him I did: Angus Cameron. He knew of Angus and said he thought we would make a great team. At this point David announced that seven of the nine members of the board of directors were resigning. He explained that although they were progressive, decent people—lawyers, accountants, business executives, and the like—they could not afford to be linked to a left-wing outfit. Thus Alex Munsell and Howard Fast were the entire board. I asked about the role of the Communist Party. David indicated that, through Howard Fast, the party exerted considerable influence. However, he pointed out, Alex Munsell was not a party member and he was the major stockholder. If Angus and I took the job, we would be in complete charge with no strings attached. "What about you?" I asked. "I was Alex's attorney and I helped set up the book club. Since he went broke I have been his legal adviser, and Liberty's, *pro bono publico*."

Angus Cameron was one of the top book editors in the United States, editor in chief at Little, Brown & Co. until 1951, when he resigned over an issue of FBI censorship. Angus was blacklisted during the McCarthy era, whereupon he got together with Albert Kahn. Kahn was a distinguished investigative reporter, the author of several books exposing domestic fascists and their ties abroad. He was the editor of *The Hour*, a newsletter of the American Council Against Nazi Propaganda, chaired by William E. Dodd, former U.S. ambassador to Germany. Angus and Albert set up Cameron & Kahn in 1952 to publish pro-labor and left writers, many of whom had been blacklisted. They had planned a book club for trade-union members with the low price of four paperback books for $2. The unions would guarantee a certain number of members, and do all the promotion.

The UE was the first customer of the Union Book Club; the *UE News* and the *UE Steward* were the main promotion channels. That's how I got to know Angus Cameron and Albert Kahn. Albert, who was born in England and had a bit of an accent, was strong on salesmanship and promotion. Angus, born in the Midwest of Scottish descent, was an erudite man of grace and wisdom who knew every aspect of publishing. I liked him and felt we were compatible. Cameron & Kahn was a viable conception: there were many well-known writers available, and the left-wing unions, though battered, still mustered members in the hundreds of thousands. The firm, though, had made one mistake, which turned out to be fatal. It had opened for business prematurely with no books ready (it had two manuscripts), so its small capital was steadily depleted—on rent and a secretary for several months, advances to authors, a copy-editor for the two manuscripts, composition for both, and paper, printing, and binding for one. Their first book was *Mill Town*, by Bill Cahn, which was a largely photographic essay on the struggle for unions in the early days of the textile industry. By August 1954 the firm had exhausted its capital as well as the advance monies from Union Book Club members. Members had received *Mill Town*, but had three more books due to them.

I got together with Angus and Albert and laid out all the facts that David had given me. They were attentive. They had debts and no money; Liberty Book Club, while in decline, was solvent and had good credit. Albert said he had a project in mind (not further specified), which he was eager to explore. If Liberty would assume the responsibility of three books apiece for a thousand or so members of the Union Book Club and debts of several hundred dollars, he would relinquish the Cameron & Kahn contracts for *The Ecstasy of Owen Muir* by Ring Lardner, Jr., *The Judgment of Julius and Ethel Rosenberg* by John Wexley, and *Labor's Untold Story* by Richard Boyer and Herbert Morais. But he thought it only fair that these books should carry the imprint of Cameron & Kahn.

I thought Albert had chutzpah, but I said nothing. If his firm went out of business, the contracts were of little worth. The firm had the galleys of Lardner's book, but the compositor would not release the type until he was paid in full. On the other side of the ledger were two or three thousand dollars of debts. I waited for Angus to speak. Angus expressed concern about their secretary, Athene Ryan, widow of a UE organizer. I was sure she would be of use and reminded Angus of what David had said: we could write our own ticket. We just had to increase income. Angus was willing to give it a try and Albert's proposal was accepted.

Angus, Athene, and I went on Liberty's payroll in mid-October, 1954. The November and December selections, *The Neurotic* by Joseph Furst and *My Mission to Spain* by Claude Bowers, had already been made—I assumed by the office manager Tillie Goldway. She was a very able person who had kept the place running after Charles Collins had quit. In addition to Tillie, the staff consisted of a bookkeeper, a shipping clerk with an assistant (Joe Betro would replace both in 1958). Rosalie Sinkler and the newly arrived Athene Ryan were both secretary–typists and clerical workers. Dorothy Kaplan and Zelda Howard dealt with membership. (Zelda's husband, Milton, was co-editor with Sam Sillen of *Masses and Mainstream*, a magazine sponsored by the Communist Party.)

Tillie told us that Zelda had been in charge of asking publishers for books. It was thus Zelda, not Tillie, who had chosen the November and December titles, and indeed it became apparent that she had made all the selections during the Collins tenure. I doubt that she had done so under Sidney Russell. I happened to be standing by when Angus asked Zelda to request for him a certain book and Zelda said, "Oh, that's not for us." "How do you know?" said Angus. "I've read the book," said Zelda. "But I haven't," said Angus. "Please get it."

Liberty functioned like other book clubs at that time. A newsletter was sent out each month describing the coming selection and the member had to say no by a given date. If there was no answer, the selection was sent and billed. Unless told to stop, we would send three selections, each with the balance due and a different letter. Thereafter we would send no more books, but a series of reminders playing on a member's conscience, ending with a letter indicating this was a final request. Though there were collection agencies, we did not believe in using them. The letter also said that we took for granted the member had joined in good faith and was having financial problems. We would welcome payment at any time, with or without renewal of membership.

We sought books that subverted the status quo. Among those we went on to publish were C. Wright Mills, *The Power Elite*; Joachim Joesten, *Oswald: Assassin or Fall Guy?*; Robert Williams, *Negroes With Guns*; Fred

Cook, *The FBI Nobody Knows*; Rex Tugwell, *The Democratic Roosevelt*; Avro Manhattan, *The Vatican in World Politics*; John Wexley, *The Judgment of Julius and Ethel Rosenberg*; Harvey Matusow, *False Witness*; Eve Merriam, *The Double Bed*; Isaac Deutscher, *Stalin: A Political Biography*; Ring Lardner, Jr., *The Ecstasy of Owen Muir*; Richard Boyer and Herbert Morais, *Labor's Untold Story*; William Appleman Williams, *Contours of American History*; Curtis MacDougal, *Gideon's Army*; Dalton Trumbo, *Johnny Got His Gun*; Alexander Solzhenitsyn, *One Day in the Life of Ivan Denisovich*; W. E. B. Du Bois, *The World and Africa*. In all, we published nearly two hundred books, totaling over a million copies.

Our pamphlets were also calculated and timed to distress the power elite. Usually initiated by us, the minimum press run was 10,000 copies, often repeated more than once. *Cuba vs the CIA* sold around 60,000 copies, a third of them in bookstores in the Miami area where anti-Castro Cubans were concentrated. Other titles included *The Gaps in the Warren Report, Critical Reactions to the Warren Report, Montgomery, Alabama, The Shelter Hoax, The Silent Slaughter* (about Indonesia), *The Unspeakable War* and *Withdraw!* (about Vietnam), *Concentration Camps, USA, German Hands on the Nuclear Trigger, Goldwaterism, Jews and the National Question, Peace by Finesse, The Open Marxism of Antonio Gramsci,* and *War and Peace in Vietnam*. As Angus reminisced much later: "We did strike a few blows." My reaction was more personal: a thousand copies of "subversive" books in the country for each of my thousand days in jail.

Our first selection, January 1955, was *The Ecstasy of Owen Muir* by Ring Lardner, Jr., a brilliant satire targeting many facets of American society including Catholic ideology. In the process of marrying a Catholic, Owen Muir converts and his zealotry is priceless. Another target is the political informer racket of the FBI and the Department of Justice, abetted by the judiciary. Angus drew up the newsletter. Tillie Goldway was enthusiastic, and predicted a sharp rise in the acceptance rate. Angus had a way of describing a book which made you yearn to read it. The camera-ready mechanicals were on my desk when Howard Fast happened to stop by the office to see Angus, who was not in. Howard looked over the layout and gathered that Ring's book was a satire on Catholicism. He was wary of the subject matter and said he'd like a copy. I said that we wouldn't have books until mid-December but I had a set of galleys. He took them and told me to hold off printing the newsletter. It was mid-November; I reminded Howard our members should have it by the first week in December.

Two days later, Howard called. Angus took the call, listened for quite a few minutes, and said he would call back. Howard, Angus reported, was very agitated about the novel. It was divisive, anti-Catholic, politically wrong, and would be offensive to our members. He wanted a board meeting the next day. "He's nuts," I said. "The board meeting won't do him any good. Alex will vote with us." I called Alex, who was free to join us, and Angus so informed Howard. Alex had not read *Ecstasy* either but he trusted our judgment as against Howard's. Also, he had promised, via David Freedman, that Angus and I would be in complete charge.

The board meeting was stormy. Howard was very emotional about the book. It was utterly wrong, he said, for Liberty to offer *The Ecstasy of Owen Muir* as a selection. It was grossly anti-Catholic, ridiculing Catholic priests and Catholic rituals; even he, an atheist, had found it offensive. He had no brief for Catholicism, but the tenor of the book was as divisive as anti-Semitism, racism, and ethnic prejudices. He would not have published it, but that was the business of Cameron & Kahn; however, its selection by Liberty Book Club *was* his business. The novel was not only wrong politically, but would harm the club financially, he claimed. The rejection rate was bound to be high and many members would resign.

Howard spoke with passion and increasing heat. I said, placatingly, that Howard was emphasizing one aspect of the novel, but that Ring Lardner had dealt with many other issues. Our members would delight in the portrait of an informer who boasts of his patriotism—do you think it's easy to turn in your own mother?—and waves newspaper clippings extolling his actions. I argued that Lardner used a stiletto not a bludgeon, and that Catholics who were Liberty members would probably enjoy the satire.

The board meeting went on for over an hour, but after fifteen minutes the pros and cons had become wholly repetitious. Alex didn't speak at all; he listened closely, nodding several times as I spoke. Alex was otherworldly, but he was no fool and on practical matters depended heavily on David Freedman. David had assured me that Alex, who was the majority stockholder, would be solidly behind us. Angus made several brief comments, designed to soften the growing acrimony. Amicably, he would say: "Come, Howard, you know that's an exaggeration," or, "Now, Howard that is not the case."

Howard knew he could not convince Angus, who had accepted, edited, and published the novel. I suspect Howard also knew of Alex's commitment to David. Howard was directing his arguments at me, using the twin tracks of political conscience and financial responsibility. Finally, in exasperation, I said: "Look, Howard, we're both atheists—you're a Jewish atheist, I'm a Catholic atheist. You worry about our Jewish members, I'll worry about the Catholics. The vote is three to one and we should adjourn." There had been no vote, of course. The mechanicals of the newsletter went to the printer.

A few days later I received a telephone call from Sam Sillen, in charge of cultural affairs for the Communist Party. He'd like to have lunch with me. We met at the Oyster Bar in Grand Central station the following day. I am very fond of oysters and was in a good mood; this Sam quickly altered. The party, said Sillen, thought that the publication of *The Ecstasy of Owen Muir* was a political error of the first magnitude and would wreck Liberty Book Club. I blew up. "Bullshit," I said. "You haven't read the book, the party hasn't read the book." Sillen bristled. "I have read it. Howard gave me the galleys. And we have discussed it at the state level." "Okay," I said, "I was wrong to say you hadn't read it." However, I went on, the newsletter was being printed and Liberty's selection stood. Howard had represented the party's point of view and we welcomed having it. Angus and I were not at all antiparty; on the contrary, we had respect and affection for it. There should be no hostility between Liberty and the party, which was highly regarded by many of our members. I was sure that most selections would be acceptable. I told him that the next two selections were *Silas Timberman* by Howard Fast and *Soviet Civilization* by Corliss Lamont. Sillen was not to be mollified and we ate in silence. At the end we split the check. As we parted, I said, "One other thing, Sam. Angus and I are partners, and I am not going to have this kind of talk without him. No hard feelings, okay?" I held out my hand and Sam took it.

(Howard Fast mentions Liberty Book Club in his memoir, *Being Red*, published in 1990. He writes: "I organized a left-wing book club, the Liberty Book Club, and left it to Angus Cameron to run." Fast writes as if that took place at the end of 1952, but his memory plays him false. He organized the club almost five years earlier, in the spring of 1948. Howard's book *The Children* was an alternate selection for August of 1948, and his *My Glorious Brothers* was the selection for January, 1949. My book on the Cold War, *We Can Be Friends*, was the selection of September 1952, when Howard says he was organizing the club.) The four-page printed newsletter was sent with an announcement of the new directors. It was a single sheet, very elegant, with biographies of Angus

and myself, a statement that we had formed a new firm, Cameron Associates, and a request that members send in names of people who might
join the the book club. Liberty had about eight thousand members at the
time; some five thousand lapsed subscribers also received the mailing.

The results were stunning: Tillie's enthusiasm was justified and
Howard's worries groundless. The acceptance rate, normally 45 to 55
percent, soared to nearly 70 percent. More important in the long run,
we picked up over four hundred lapsed subscribers and got several
hundred names of friends from the members. A mailing to those names
brought another hundred new subscribers. Increased income removed
any concern about Athene's pay. In fact, we did so well that Angus and
I opened a charge account at Anchor Inn, a modest but excellent fish
restaurant on our block of West 23rd Street. Perks, said Angus, are
better than a raise in pay.

——4——

Death of a Racket

On April 2, 1955, the *Saturday Review of Literature* ran a full-page editorial signed by the writer John Steinbeck (he would receive the 1962 Nobel Prize for Literature). Steinbeck was commenting on a book, *False Witness*, by Harvey Matusow, published on March 15 under the imprint of Cameron & Kahn. (This was the project Albert Kahn had in mind, but didn't name, when he, Angus Cameron, and I had met in September. It became a reality at the end of October, when Matusow agreed to do the book.) Steinbeck wrote in his editorial:

> The Matusow testimony to anyone who will listen places a bouquet of forget-me-nots on the grave of McCarthy....
>
> Matusow, swearing he was a Communist, was employed by various parts of our Government to swear that hundreds of other people were Communists. And now, he says, he lied. He swears that other professional Government witnesses also lied. Now a wave of hysteria has swept over the investigators. Senators who are personally involved cry out that Matusow lies now but didn't when he testified for them and against their enemies. A certain Senator not notorious for telling the truth himself says very sharply that he pays no attention to liars. And yet this liar campaigned for this Senator in a happier time....
>
> I suspect that Government informers, even if they have told the truth, can't survive Matusow's testimony. He has said that it was a good racket. Well, Matusow has ruined the racket. It will never be so good again.

The *Saturday Review* editorial was entitled "Death of a Racket." The bluntness of the title and the prestige of its author testify to the explosive effect of the book on the American political scene. Steinbeck's comments climaxed ten weeks of television news and press stories, columns, and editorials, beginning on January 20, when Stewart Alsop obtained the "confession" of Harvey Matusow. In that period, the FBI and the Department of Justice tried to prevent the book's publication. Their efforts only created more publicity.

False Witness was shocking even to me—one who knew firsthand from his trial, eight years before, the shameless use of professional informers by the Department of Justice. Matusow's range of lies was spectacular, as was the roster of his employers—the FBI; federal prosecutors; House and Senate committees; William Jensen, superintendent of schools for New York City; and John Theobald, president of Queens College. Hundreds, indeed thousands, of lives were injured and scores of people went to jail. Matusow's recantation crimped pending prosecutions. Four convictions were voided and new trials ordered for Clinton Jencks, Elizabeth Gurley Flynn, George Charney, and Alexander Trachtenberg—all of whom were eventually acquitted.

One of Matusow's important revelations was that he became an informer because of the Cold War. The Acheson–Vandenberg strategy to gain support for the Truman Doctrine was to scare the nation and its Congress with the specter of Soviet military power. Though the Soviet Union was prostrate and busy repairing war damage, the media portrayed it as a threat, obscuring the huge superiority in the armory of the United States. The country had a monopoly of atomic weapons, a vastly larger navy and air force with aircraft carriers and long-range bombers. The domestic corollary of this strategy was repression of dissidents (I was indicted January 7, 1947).

The Korean war in mid-1950 created a national "war hysteria" (the characterization was made by the Republican ex-president, Herbert Hoover). Matusow, who in 1950 was in his twenties and a Communist Party member, was frightened that he might be jailed if war with Russia took place. He called the FBI and volunteered to be an informer. In 1951 his comrades caught on and Matusow was expelled from the Communist Party, whereupon he made his debut as a paid witness. He was twenty-six, personable, dramatic, imaginative, and with his glib tongue he rose quickly in his profession to become an aide to Senator Joseph McCarthy. It was a good racket, said Matusow to his publishers, Angus Cameron and Albert Kahn.

Matusow's trajectory over ten years, from entering the U.S. Army at nineteen to writing a book for Cameron and Kahn at twenty-nine, is an engrossing psychological tale. The story was given life and shape by Albert Kahn in *The Matusow Affair*. The manuscript of this book was finished in the late 1950s, but, although Kahn was a well-known author and personal friend of several publishers, it was rejected everywhere. The consensus was that the book had great merit, and would sell well, but the wrath of the FBI and the Department of Justice was not to be taken lightly. In a real sense, the content of the manuscript cautioned against acceptance, as it described the vindictiveness of the government and its powers of harassment.

Albert Kahn died in 1979. His wife Riette persevered, and *The Matusow Affair* was published in 1987 by Moyer Bell, with an introduction by Angus Cameron. The introduction made clear the political background, stressing Truman's apostasy from FDR's vision of a friendly postwar world, the start of the Cold War, and the concomitant domestic reaction. Angus ended his introduction: "The politics of those days lay a heavy hand on the present." *The Matusow Affair* is written in a robust prose and an easygoing style. It details how *False Witness* came about. Albert Kahn had written extensively on civil liberties and kept good files. He had clipped an article dated June 7, 1954: at a Baltimore conference of the Methodist Church, Bishop G. Bromley Oxnam related that Harvey Matusow had come to apologize for slandering him. He indicated that he had lied also about many other people, whom he was similarly going to see, and that he might write a book about blacklisting.

Soon after, the House Committee on Un-American Activities held a special session and summoned Matusow (who had worked for the Committee) to talk about Oxnam. Matusow flatly denied the press reports: if the bishop had been quoted correctly, he was "dishonest." However, a prominent Washington attorney, Russell Brown, then made public the fact that Matusow had visited him, confessing his lies as he had to the bishop, and saying he was thinking of writing a book. Albert Kahn was interested because Matusow's testimony had been key to the conviction for perjury in 1954 of an old friend, Clinton Jencks. Clinton Jencks, an official of the Mine, Mill and Smelter Workers Union, had been indicted under the 1947 Taft–Hartley Act, a law tailored to break up unions that opposed the Cold War. The National Labor Board was a New Deal agency designed to facilitate unionization by mandating elections upon request of the workers. Under Taft–Hartley, only those unions and their officials who had filed non-Communist affidavits could participate in elections. In response, trade-union officials who were Communists resigned from the party. They were prosecuted for perjury on the basis of false testimony by paid witnesses. For instance, Matusow had testified that Jencks had told him he was still a Communist. Without the false witness racket, and complaisant judges, the law was useless.

Early in September 1954 Jencks visited the Kahns. He had been sentenced to five years in prison and was out on bail. If Albert could find Matusow and persuade him to write a book about his lies, Jencks might obtain a retrial. In advance, the Mine, Mill and Smelters Workers Union would order (and pay for) two thousand copies. Albert and Angus talked about the idea: the chances of success were slim, but the importance of the issue warranted every effort. Over several weeks Albert traced Harvey Matusow from address to address, finally drawing a blank. He then left a message (and telephone number) with Harvey's parents that Cameron & Kahn were interested in Harvey's book. During his search Albert discovered that the FBI were also looking for Matusow. (It turned out that Matusow was on a bicycle tour of the southwest, going from town to town as the spirit moved him. The FBI, with all its resources, kept missing him by twenty-four hours.) On October 23 Matusow called Kahn from Taos, New Mexico, and agreed to come to New York. Albert said there would be a ticket for Harvey at the airport. When the FBI got to Taos, Harvey was up in the skies.

On October 25 Matusow met with Albert and Angus for lunch at the Delmonico Hotel. After lunch the discussion continued in a private room. Harvey had brought some clippings, documents, and the outline of a book, *Blacklisting Was My Business*, with a preface and two chapters. "The first chapter is bad," Angus said when he brought me up to date, "prolix and dull. The second chapter is a lot better. It's about meeting McCarthy and the prose is swift and colloquial. I'm convinced he can do a book." (Matusow was euphoric when Angus said he wrote well.) "He is an insecure man," said Angus. "But he's smart. He knows he has to be straight with us. After all, he said he was having lunch with us only because of my reputation." Angus smiled wryly. Matusow had said he'd seen the FBI dossiers, and he looked straight at Albert when he said it. The implication was clear. He was saying, I trust Cameron but I don't trust you.

Angus thought Harvey was sincerely repentant, but was torn between the love of publicity and fear of governmental reprisal. "I emphasized," said Angus, "that he had to overcome a reader's hostility." Why should a reader believe a liar? Harvey could convince only by stressing the political hysteria and by revealing *himself*, his thoughts, and feelings at the time. The three had discussed finances: Harvey would receive rent, food, and spending money for the next six months—an estimated $1,500. The three also signed as a preliminary contract a letter drawn up by Albert, stating *inter alia* that Harvey wished to undo the harm he had done by testimony which "was not a true and complete reflection of the actual facts."

Reading his book, I began to realize the amount of work Albert had done. He went over hundreds of pages of transcripts, news stories, profiles, letters, and documents. Each day he had compiled a series of questions for Matusow to answer. Everything was taped, transcribed, and edited. *The Matusow Affair* made me revise my opinion of Albert. I had known him for several years, had visited his home, played with his children and dried dishes with Riette after dinner. It was a fine family but, hitherto, I had given Riette all the credit for it; I thought Albert extremely self-centered. He was that, but the book revealed a man of considerable compassion. Nevertheless, it was Riette who transformed Harvey Matusow. When she saw how hard he was trying to cast off his past, she overcame her initial revulsion and brought him within the warmth and security of her family circle.

The last taping session was on December 14, 1954. A couple of days later Harvey began writing his book, dictating twelve to fourteen pages a day. Angus, who maintained a firm editorial hand, soon overcame his skepticism about Harvey's ability to dictate a book. After some sixty pages, Angus thought the book was going well but urged Harvey put in more of himself. Publication was set for May; this required a tight but not impossible schedule.

While Matusow was writing on his testimony against Elizabeth Gurley Flynn, one of the Communist leaders convicted under the Smith Act, he asked Albert to procure a transcript of the case to refresh his memory. When Albert went to do so, the sky fell on him. The attorney in charge of the cases, Harry Sacher, informed Albert that the petition for retrial for Ms. Flynn had to be filed by February 3, 1955, and that for Clinton Jencks soon after. According to the law, it emerged, petitions for retrial had to be filed within two years of the date of conviction. Thus, to repair the harm he had done, Matusow would have to give affidavits of his lying by February 3. The news stunned Albert—why hadn't he and Angus been informed? Sacher had no idea; he had come into the case only recently, but the two-year limit was well known among lawyers.

On Thursday, December 30 Albert phoned Angus at about four o'clock with news of a crisis. They arranged to meet at Grand Central Station. (Angus usually took a 5:30 train to upstate New York. Preferring the country to the city, Angus, his wife Sheila and their two children lived in the Adirondacks. Angus took long weekends, taking a bulging briefcase.) Over stiff drinks in a bar lounge, Albert gave Angus the bad news. The problem was they had promised Harvey that nothing would be asked of him until after publication. Harvey would then have time to consider any requests from the defendants he had wronged. Albert and Angus feared that Harvey might think they had been stringing him along just to get the affidavits and walk out. Angus said they just had to live with the situation. They would have to present the issue to Matusow and reiterate that Cameron & Kahn would publish his book, period. Whether or not to provide the affidavits was obviously Harvey's decision. If he decided no, they would keep to the May schedule; if yes, they would strive to get the book out quickly. After all, in a ten-day period, Harvey had completed about a third of the book; he felt he could finish the manuscript in three weeks. Furthermore, what he had done thus far was well written and the process of editing could begin.

As they parted, Angus jolted Albert with a weighty observation. Angus said he naturally hoped that Matusow would give the affidavits; however, if he did, sales of *False Witness* would be drastically reduced. From what he had read, he was convinced that the book would be a sensation and generate a tidal wave of publicity. Yet, publicity could make a book into a bestseller, or it could kill it. Everything depended on the timing. If the work was in bookstores when the publicity broke, its sales would soar in the first few days. Thereafter the combination of word of mouth and continuing publicity would keep the sales high. Half a million copies could sell in the first three months. However, were the book not available for a week or two, the publicity would convince people they knew what was inside the book—why, then, should they buy it?

There was no way, Angus gloomed, that *False Witness* could be available by February 3. However hard one drove Matusow, he would need at least three weeks to finish. With another week for copy-editing, the manuscript would, at best, be going to the printer on February 3. Thereafter it was correction of galleys, printing and binding. If nothing went wrong, they might have copies by mid-March—that would mean six weeks of publicity with no books to sell. Furthermore, said Angus, in this instance, the natural constituency of the book—readers on the left—would be hostile to the author and not wish to add to his royalties. As it turned out, Angus was prophetic.

It was a tribute to Riette and Albert that Harvey Matusow had no doubts about Cameron & Kahn's good faith and decided to provide the affidavits. Albert swung into action. He took two rooms at the Chelsea Hotel on 23rd Street near Seventh Avenue, installed Harvey and his typist in the smaller one, and told them to push for twenty pages a day.

In the other room, an editor worked on the written pages, which had been peppered with Angus's comments. The edited pages went to a second typist, who put them on mimeograph stencils, which were checked by a copy-editor. From time to time, the accumulated stencils were taken to a shop and copies run off.

Within a week of Harvey's finishing the book, the publishers had fifty mimeographed manuscripts at their disposal. One of those copies went to a copy-editor to be readied for the printer. Another copy went to Stewart Alsop, whose nationally syndicated column broke the story on January 20. A torrent of editorials, news stories, and columns followed; these increased when, a week later, the petitions for retrial for Flynn and Jencks were filed in the respective courts. Matusow's affidavits were filed with the petitions. Immediately, the government and its apologists presented a theory that Matusow had remained a secret Communist, infiltrating the ranks of professional witnesses, planning to recant and discredit the FBI and the Department of Justice. Scores of FBI agents scoured the country, particularly the small towns of the southwest visited by Matusow, looking for anything to bolster the theory of a Communist conspiracy. Meanwhile, the obvious was overlooked: Cameron's association with Carl Marzani, that convicted Communist infiltrator into the intelligence community. The government theory was puerile but its motivation was not. It was damage control: keep other informers from defecting, and give compliant judges, editors, and columnists a rationale for discrediting Matusow.

The phone calls and clamor for interviews and information were such that Angus, Albert, and Harvey concluded that a press conference would be most useful. An announcement was made that Cameron and Kahn and Harvey Matusow would meet the press at the Biltmore Hotel at two o'clock in the afternoon of February 3. By agreement, television stations conducted brief interviews in their studios beforehand and did not come to the Biltmore. The conference was held in one of the hotel's large meeting rooms. Several rows of chairs, flanked by potted plants, faced a table for the speakers. By two o'clock some fifty people were seated, with perhaps as many bystanders, including me. Promptly, Matusow and his publishers entered, and seated themselves, with Harvey in the center, as flashbulbs popped from several cameras. Then Angus stood and read a brief statement:

> I want to state at the outset that if it hadn't been for Judge Dimock's ruling postponing Matusow's grand jury appearance, the Justice Department would have prevented him from being at this press conference. As the publishers of

Matusow's book, we think it's pertinent to note that while other informer-witnesses have been proven to have lied under oath, the Justice Department has taken no legal action against them. But when a man tries to publish the truth about his former false testimony, the Department goes all out against him. Anyway, Mr. Matusow is here now and ready to answer your questions.

As Matusow got up to speak, six or seven men in the back row stood up and tried to turn the conference into a circus, shouting provocative questions: were Cameron and Kahn Communists; did Harvey miss the dead Stalin; what did he think of the Nazi–Soviet pact; and so on. The questioners were long-time redbaiters including Victor Riesel—anti-labor, anti-Semitic, anti-black. Harvey knew most of them; they had printed his false testimony, and had collaborated, as he reminded them, in concocting stories. At one point Riesel wanted to know when McCarthy had said such and such. Matusow replied: "You know when, Victor. You were with us that evening."

Harvey Matusow never lost his cool. A photograph on the cover of *The Matusow Affair* shows him the way I remember him on that occasion. He is standing solidly, leaning slightly forward, his arms stiff, his hands resting on the table. On one side is Albert, scribbling; on the other side is Angus, bemused, gazing at Harvey, who looks like a young bull about to charge. Under all the din, I could hear I. F. Stone repeating like a mantra: "Shut up, you sons-of-bitches!" ("Izzie" Stone was famed for his columns and for his *Weekly*, a widely read muckraking newsletter.) He finally stood and faced the hecklers: "What the hell's the matter with you bastards?" he shouted. "Why don't you let him speak? You call yourselves newspapermen? I have never seen such a shameful exhibition." There was silence; other reporters then began asking questions.

Apart from this press conference the only other time I saw Matusow was a chance encounter on 23rd Street, which only lasted a few minutes. Albert introduced us and as we shook hands Harvey said: "I know all about you. I was in the party when you were in jail and I kind of looked up to you." I refrained from commenting that while I was in jail, Harvey became an informer for the FBI; I said I was flattered.

Staying away from Matusow was by design. For, by the time Harvey contacted Albert and flew to New York in October, Angus and his secretary Athene, were at Liberty Book Club–Cameron Associates. The office of Cameron & Kahn in Greenwich Village had been closed, its furnishings dispersed. Athene's desk and a four-drawer file had come with her, and a small couch on a wrought iron frame was in the office shared by Angus and me. But the firm had not been officially dissolved and its mail was being placed in a P.O. box at the Greenwich Village post office. By focusing attention on Cameron & Kahn, we hoped that Angus's connection with me and Liberty Book Club would be minimized, even obscured. I would stay away from Harvey, and Albert would stay away from our office, meeting Angus in restaurants.

Angus rarely saw Matusow, who was under constant, and open, FBI surveillance. The ploy succeeded. At the subsequent proceedings of the Department of Justice—both men were subpoenaed on February 7— Albert would be called ahead of Angus. The subpoena had demanded all the notes, tapes, manuscripts, and any other material relating to the book. The idea was to impound them, thus preventing publication. Albert refused, was brought into court, cited for contempt, and sentenced. Execution was stayed pending appeal. Angus and Albert had a bright idea: release all the material to the press and public. The grand jury was part of the public. Angus, who was called as witness, handed over the material requested. The sentence was vacated. The government's scheme had backfired; it had wanted the material in order to keep it from the public, but had accomplished the opposite.

After the publication of *False Witness*, Cameron Associates became the distributors, filling orders, billing, and so on. Unfortunately, Angus's analysis was accurate: publicity without books kills sales. For example, the American News Company, which owned a large number of news-stands and serviced many more, ordered 2,000 books; these were dis-patched in cartons, each containing fifty copies. Six weeks later they returned thirty-nine cartons out of forty—unopened. The conservative executives of the company had not distributed the books, waiting to see if there was a strong demand. Requests were few.

The Matusow affair was a severe setback for the Department of Justice, which sought to limit the damage by indicting Matusow for perjury. A conviction would salvage some credibility and warn would-be defectors (in fact, within three weeks two other professional liars, Marie Natwig and Lowell Watson, had recanted). In the last days of September 1956, twenty months after his recantation was made public, Harvey Matusow went on trial in New York City. The perjury was not about any of the numerous lies in Harvey's career as an informer but about his statement in a sworn affidavit of recantation that Roy Cohn had coached him in false testimony.

Roy Cohn, counsel to Senator McCarthy's subcommittee and active in the Rosenberg case, had been an Assistant U.S. Attorney in the Smith

Act trials and worked with Matusow in preparation for Harvey's appearance as a witness. In the presence of four Justice Department attorneys and one FBI agent, Cohn had brought up a book, *The Law of our Soviet State* by Andrei Vyshinski, which, said Cohn, contained directives for the overthrow of capitalism. Although Matusow had never heard of the book, he nevertheless testified that one of the defendants, Alexander Trachtenberg, had talked to him about it.

It was expected that Roy Cohn would assert that Matusow had lied in his affidavit. The five other individuals involved would be called as witnesses and would, under oath, back up Cohn. The jury was bound to believe the words of six sterling civil servants as against the word of one self-confessed liar. The only chance for Matusow (in Albert's opinion, shared by Angus, me, and defense attorney Stanley Faulkner) was to put the Department of Justice on the defensive and show the jurors what it had been doing. Matusow would have to recount, and document, the highlights in *False Witness*. Harvey balked. He was sick of regurgitating a past that he knew the Justice Department would not give up; if it lost now it would try again—and again. It was, he felt, better to get it over with.

Cohn and his five co-workers duly stated under oath that Matusow had lied. The jury deliberated for less than two hours and found Harvey guilty. He was sentenced to five years. Cohn went into private practice. Harvey Matusow, with good behavior, served the customary four years and a few days. Released from prison in 1960, he first worked in publishing, then lived in England from 1966 to 1973, working on documentary films. In 1987 he became director of the Gandhi Peace Center in Massachusetts, a nonprofit organization helping various disadvantaged groups.

The sordid machinations to suppress *False Witness*, followed by the legal frame-up and conviction of Harvey Matusow, exposed the extent to which the anticommunist hysteria of the Cold War served as a cloak for the government's subversion of democracy. Government repression, clearly seen at my trial in 1947, had steadily increased in ferocity and effrontery. The government used three perjured witnesses at my trial, one of whom was a government official; it used six against Matusow, all of whom were employed by the government (the principal liar, Roy Cohn, had recently resigned).

More significant, and sinister, was the spread of repression through all branches of government. In my case there had been no legislative involvement and only partial judicial collusion. In the Matusow affair all branches were put to work—the executive branch with its Department of Justice orchestrating the job, the legislative branch with its hearings, the judicial branch with its injunctions. What was their purpose? In a betrayal of their oath of office, they violated the spirit and very structure of the Constitution. The Founding Fathers had worked hard to create a system of checks and balances to limit and restrain the power of government over individuals and their liberties, spelled out in the Bill of Rights. In the Matusow case these checks were subverted; the guardians of liberty joined hands *to prevent the publication of a book.* It is difficult to imagine a more direct and pernicious assault on the expressed purposes—in spirit and wording— of the Constitution of the United States.

The Matusow affair is symbolic of the times. In one way or another, there were thousands of cases of individual repression at all levels of society. Arrogance in government grew apace, leading to Watergate and Irangate, and the ineffable Nixon Doctrine: whatever a president does is legal!

The Matusow affair also illustrates a major contention of these memoirs: democracy is more strongly rooted in the American people than cynics believe. It sprouts such unlikely places such as Harvey Matusow's conscience. Similarly, editors in various media hitherto usually subservient to the interest of the owners saw in Matusow's recantation an opportunity to vent their true feelings. I am not unmindful that most editors and columnists knew about the racket; nevertheless, only a few protested before the recantation of Harvey Matusow.

What then? Left victories are always shadowed.

——5——

Prometheus Paperbacks

The 1950s were hard years for the Left. Although Senator Joseph McCarthy had been brought down when he overreached and went after the army, the Truman-initiated repression increased in scope and power. A visitor from Mars would have been amazed to see a huge nation with a mighty army, navy, and air force, and police officers galore, expend all its efforts hunting some little-known individual, using all the might at its disposal—corporate power, the media, universities, and so on. Dalton Trumbo, the screenwriter, defined this period as "the time of the toad," meaning that to survive each day, a person had to swallow a toad in the morning.

As if the wrath of the Establishment were not bad enough, the forces of repression got a mighty assist from Nikita Khrushchev. In 1956, at the Twentieth Congress of the Communist Party of the Soviet Union, Khrushchev revealed in full detail the extent and horror of Stalin's crimes. Comrades were overwhelmed. Dorothy Healey, a top party leader and an old friend, said that she went home and wept. The group that was hardest hit was, of course, the Communist Party of the USA, which almost overnight lost the majority of its members. But all left groups were in some state of disarray. Perhaps it was fortunate that in the last three years Angus and I had been independent publishers; we thought of ourselves as unaffiliated Marxists. Nevertheless the result of the Truman–McCarthy repressive measures was that Liberty Book Club lost many members. (Julius Emspak and I had a long discussion about the Khrushchev speech. Whether Julius was a member of the Communist Party at that time I doubt. I certainly wasn't. We talked as comrades, as people to whom these events mattered. Neither of us had hard and fast positions, but Julius tended to think that Khrushchev had gone too far—after all, said Julius, his action had dealt a considerable blow to the U.S. Communist Party. I didn't disagree with him. I suspected Khrushchev had no choice; he was probably facing a struggle inside his party. If he had compromised with his opponents, they might very well have won: so I think he went for broke. The more important issue, however, was whether he was serious about recasting the whole society.)

* * *

A footnote to the history of this period involved me in the life of Dr. W. E. B. Du Bois. One of the consequences of Khrushchev's speech was a rejuvenation of small left groups interested in discussing the Twentieth Congress. The individuals invited were paid as little as $15 to speak and to answer questions. I was invited to one such meeting on 23rd Street, along with several other speakers, including Du Bois. During the question period Du Bois was so obviously tired that I volunteered to answer the questions directed to him.

At the end, as was his wont, Du Bois sat in his chair until the hall was vacant. This way, he could leave at his own pace. I kept him company. As we got into the street, I looked for a cab; he, I noticed, was walking away. I said "Where are you going, doctor?" He said "I'm going to the subway." Thinking quickly, I said "Oh no, the organizers gave me money to see that you get home by cab." Walking home, it occurred to me that this man, close to ninety, had only come to the meeting for the $15! Next day I called his wife, Shirley Graham. "Shirley," I said, "tell me it's none of my business, but are you folks in trouble financially?" There was a long silence, and I was sure she was offended. Then there was a sigh. "I wondered," said Shirley, "how long it would be before someone noticed. Yes, we are in trouble, but the Doctor will not let me talk about it." "Well," I said, "clearly something has to be done."

When Angus came in, I described the situation and suggested that we have a meeting in Du Bois' honor on the occasion of his ninetieth birthday, going by the year, not by the date. We made up a word derived from the Roman numerals XC and called it the DecaCentennial. We reserved a meeting hall at the Hotel Roosevelt for March 2, 1958, and began to send out invitations. Shirley Graham and the writer John Killens drew up a list of prospective speakers. The meeting was a great success: we raised $15,000 for the Du Bois. Dr. Du Bois had always been very generous with his time. It was an honor to return the compliment.

Later, when Shirley came back from China, they brought me a little present, a 9" x 11" photograph of Dr. Du Bois and Mao Tse-tung standing about two feet apart, face to face, deep in a a belly laugh, looking for all the

world like two boys playing hooky. Nevertheless, Du Bois was very despond-
ent when he came back from China, feeling that the United States was
doomed. When I quietly remonstrated, Shirley cut in with her loud voice:
"Give it to him, Carl, give it to him! He won't make his bed anymore." It
turned out that making his bed was his prescriptive exercise for the day.

* * *

The attrition of Liberty Book Club's membership continued. Because
other left institutions were shrinking, we had fewer places to put ads or
do mailings. A tactic of the Establishment was to embroil left groups in
lawsuits, so that time, money, and energy would be spent in self-defense.
Our own parameters were fairly clear. Unless we could sell four thousand
copies of a selection per month, we could not function. We were approaching that watershed, even though our acceptance rate remained
fairly high, at around 60 percent. But as the membership shrank, the
sales dropped.

Angus and I discussed the problem. It was clear that unless we found
a solution, we would have to close shop. One possible saving was in print
costs. Angus had always been partial to quality paperbacks, in which the
sheets are folded and "Smythe-sewn," rather than glued in, where there
is a tendency for the pages to to fall out. Another was to reorganize the
book club. A lot of money and energy went into the business of sending
out notices, processing acceptances and rejections, mailing the books
out, and often having to bill members. Our new idea was to abandon the
principle of choice. Instead, members would receive eight books a year,
chosen by us, for $10, including postage. We called the new operation
the Prometheus Paperback Book Club.

This change in the operation did reduce the paperwork considerably,
saving a good deal of money. It was a bold gamble. We picked an important book, *The Power Elite* by C. Wright Mills, and sent it out free.
We were, in effect, asking people to join Prometheus Book Club on the
strength of the quality of the Mills book in their hands. We raised some
contributions (Corliss Lamont gave us $1,000) and we printed 30,000
copies of Mills's book as the first Prometheus paperback. We dispatched
a mailing to our own membership, to former members, and to readers of
the *National Guardian*. As it turned out, our predictions regarding response were fairly good. We got 80 percent of our own membership,
about 4,800 people; 20 percent of former members, about 1,600; and a
whopping 18 percent of the *National Guardian*, making a total close to
10,000.

The need to cut costs left us no choice but to lay off practically all our staff. But still the numbers weren't there. Then fate intervened in the person of the publisher Alfred A. Knopf. Out of the blue, Knopf invited Angus to be a senior editor. His re-entry into mainstream publishing was a serious blow, perhaps even a mortal wound, to the blacklisting within the publishing industry. We were overjoyed.

Our payroll was now four people: Aspro Betro, shipping clerk, on $110 a week; Charlotte Pomerantz, part-time editor, on $80 a week; Rosalie Sinkler, office manager, on $120 a week; and me, the big boss, on around $60 a week. We had also at the time two volunteers: Mickey Pilsudski, who was working on the manuscript of *Gideon's Army* by Professor Curtis MacDougall; and Sema Sverdlove, wife of Leon, whom I had known as a trade-union official on the East Side.

As we were so few, we worked closely together. Both Charlotte and I liked to work late, so we saw quite a bit of each other. Charlotte possessed a unique sense of humor, which later served her well as a writer of children's books. A top-flight editor, she had a habit of getting lost in statistics. When I disputed her facts, she would shrug. Once in a while she would dig in her heels and say "I'll bet I'm right—I'll bet you dinner and the theater." Well, it was a little bit like taking candy from a baby. On the other hand, she was making more money than I, and dinner and the theater were very pleasant ways of spending time. Ultimately, this innocent pastime led to a completely new life.

We were a small group, but we had volunteer help: copy-editors, artists, book designers—all friends of Angus Cameron. And he was available to me for counsel over the phone. So I thought we could manage. After five years under the tutelage of Angus, I felt competent to run the book club and Cameron Associates, now renamed Marzani & Munsell. I learned from Angus the many aspects of publishing. Above all, I had learned what I can only call a certain reverence for books. To see Angus with a new book in his hand reminded me of an Anglican bishop caressing his prayer book.

While all this reorganization was going on, a small incident occurred which was to have substantial repercussions. I had an American friend, John Crane, living in Italy, who would return home from time to time. He picked up at a newsstand in Rome a new book about Khrushchev called *La Grande Svolta* (*The Great Turning*), as a present for me. I started to read it, was very impressed, and decided to translate and publish it. It was written by a correspondent of the Communist daily *l'Unita*, Giuseppe Boffa, a historian, high in the ranks of the Party (he later became a Communist senator). The book was a serious analysis of Krushchev's policies. I wrote to the publisher and was granted permission to translate and publish the work. This was around August; Angus had just left, and it would be my first venture as an independent publisher. I felt good about the choice and planned to translate the book in a leisurely manner during the summer. It would be published under the title, *Inside the Khrushchev Era*.

Then all hell broke loose. I was having breakfast with Angus the morning of August 31, primed to tell him about this new book, when the headline in the *New York Times* screamed, "Khrushchev arriving U.S. September 29th." "Son of a bitch," I said to Angus, "Why couldn't he wait another month?" Angus agreed that the book was right for the book club, but of course it was impossible to get a book out in a month—a book that wasn't even translated. Angus surprised me by saying: "Well, Carl, if anybody can do it, you can!" I immediately went back to the office and called our printer, McKibbon, who owed me a big favor.

* * *

When Cameron & Kahn published The Judgment of Julius and Ethel Rosenberg *by John Wexley, the government went to extraordinary lengths to suppress it. They behaved like the cheapest of conmen. FBI agents went around to printers issuing threats that the government would be displeased if this book were published. The same thing happened with Harvey Matusow's* False Witness. *The vice-president of McKibbon, Mr. Stein, called me and said they were taking the type off the press because of FBI pressure. I said: "I take it you don't value our business." "No sir," said Mr. Stein, "we do value it. It's our bread and butter. You're steady, regular, and you pay on time. But I cannot ignore the threats. Government agencies can make things very difficult for us." I said: "Mr. Stein, what kind of a country do you want for your children?" He was practically weeping on the telephone. "Mr. Marzani," he said, "I am as liberal as anyone I know and I think this whole matter is shameful, but I am an officer of the corporation and I have an obligation to protect it. I beg of you, forgive us this time and I promise that somewhere down the line, I'll make it up to you."*

We found a printer for The Judgment, *in Philadelphia; he was an old Republican curmudgeon. When the FBI came to see him, he asked: "Is there anything illegal about this book?" When the agents said "No," he exploded: "Get the hell out of my office, you socialist New Deal bastards! Trying to tell American businessmen how to run their affairs! Get out!" The printer asked his lawyer to look over the manuscript of* The Judgment *to see if it slandered the government. The lawyer laughed in his face. "Hell, the whole thing is one huge slander; but don't worry, they won't come near it with a ten-foot pole. Just go right ahead and print it." The lawyer was William Kunstler, who went on to a great career as defender of civil liberties.*

* * *

When I called McKibbon about the Khrushchev book, I didn't have to remind them that they owed me one. I told the production manager that I had a manuscript of about three hundred typewritten pages. Could he set it up in type in five days, print it, bind it and deliver to bookstores in thirty days? "Give me a minute," he said. When he returned he said: "It will take us a couple of days to get the typesetting arranged, but I think we can make it." I sat down at my typewriter and started typing. When he called me two days later, I had over 150 pages to send him. As the galleys came back, I sent more. By the end of five days, the book was all set in type. Meanwhile, our volunteer copy-editor returned the corrected galleys. Miraculously, every step fell into place. These included unexpected aid from the old wartime days. I ran across Si Nydorf, an artist from Presentation Division, who was running a small graphics shop. He was outraged at the stories of government interference. He thought that Liberty Book Club was doing a great job and wanted to help. "Well," I said, "I need a jacket for a book in the next couple of days." At lunch two days later, Si presented Angus and me with three clear sketches. We chose one, and he went ahead with the cover.

On the morning that Khrushchev arrived, the book page of the *New York Times* was dominated by a large ad from Marzani & Munsell that proclaimed, "Welcome, Mr. Khrushchev" and described *Inside the Khrushchev Era*. There were also other ads for books on Russia, but ours was the only one courteous enough to say "welcome." The Soviet Delegation at the United Nations bought two copies of *Inside the Khrushchev Era* for each of the other U.N. delegations, and this money paid for the ad. *Inside the Khrushchev Era* served as my final exam in publishing, and it was Angus's opinion, shared by others, that I had done very well. Thus I felt satisfied that the daily business of running Prometheus Paperbacks was something I could handle.

Several days later, Angus narrated a story of the day Khrushchev arrived. It was lunchtime and Angus was going down the elevator at Knopf. Another editor said to him slyly, "I see your former partner sent up quite a rocket today." "Indeed he did," said Angus. Whereupon the other editor said to him, "He must have had quite a bit of advance notice. How much earlier did he know that Khrushchev was coming?" Angus told me, "I took great pleasure in telling him that, believe it or not, he got it from the same source as everyone else, the morning newspaper. I couldn't resist adding: 'Not only that, but he began to translate the book that very morning.'" The book sold well, and while we didn't get rich, we didn't lose money. The importance of the book was the insight it provided into Khrushchev's attitudes. Recalling my conversation with Julius Emspak, at the time of the Twentieth Congress in 1956, it was clear that Khrushchev's speech on Stalin signaled a thoroughgoing change in Soviet society. Nevertheless Khrushchev would have to deal with a lot of obstructionism. Indeed, there came a point when Khrushchev was voted out of the Politburo. He challenged the vote on the grounds that only the Central Committee had the authority to remove him. With the help of the army, which flew to Moscow members of the Central Committee from all over the Soviet Union, Khrushchev was able to reverse the Politburo decision. Thus in one stroke the supremacy of the Central Committee was reestablished. For me, the awareness that Khrushchev meant business was of the utmost importance: it got me thinking again about the Cold War.

I had been interested in the Cold War ever since I wrote *We Can Be Friends*, but the UE, then the book club, had occupied me such that I remained more an observer than a participant. Now I felt a need to think seriously about solutions and my possible contribution. I thought it important to present a picture of where the world stood at the moment. I called an old friend, Victor Perlo, to suggest that we do a book together. He would do the economic side and I would do the military and political analysis. The book became *Dollars and Sense of Disarmament*. I was back in the business of doing battle with the powers that be.

—— 6 ——
The Threat of War

The Cold War was anything but cold. What Walter Lippman meant by "cold" was that the two powers were not firing at each other directly—a crucial restraint given the existence of nuclear weapons. Outside the dubious area of nuclear deterrence (appropriately known as MAD—mutually assured destruction), actual wars, large and small, filled the headlines. From the American airlift of Kuomintang troops to North China in 1946 to the Soviet evacuation of Afghanistan in 1988, there was hardly a year when blood was not being shed as a result of the "cold" war. Even when conflicts were not caused by it, as in the case of the Arab–Israeli wars, they were fed, and the UN was paralyzed, by the rivalry of the two great powers.

The cost to the world in blood was high: millions of dead and wounded. The United States paid a stiff price. Half a million casualties in Korea and Vietnam—half as many as the country's casualties in World War II. The total cost to global society in value of labor and materials was stupendous, beyond comprehension: sixteen trillion dollars—that is, sixteen million million, $16,000,000,000,000 (the U.S. eight trillion; the USSR four trillion; and England, France, and the other 157 nations four trillion). In the forty years between 1949 and 1989, the United States came close to apocalyptic disaster on six occasions: two good-sized wars, in Korea and Vietnam, which might have spread; one aborted invasion at the Bay of Pigs in Cuba; and three major confrontations in Berlin, Suez, and Cuba. In addition, there were numerous smaller interventions, some covert: Guatemala and the elimination of Arbenz; Chile and Allende; the Dominican Republic and Bosch; El Salvador; Indonesia; Angola; Nicaragua.

While the violence of war—of trained troops and lethal equipment—was endemic in news from abroad, another kind of violence—that of police and vigilantes—erupted at home. This violence came from white supremacists in the segregated South, who were hard pressed by the freedom campaign spearheaded by Black college students and by the Montgomery bus boycott. The heavy artillery of that campaign was the unanimous decision of 1954 by the Warren Supreme Court against segregation. The civil rights struggle revolutionized the South and, merging with the antiwar movement, shook the country. President Johnson was forced to retire in 1968. The tensions of those years were reflected in the series of assassinations and murders, from those of John and Robert Kennedy, Malcolm X, and Martin Luther King, Jr., to scores of lesser-known crimes such as the killing of Medgar Evers in Mississippi and of the Neshoba County trio of James Chaney, Michael Schwerner, and Andrew Goodman. (This last touched Edith and me directly: the Goodmans were close friends and we had seen Andy grow up.)

In those decades I was immersed in both foreign and domestic policies by virtue of my daily activities. Besides publishing, I was writing—books, pamphlets, articles, reviews. I also wrote a weekly column for *Romania Libera* in Bucharest. Throughout the 1970s, I did a column for *Ethnos*, the leading newspaper in Athens, Greece.

Overlapping the writing and publishing, was a monthly meeting of the Advisory Committee of the L. M. Rabinowitz Foundation, which functioned from September 1960 to June 1976. The foundation played a substantial role within the left, supporting writers and activists. I also did a good deal of speaking at meetings in, or close to, the New York City metropolitan area, as well as tours in other major cities. (The most memorable speaking engagement was one that did not take place. In January 1953, when I was on the UE staff, there was a Moscow announcement of a doctors' plot against Stalin. An American Labor Party club asked me to speak on the plot, and, without thinking, I said I would. In a day or two it struck me that I didn't know beans about the plot, and I canceled my speech. On the Monday following the non-meeting, I ran across Albert Fitzgerald, president of the UE. "I see you spoke on the doctors' plot," was his greeting. "Who says?" I countered. "The *New York Times* had an announcement." "Fitzie," I said, "you know better than to trust the *Times*!") Modest grants were made by the Rabinowitz Foundation to writers and activists. Tens of thousands of dollars went to the Students Nonviolent Coordinating Committee (SNCC). Started mostly by Black college students, SNCC "quickly

became the militant thrusting point of the civil rights movement"
(*Encyclopedia of the American Left*).

* * *

The period following my release from jail in 1951 was to see a gradual
deterioration in my marriage. Among the reasons was a certain distance
on Edith's part, which I attributed to the worsening pain of her illness.
In response I found solace in a deepening friendship with Eve Merriam.
Married with two small children, she owned a summer home on Fire
Island, where I was building a house. Eve, a published poet, had written
several stirring poems on the Montgomery bus boycott and other events
in the South. Angus and I thought they would make an effective pamphlet. We would meet in Eve's studio, and there pulled the material into
shape. We eventually produced the volume *Montgomery, Alabama, Money,
Mississippi and Other Places*. Eve was attractive, witty, and uninhibited;
we fell it love. Over the next five years our attachment deepened; I felt
it was permanent. When, in mid-1960, Eve divorced her husband. I had
misgivings, as I was afraid this would destabilize our relationship. But
our break-up, when it came, would be a great shock.

* * *

In September 1960 I travelled to Europe to visit the Soviet Union and
the Eastern European countries, where I had accumulated royalties from
my novel, *The Survivor*, and other books. Eve met me for a week in
London. We returned home to disturbing rumors of a pending invasion
of Cuba. In November the Hispanic American Report from an institute
at Stanford University revealed that the CIA had a camp in Guatemala
where a couple of thousand Cuban exiles were in training. Presumably,
the United States would take action after the inauguration of President
John F. Kennedy.

At that time, *We Can Be Friends* was being translated in Havana; on
its completion I would go over to do the checking, and Eve would go
with me. I had been in touch with the Cubans at the UN, who were
making arrangements for our trip. In mid-January, on a Friday evening,
Washington announced an embargo on Cuba, effective Monday. On
Saturday morning my Cuban contact called me: a Cuban plane that had
been undergoing repairs in New York would leave for Havana at two
o'clock and had instructions to take me and Eve. I called Eve; she had
left the house. I tried desperately to locate her, but to no avail. I decided
I would go alone.

The big four-engine plane was empty of passengers except for me and an aloof American woman, the wife of a Cuban writer. At the airport in Cuba I was arrested: I had no visa. I explained the circumstances. The publishing cooperative was called: fortunately, although it was Saturday, there were people working. Having been vouched for, I was soon ensconced at the former Havana Hilton, now the Havana Libre. When I called Eve she was cold and angry, and faulted me for not trying hard enough to find her. Nothing I said would mollify her. She'd get over it, I thought. But she didn't.

Havana was a city in revolution. It reminded me in many ways of Barcelona twenty-five years earlier, not least in its ubiquitous slogans, particularly those of the workers in the food trade. Now, as then, streamers hung from buildings and were strung across streets, dominating the scene. One might have thought that food workers had spearheaded the revolution. Cedric Belfrage, an old friend, confirmed that the Sindacato Gastronomico was a pretty aggressive union with a Communist leadership. Cedric was one of four friends I unexpectedly met up with in Havana. The English-born editor of the *National Guardian*, he had been deported from New York as a subversive and was now that paper's correspondent in Cuba. The other three were Joe North of the *Daily Worker*; Joe Newman of the *New York Herald Tribune*, a classmate at Williams College; and Eddie Boorstein, an economist who had been in the OSS and was now on the staff of Che Guevara and the head of the National Bank (the fiery revolutionary as banker tickled left-wingers). Thanks to the presence of these four, my circle of acquaintances now went beyond the publishing cooperative and the film community for whom I had brought *Deadline for Action*. Joe North vouched for me to Carlos Rafael Rodríguez, probably the most influential Communist in Cuba and close to Castro. Boorstein set up a night meeting with Che Guevara and arranged for me to join a small group of students from Latin America who met with Fidel. Cedric, for his part, introduced me to a top aide of the foreign minister, Raul Roa. He also took me to visit Colonel Jacob Arbenz, former president of Guatemala, overthrown by a CIA coup in 1954.

Arbenz was a small, trim man of great charm. He was a reformer not a revolutionary. Astute politically at the level of votes and elections, he had, for a socialist, been a little naive in the past about imperialism; he wasn't now. There was no revolution in Guatemala, said Arbenz: the old army had not been touched; productive capitalists, whether industrial or agricultural, were not threatened; and the expropriated land of the

United Fruit Company was to be paid for. Cuba, of course, was different: here a true revolution was taking place, though not in the Soviet style. Arbenz saw Cuba's economic structure as being in flux. It was a combination of state ownership in large enterprises such as utilities, oil refineries, and sugar cane; a strong sector of family farm cooperatives; and an equally strong sector of small entrepreneurs. Cedric agreed—as, significantly, did Rafael Rodríguez.

Carlos Rafael Rodríguez was impressive, a former professor of economic and political science. He spoke excellent English and was widely recognized, even by opponents, as a brilliant social thinker. At thirty he had been the youngest member of the Central Committee of the Union Revolucionaria Comunista (soon changed to Partido Socialista Popular—PSP) and, in contrast to the hostility of older party leaders, had been an early supporter of Castro. "They could accept Mao and his peasant army," Rafael told me, "because Mao used Marxian terminology, but they couldn't see that Fidel was doing the same thing."

Rodríguez and I quickly took to each other, as *aficionados* of Isaac Deutscher, whose clear-eyed biography of Stalin we both had read when it was first published (1949). (I had been to dinner at Deutscher's home in England only two months before I went to Cuba.) By the end of our two-hour meeting Rodríguez and I had reached a degree of political intimacy that was unusual. The ground for this friendship had been well prepared. The *Monthly Review* editors, Leo Huberman and Paul Sweezy, had visited Cuba twice in 1960 and had spoken to me of Rodríguez in superlatives, while Joe North had talked of me enthusiastically to Rodríguez. Joe was an old friend and long-time party member. His vouching for me, a nonparty person, was important. And my own personal credentials were not negligible: *We Can Be Friends*, my fighting with the Durruti Column in Spain, three years in jail, and my early espousal of Gramsci.

In the four weeks I was in Havana I saw Rodríguez perhaps a dozen times. I valued his comments on the gossip, information, and opinions I was picking up from many different quarters—from the waiters at the hotel to Che Guevara. I spent three hours with Che in a midnight tête-à-tête, just one night after I had been with a small group that spent five hours with Castro. I had definite reactions to the two men, and Rodríguez was amused by my views. Both were extremely self-confident, but Fidel was a better listener—his mind was more open, whereas Che was more doctrinaire. I had also felt an element of posturing in Che (living up to a romantic image of a revolutionary), which was totally lacking in Fidel.

Rafael said that Che could be irritating but thought I was too harsh on him. Yet he found the overall comparison of the two men valid.

I had intended to talk economics with Guevara but never got to the subject. My OSS buddy, Eddie Boorstein, had ushered me into Che's office. Che, at his desk, waved his cigar in greeting. Without preamble, Che said in Spanish: "Will there be an invasion?" I said "Yes," and he said, "When?" I said, "Tomorrow morning... a week... a month... as soon as Kennedy gives the word." "That's what we think, too," he said, his tone noticeably warmer, as if I had passed a test by my prompt answers. I said that Kennedy, who had just been inaugurated, might take his time, and Guevara nodded. He said, "Eduardo tells me you fought in Spain and that you worked with the Joint Chiefs of Staff in the war." That was correct, I said, but I was no military expert. Che waved his cigar as if my lack of expertise was irrelevant, then asked what I thought would be the size of the invasion. I said I thought the force might be two Marine divisions, one attacking and the other in reserve, with plenty of air cover from an aircraft carrier. "That will not be enough," said Guevara sharply.

I demurred. A Marine division of twelve thousand men was a formidable force. Che's experience, I pointed out, had been fighting Batista's excuse of an army—half-trained, demoralized and poorly led. (Che Guevara's column had been less than two hundred men.) In contrast, U.S. Marines had high morale, well-trained officers, and tremendous firepower. Most crucial in this case, they had unlimited ammunition. Modern warfare devoured ammunition at an incredible rate. I said I would wager that all the artillery shells in Cuba, including those for tanks, would be used up in one day of heavy fighting. The Americans could deliver that amount by air every day! Our discussion went on for three hours. I am not sure I convinced him, but he became much less combative as we talked. We agreed that the force of Cuban exiles being trained by the CIA in Guatemala, which he put at fifteen hundred men, was a fig leaf to seize and hold a beach under the protection of air power. This would allow the "government-in-exile" to land, be recognized by the U.S., and ask for military aid. It never occurred to either of us that when the Bay of Pigs invasion did take place there wouldn't be U.S. Marines in Navy ships offshore ready to go. Nor, of course, did it occur to Rodríguez when I reported the conversation. Fidel, he said, was more realistic than Che about American military power. Invasion would be a disaster.

I didn't get an opportunity to discuss the invasion with Fidel. Questions and answers in his meeting with the students were more oriented to politics and ideology. It was very obvious that Fidel had not been a Communist when he was in the Sierra Maestra; nor was he one now. His only program had been to overthrow Batista and carry out a thorough agrarian reform. I wrote a summary of my impressions of Castro for a special Cuba issue of *Mainstream*, May 1961.

I spoke to a great many people while I was in Havana, but I should emphasize that my encounters were almost wholly random. I had not gone to Havana to study the revolution, or to write about it, but to approve a translation of my book. However, I did have a little background. I had read up on Cuba, particularly *Cuba: Anatomy of a Revolution* by Leo Huberman and Paul Sweezy, so I was aware that Cuban society was very much in a state of flux. Many political currents were competing to shape emerging institutions as well as current *ad hoc* policies—for example, what should be the role of heavy industry. I found an astute guide in Roa's assistant, Manuel. Manuel had a certain proprietary interest in me because *We Can Be Friends* was being translated for publication in Cuba on his initiative. He was in his mid-thirties, a former academic whose field was international relations; he had a good command of English, and was enthusiastic about my book. He and his wife took me to parties and gatherings, thereby widening my circle of acquaintances. My Spanish was fluent (if erratic), and it struck me that people like Manuel, who spoke both English and Spanish, would criticize Castro's policies more freely when speaking in their native tongue. This may account for the difference in interpretation between Joe Newman of the *New York Herald Tribune* and myself.

I had not seen Joe since Tokyo in the spring of 1939 when he had been a fledgling reporter and I had been a member of the British Communist Party. At that time he still retained a touch of his college radicalism. Now, he had become a seasoned newspaperman with his share of professional skepticism, allergic to Marxists as know-it-alls, but without ever being a redbaiter. We were in solid agreement on two fundamental issues: that Fidel had not been a Communist but had been pushed further to the left by American policies, and that he was supported by an overwhelming majority of the population. His newly minted army was well equipped, a very large militia was well armed, and both were highly motivated—*Patria o Muerte* was more than a slogan. An American invasion would meet with fierce resistance.

Joe was a good observer. Where he and I differed was on nuances of interpretation. Joe felt that Castro had a big ego. It was no bigger than that of FDR or JFK, I said. Joe saw oratory as Fidel's weakness and his drug. Speeches of four, five, even six hours were marathons of boredom. My response was: for Joe Newman, but not for his audiences. Fidel was teaching an audience with an illiteracy rate of 40 percent—even higher among his basic constituency of *campesinos*.

Some of our differences were important. Joe considered Fidel to be in complete control of the revolution. I thought this was true in the sense that the old economic structure was gone, and that Castro was the undisputed center of power. But Fidel and Cuba were in a state of ferment; the revolution and Fidel's thinking were continually evolving. There were contending forces which could shape the revolution in different ways and the United States could play a substantial role. To give the impression that the revolution was a monolith was to play into the hands of the American interventionists. Joe was not persuaded.

Carlos Rafael Rodríguez was persuaded, however. He knew exactly what I was talking about and was aware all of the various currents and pressures, from Che on one extreme to Raul Roa on the other. It was Fidel who had to make the pragmatic decisions. I told Carlos that I could try to get this picture across in the United States, but I would have to say that I had been authorized to do so. Without his authorization my opinions would have no weight.

Rodríguez listened carefully, and questioned me closely as to my entrée to the White House. I said it was a tenuous thread via Arthur Schlesinger, Jr., who was expected to be the historian of the Kennedy administration. I had known Schlesinger in the OSS: while there was no trace of amity between us, there was courtesy. During the Kennedy campaign I had written Schlesinger about reaching voters on the left, and he had passed me on to Professor Archibald Cox, who was screening suggestions and people potentially useful in the election. I told Rodríguez that I thought Schlesinger would see me. Rodríguez said he'd have to discuss my suggestion and he'd see me the next day. He duly gave me the go-ahead. I did not ask whom he had consulted, but I assumed it was Castro. I returned to New York on February 10, a Saturday, planning to start my small operation on Monday.

My plan was derailed. On my return, a glacial Eve Merriam informed me she had fallen in love with a man named Leonard Lewin and was holding an engagement party in two weeks. I was stunned. It was two days before I rallied enough to think about Schlesinger, only to find he had just left for a tour of Latin America. That left me with the misery of Eve's rejection. This was abruptly doubled: Edith ordered me out of the house—permanently.

* * *

Arthur Schlesinger returned from Latin America on March 4, which only came to my attention a week later. Because I was in a serious depression over my personal life, I procrastinated until a series of articles by Joe Newman pricked my conscience. On March 24 I finally wrote to Schlesinger. I indicated that I had been in Cuba at the same time as Joe Newman. I thought Joe was badly mistaken "in assuming the irreversibility in events there, and in the extent and character of Communist Party and Soviet influence." Schlesinger answered courteously on April 5; he would be glad to hear anything I had to say, but Kingsley Martin and I. F. Stone, who had been in Cuba recently, supported "the salient features of the Newman series." These two observers, the first British and the second American, were well-known writers on the left; however, their views did not faze me, as mine had the imprimatur of Carlos Rafael Rodríguez. I should have gone down to Washington immediately but accidie was at work and I postponed the trip from day to day. On April 17 the invasion began at the Bay of Pigs. I experienced a strong sense of guilt over my procrastination, though this was tempered by an awareness that nothing I had to say at this stage would have made any difference. The Bay of Pigs invasion was a fiasco. One congressman who knew the background of the operation said it was "a case of cumulative stupidities." Though this observation was correct as far as it went, it did not indicate *whose* stupidities—those of the CIA wonks who drew up the plans; the CIA director, Allen Dulles; the Joint Chiefs of Staff, who authorized an improbable scheme as "viable"; and Secretary of State John Foster Dulles, who sold it to President Eisenhower.

By all accounts, Ike never looked at the plans; and, in fact, he held back the go-ahead to give Kennedy a chance to review the operation. Kennedy was dubious and made it very clear that American forces—ships, planes, men—could not be used. The CIA assured him that they would not be needed. This was a barefaced lie, since the scheme was to establish a beachhead, then fly in a "provisional government" which would be recognized as legitimate and entitled to the help of U.S. armed force. It was the Caribbean version of Franco's Spanish war.

The flawed plan was further bungled in execution. Intelligence was puerile. There were reefs in the landing area that no one knew about. Castro's air force of six planes, reportedly destroyed by an air bombing, turned out to be intact. Castro's planes controlled the skies, blew up the ammunition ship, crippled another, and shot up tanks. In seventy-two hours, it was all over: 1,214 invaders (out of a maximum of 1,700 men) were prisoners. Robert Light, a reporter for the *National Guardian*, called me and suggested we collaborate on a pamphlet. He had followed events closely and had accumulated clippings from many sources. *Cuba vs. the CIA* was published in two weeks: 72 pages, selling for $1, with big discounts for bulk purchases. The UE bought 10,000 copies at 70 percent discount. Royalties, ranging from 6 percent to 2 percent, were split between Light and me—over $700 each. (This windfall would pay the $600 fee for the three eight-hour sessions I would with psychiatrist Dr. James Watts, under whose care I experimented with hallucinogenic drugs.)

* * *

October 22, 1962, was a historic day in the Kennedy administration. On that morning, I picked up the *New York Times* at my usual newsstand. The headline on the right-hand column said that President Kennedy would address the nation on television that evening. The subhead and lead paragraph spoke of a somber mood at the White House and an atmosphere of crisis. I suspected right away what the crisis was: the Soviet Union was placing nuclear missiles in Cuba. Senator Kenneth Keating of New York had been right. (Throughout September, Senator Keating, a Republican from New York, had been clamoring that missile bases were being built by Russians in Cuba. His informants were recent arrivals from Cuba. The CIA had no official comments but discreet leaks reassured the public. The agency knew about the construction: these were bases for anti-aircraft SAMs (surface-to-air missiles); they were not a surprise and held no offensive threat. Commentators dismissed Keating's claims: it was inconceivable that Khrushchev would challenge the United States in its own backyard.

The events of October 1962 were a sequel to the CIA operation against Cuba in April 1961—the Bay of Pigs invasion. According to *Khrushchev Remembers*, the Cuban and the Soviet leaderships were both convinced that the United States would try to avenge that failure and destroy Castro. How could they prevent it? A solution took shape. If several dozen nuclear missiles could be secretly deployed in Cuba, the Pentagon could not be sure of destroying them all in an air strike. If only one missile survived, it could devastate an American city, and this was a sufficient deterrent to invasion. The tactic was essentially a gamble that the sites would be built and Soviet missiles installed before the United States caught on and took action. Deployment of the missiles was Khrushchev's decision, and he was a gambler. (After all, his famous speech to the Twentieth Congress of the Communist Party of the Soviet Union exposing Stalin's crimes had been a huge gamble. He had done it without the consent of the top ruling body, the Presidium, also known as the Political Bureau or Politburo. It was a tremendous shock to the party and the Russian people. It was Khrushchev's way of cutting into the power of the bureaucracy.)

The *Times* story didn't talk about Cuba, which confirmed my worst fears. The president's speech was set for 7:00 P.M. What would he say? Would he issue an ultimatum? To whom? Sending one to Castro would be useless; sending it to Khrushchev was to invite a rejection and possibly escalate the confrontation. My fear was that President Kennedy would announce a bombing of the missile bases in Cuba. Then what would Khrushchev do? Move in on Berlin? How could Kennedy respond—nuke a Soviet silo, *one silo?*

My thoughts raced. The sunny autumn morning seemed peculiarly fresh, clear, alive, and inviting. It brought a constriction in my throat, and I gulped air to offset it. The mind needed oxygen to think, to face the possible and probable consequences. The world was teetering on the edge of nuclear war. My thoughts recoiled, became jumbled, disoriented.

* * *

In fifty years of living, only twice had I experienced such dread of the future. The first time was in Prague at the time of the Munich pact in 1938. Europe had united behind Nazi aggression; war against the Soviet Union was a certainty, with Japan in cahoots and the United States in furtive support. The Soviet Union was doomed and so would social experimentation be for a hundred years. The lives of millions of people, including mine and Edith's, would be affected in ways beyond our imagination. I recall how at the time we had decided not to have children. The second time was in Lewisburg Penitentiary during the four months I was in isolation, from the last week in October 1950 to the last week in February 1951.

* * *

With the *Times* rolled up, I walked down to the office of Marzani & Munsell at the corner of 23rd Street and Sixth Avenue. No one at the office seemed as upset as I. There were five on the staff, all politically active. Rosalie Sinkler was now the only person left from the staff of seven which Angus and I had inherited from the previous management of Liberty Book Club. We had one editor, Charlotte Pomerantz, and two subeditors, Steve Vartinsky and Sema Sverdlove. Sema and Charlotte were close friends and shared an interest in music, literature, and yoga. The shipping clerk, Joe Betro, followed foreign-policy matters more closely. When he saw me he said, "Hey, Carl, what's up?" I told him I didn't know, but my guess was that Kennedy would talk about Cuba.

I paused at Charlotte's desk to say good morning. She was working on *A Quarter Century of Un-Americana, 1938-1963*, a satirical compendium of quips, cartoons, and opprobrium about the House Un-American Activities Committee (HUAC). The book was Charlotte's idea, and entailed an enormous amount of research, with considerable help from Sema. Charlotte had written profiles of each of the six HUAC chairmen: "The Reign of Martin Dies, 1938–45," "The Regency of Rankin, 1945–47," "The Term of Thomas, 1947–49," "The Blacklists of Wood, 1949–53," "The Piety of Velde, 1953–55," and "The Realpolitik of Walter, 1955–?" There was a foreword by H. H. Wilson, Professor of Politics at Princeton, an envoi by the novelist James Baldwin, an Editor's Note, and an essay which I wrote: "Free, with an Eye to See Things as They Are." The cover by Si Ross was a carnival of burlesque, in many colors with a border of witches.

The book, published by Marzani & Munsell in 1963, was a great success, with blurbs from Archibald MacLeish, Norman Thomas, Dagmar Wilson, Carey McWilliams, Alexander Meiklejohn, Rev. Fred Shuttlesworth, and other eminent guardians of civil liberties. Because I thought a popular book did not need scholarly armory I decided to drop the footnotes. Charlotte, who had meticulously documented every quotation never forgave me or herself for letting it happen.

* * *

Historic events rolled on at home and abroad. On the same calendar, day after day, one's personal history also rolled on, and some important dates in my personal life were directly related to historic incidents. The Cuban missile crisis sparked the beginning of a romance with Charlotte Pomerantz, which culminated in our marriage in 1966. Charlotte and I have been married almost thirty years as I write this. In October 1962 we both would have considered such an eventuality preposterous. I was fifty; she was thirty-two, and looked even younger. Though separated from Edith for two years, I was still married (March 12, 1962, had been our twenty-fifth wedding anniversary) and had two teenage children. Charlotte had been divorced for six years and led an active social life. At that time I had a wonderful woman companion, Anne, close to my age, with a boy of nine of whom I was very fond.

Charlotte was a graceful woman of intelligence and wit. She had been hired by Marzani & Munsell on the recommendation of Otto Nathan, the literary executor of Albert Einstein. Otto and I had known each other since 1939, when he was a professor of economics at NYU and I was an instructor. Otto was a Marxist of the Austrian persuasion—too revolutionary for the socialist Second International and too democratic for the Communist Third. Charlotte had assisted Otto and Heinz Norden in the production of *Einstein on Peace* (Simon & Schuster, 1960). In the editor's note she was thanked by them for her "keen and intelligent analysis of the material and great editorial skill in the final revision of the manuscript"—Otto told me that Charlotte should have been listed as a coeditor. I had known Charlotte slightly before we hired her: her parents were our neighbors. They lived on 87th Street and Riverside Drive; in 1956 our family had moved into a double brownstone on the same block. As Edith's multiple sclerosis progressed, she was increasingly bound to a wheelchair; hence living on two floors became impossible. We had sold our house on 88th street and bought the double brownstone where the family could live on one floor.

Charlotte lived in a very cheap apartment ($18.25 a month) on West 55th Street between Ninth and Tenth Avenues. It had one bedroom, with a bathtub in the kitchen, and a claustrophobic toilet. When Edith and I separated, Charlotte found a similar apartment for me on 56th Street, except that my toilet was in the hall. My rent was higher than Charlotte's—$23.50 a month.

It was to this apartment that I repaired when I left the office early at four o'clock on October 22. We closed at five, though I often stayed later. On this day, however, my anxiety had been growing and I had to get to a television for the president's speech. The problem was that I didn't have a set, as I had never got into the habit of watching television. So on the way home I stopped at a repair shop. I told the man there that I was looking for something real cheap, just to hear the president's speech. He waved at a small set on a messy bench. "There's that," he said. "It ain't worth fixing, but one channel works." Would it get the president? I asked. Sure, he replied, he'd be on all stations. He plugged it in; the picture was terrible but the sound was clear. He charged me $15, my ticket of admission to the apocalypse.

Seated at the kitchen table, with beer, bread, and cheese, I ate and wondered where to put the set. The kitchen table had no convenient outlet; the handiest was the one near the head of the bed, where I had a bridge lamp. I could place the television on a chair, prop myself in bed with a couple of pillows, pour another beer, and get scared in comfort. I finished eating, made the arrangements, plugged the television into the upper half of the outlet and clicked the power switch. Nothing happened: the set didn't work. I fiddled with the switch, but to no effect. The lamp was on, so the outlet was working. To make sure, I switched the two plugs in the outlet. The lamp functioned. Damn it, that piece of junk had chosen this moment to expire—it had obviously been *in extremis*. I wasn't going to buy another set; I'd just go to a bar. Then I thought of Charlotte: surely she would have a television. It was a little after six o'clock when I called. Yes, she had a set, yes, she was going to hear the president and yes, I would be welcome. She used her tiny bedroom as a study and slept in the living room. We sat on her couch, snacks and drinks on a table, amused at the tale of my set's demise. She asked me to speculate on the nature of the president's address and I told her about Senator Keating's alerts on Cuban missile sites, of which she was unaware. What could happen? An ultimatum, if rejected, would heighten the confrontation. Having bottled up my anxieties, I now poured them out. The military would demand action; Kennedy, after the failure of the Bay of Pigs, couldn't afford to look like a wimp. They would bomb the sites, I suggested, and possibly invade Cuba. The Russians were bound to retaliate—how, where, and at what level God only knew. Then what? Escalation to nuclear weapons? I managed to thoroughly frighten both of us.

At seven o'clock, President John F. Kennedy spoke. He looked very grave; his voice was calm and authoritative. Within seconds he gave the bad news: the United States had uncovered a Soviet military buildup in Cuba, which included missile sites whose purpose "can be none other than to provide a nuclear strike capability against the Western Hemisphere." Some sites were for medium-range missiles that could carry a nuclear warhead over a thousand miles—capable of striking Washington, D.C., the Panama Canal, or Mexico City. Others were intermediate-range ballistic missiles that could go twice as far, placing in danger "most of the major cities in the Western Hemisphere, ranging as far north as Hudson Bay in Canada and as far south as Lima, Peru. In addition," said Kennedy, "jet bombers, capable of carrying nuclear weapons, are now being uncrated and assembled in Cuba."

The president went on, giving further details; while the tone remained composed, the words were explosive—offensive missile sites, a strategic base in Cuba, nuclear capability, secret and swift buildup, Soviet falsehoods, deliberate deception, an offensive threat that could not be tolerated. "The 1930s taught us a clear lesson," said Kennedy. "Aggressive conduct, if allowed to grow unchecked and unchallenged, ultimately leads to war."

Phrase by phrase, sentence by sentence, the president had built up such a menacing behemoth that only an equally powerful response could be adequate—the invasion of Cuba. "Acting, therefore," said President Kennedy, "in the defense of our own security and of the entire Western Hemisphere, and under the authority entrusted to me by the Constitution as endorsed by the resolution of the Congress, I have directed..." Here it comes, I thought, the invasion and all its dreadful consequences. But no, what was he saying? "A strict quarantine on all offensive military equipment under shipment to Cuba is being initiated." Such ships would be turned back.

Relief flooded my being and I exclaimed, "Thank God!" Kennedy was going on, listing various diplomatic and military steps he was taking, but I wasn't really listening. I was standing up, waving my hands excitedly. . "Now," I said to Charlotte, "it's a minuet!" (It wasn't quite that simple, as Robert Kennedy would record in his account of the crisis, *Thirteen Days*, but intuitively I was on target. There would be no war. That Monday morning, informed of the quarantine by Dean Acheson, JFK's special envoy, General Charles de Gaulle, president of France, expressed his complete support. He added: "There will be no war." No war, but hard bargaining, including the removal of US nuclear missiles in Turkey. Ultimately, the shaping of the bargain was inherent in solving the crisis: the Soviet Union withdrew the missiles; the United States promised not to invade Cuba.)

Charlotte and I were suddenly in each other's arms, embracing. It was had not been love at first sight—indeed, it had taken a world crisis to get mutual attention—but the fire had been lit. Kennedy's speech had been like the book that ignited the love of Paolo and Francesca. According to Francesca's tale in Dante's *Inferno*, they were innocently reading about Lancelot and, when they looked at each other,

> La bocca mi bacio tutto tremante:
> Galeotto fu'l libro e chi lo scrisse;
> Quel giorno piu non vi leggemmo avante.

(Trembling, he kissed me:/ The book was to blame;/ We read no more.) That night of the speech, Charlotte and I went to bed together; in due time, we would be married.

——7——

Adrift

I murmur and wiggle in sheer sensual delight, the body lazily
stretching, indolent, relaxed as a cat. I cluck and chuckle, hum, sigh,
and smile as I am held enthralled, hallucinating. I am deep in a world of
exquisite colors, of intriguing patterns, ravishing juxtapositions. Actually,
I am not deep in this world, I *am* physically this world of color, a world
where color is a feeling and feelings are tactile. I am a vermillion line, an
arabesque capriciously traced on evanescent yellow; I am a swarm of
cunieform flicks dazzling white on deep magenta; I am a noble curve in
terracotta, like an arched equine neckline, edged with a crimson filigree,
and the filigree is pulsating like my blood is pulsating... so many feelings,
so many shadings...

"What are you feeling?" says the psychiatrist.

"Wonder," I say, my eyes closed. "Wonder and delight."

I open my eyes and instantly the hallucinations vanish. The darkened
room is familiar, the drawn draperies, the cool leather sofa. I tell him I
seem to become color, pattern, texture; how I feel the power of the drug
he has administered, lysergic acid diethylamide (LSD).

"Uneasy?" he asks. "Oh, no! Delighted! A child with a fistful of
circus tickets." He's walking to the hi-fi in the semi-obscurity. "Relax
now," he says. "Go with your feelings ... inside them."

Willingly, I relax, and the last thing I see as I close my eyes is the tiny
microphone pinned to the drapery above. My words, my grunts and
murmurs, my chuckles and my sighs are shimmying down the wire to
the whirring tape recorder. At times, during our sessions, we would refer
to the tapes to check exactly what I had said. When home, I wrote
copious notes.

Immersed in sensations, I barely notice that it's guitar music, steel strings twanging. I *am* that music, literally, music made flesh—female flesh in endless profusion; luscious thighs, abundant rumps, curves of clavicles and breasts, of odalisque bellies in yielding languor... a carnal carnival.

Abruptly, this largesse of sensuality is transmuted into a tapestry of baby feet, with tiny puckered toes and delicate palms, pink, enticing, with a feeling of infinite tenderness, infinite solicitude. Again, not something observed: I *am* the flesh and the feelings simultaneously. Feelings are incarnated, not as metaphor, but actually, with enormous immediacy ... and yet, and yet—some part of the mind remains observant, detached. It is an incredible drug, this LSD.

This was my second session of three, each scheduled a week apart. The psychiatrist, Dr. James Watts, had spent seven years using LSD in institutions but had found the regulations too restrictive and set up in private practice. His medical degree gave him legal access to LSD (a year later, LSD could only be legally used in accredited institutions). He required a one-hour interview to determine whether I was a suitable patient. I had sketched in my background—jail, family, writing, filmmaking. Dr. Watts took only creative people who had difficulty with their work, and did not consider himself a therapist. He was a guide to the exploration of the self, and only worked with individuals he deemed strong enough to withstand unpleasant discoveries. The sessions lasted from eight to ten hours, beginning at 8:00 in the morning with a break for a walk at 3:00. The first session was to calibrate the dosage, as the drug must be used with great caution.

The guitar music gives way to another piece, a composition with flute and orchestra. I have a happy, springtime feeling of *Wanderjahre*, of green meadows and Norwegian *skaters*—skimpy mountain pastures. There is a feeling of footloose roaming, with a hint of young medieval scholars wandering around Europe, sipping wisdom here and there... all this not in images but in actuality: I *am* the mountain pasture, the sky, the scholar. "The eternal scholar," I murmur, and hear the psychiatrist chuckle.

The melody has a lilt like the Arkansas Traveler, and the flute amuses itself, the magic touch of a Pied Piper. The orchestra takes up a counterpoint, the flute answers, and, as the dialogue goes on, the music—*which is me*—imperceptibly changes until the gaiety disappears. The undertones are somber, the scholar has matured, oppressed by knowledge... it is an austere feeling, reminiscent... "A Faustian feeling," I say and the psychiatrist queries: "What?" I repeat: "Faustian... something about Faust..." "Go with it, " he says firmly. "Deep. Explore."

I try. The somber undertones swell up, looming, and the feeling is forbidding, cold, threatening—a feeling of cowled monks, of shut-in Hanseatic façades, of jutting gargoyle spouts... "Cavernous," I am saying, "tenebrous..." I open my eyes: once again, there's the room, the psychiatrist. "Tenebrous," I repeat, "is there such a word? In Italian *tenebre* means dark shadows." He doesn't answer; perhaps he doesn't know. I sit up, light a cigarette, so does he. In the flare of the match, I see his intent features, then the face recedes into the shadows. *Tenebre.*

* * *

I was there because I could not cope with a serious depression. In the five months since my emotional upheaval, I had gone about my work like an automaton, unable to face the criticisms of the two women who knew me best. Eve and Edith both accused me of indifference and of a stultifying sexism. I thought wryly that my sins had not affected their ruthless decisions. Eve said that I didn't appreciate her writing, whereas Leonard Lewin, the man for whom she had left me, couldn't find words enough to praise it. My praise, I countered, was in publishing her work. Cold and composed, Eve refused to listen, refused to be drawn into any discussion.

Edith was more emotional: I treated her like an invalid, robbed her of her independence; she wanted me out. "With you around," she said, "I can't breathe." Eve was not mentioned, nor do I believe she was a major factor in Edith's feelings, but one rejection triggered the other. I felt ill-used. I could not deny there was a degree of truth in their indictment, yet of all the men I knew, I considered myself the least sexist. Virtues had become sins, however. My solicitude for Edith's plight was seen as stifling; concern for Eve's work was seen as derogation. Some friends on the left saw me as a man of callous selfishness. "Let's face it, Carl," said Ring Lardner over a drink, "you're the heavy." (Ring and Frances Lardner remained friends with both of us.) I also received unexpected support from my mother.

Mamma had been visiting Italy and returned in March. I dreaded telling her that Edith and I were separated—whatever the pros and cons, she would think I was selfish and disloyal. Almost fifty years old, I felt like a child. I met her at the airport; as I drove to the Triboro Bridge, I summoned up the courage to tell her. There was silence; then, "I wondered how long it would take you to rebel." Perplexed, I said: "What do you mean?" "It must have been hard on you," said mother. "But, mamma, she's ill." She shrugged and we dropped the matter. The sense of intimacy made me bold: "Mamma," I said, "why didn't you ever remarry?" She gave me a sidelong glance, a glint of coquetry in her eyes. As a child of five I had seen that glance in my handsome mother of twenty-two. Usually, but not always, it had been directed at my father. Now she said: "Don't think I haven't had offers." I was sure she had and said so. "I loved your father very much," she declared, with great simplicity. "He was a man, a good man, and no one I ever met came close to him. Not that there was much to choose from."

Mother's approbation made my depression more bearable, but inside my skin I didn't want to feel better. In Catholic doctrine, one of the cardinal sins is accidie, a state of not caring. "It became a favorite ecclesiastical word," says the *Oxford English Dictionary*, "applied primarily to the mental prostration of recluses." Its synonyms are *sloth* and *sluggishness*, but they do not carry the flavor of suspension in a void. There was no zest, no pleasure in any activity—reading a newspaper, dinner with my friend Anne, playing with her boy, Josh. I went through the motions of existence listlessly, giving little thought to the forthcoming Cuban invasion.

* * *

Anne had a friend, a composer, whose work had been blocked by a depression. This woman's three sessions with Dr. Watts had helped her greatly, and she was enthusiastic about LSD. The drug, she said, seems to weaken or remove inhibitions so that unconscious feelings rise to consciousness. LSD doesn't change feelings and sensory impressions: it only heightens them. She lent me a book on the subject, the *Joyous Cosmology* by Alan S. Watts (no relation). It has an introduction by two scientists who attempt to describe LSD and similar drugs: "It is easier to say what they are not. They are not narcotics, not intoxicants, not energizers, not anesthetics, not tranquilizers. They are, rather, biological keys which unlock experiences which are shatteringly new to most Westerners."

Dr. Watts underscored the point: "Their general effect is to sharpen the senses to a supernormal degree. The drugs appear to give a strong impetus to the creative intuition." Dr. Watts shied from words like "therapy" or "therapist." "I cure nothing," he said in our preliminary interview. "Most people I have taken on have been helped, and I can say truthfully that even in the least successful cases the depression has been

alleviated. But I promise nothing, except an honest run for your money."
He would help open doors, he said, but only those doors which I had
discovered. He scrupulously avoided putting ideas in my head, or words
in my mouth.

* * *

When I said I had a "Faustian" feeling, he said, "What do you mean?"
"I don't know," I said. "It just came." He chided me mildly. "It's your
word... Something within you." "I guess an association with scholar," I
said. "By the way, why did you chuckle at the word?" "It was a unique
response to the music. Don't change the subject. When you said 'eternal
scholar,' that phrase corresponded to your feelings?" "Oh, very." "And it
seems associated with Faust. Perhaps the Faustian feeling was there all
along?"

"But then why this forbidding feeling of austerity. Faust wanted
knowledge; to me, that's attractive."

"There are many aspects to Faust. What comes to your mind?"

"Intellectual ambition... Selling your soul to the devil for unlimited
knowledge. Isn't that it?"

"We want *your* interpretation. How well do you know *Faust?*"

"Not too well—read it once thirty years ago. Got some images...
Faust as an alchemist, black robe, retorts, a black cat... Mephisto and
Faust riding a barrel of wine through the air. And there's a girl."

"There may be a great deal more in your subconscious. When your
feelings well up, you say, 'Faustian.' I ask, what do you mean? You say
'nothing.' Then you dig and come up with overwhelming ambition,
selling his soul for knowledge. You said it—not I."

His words find resistance inside me. "You mean that's me, that my
eyes are too big for my stomach?" "I don't know," he said simply. "But
Goethe says Faust sold his soul for youth and the girl." I have nothing
to say, and he speaks: "Let it rest for now."

He puts on another record. I obey for the moment, close my eyes, and
listen. (The next day, at home, I looked up my *Faust* and Dr. Watts was
right. Reading on, at the end of the Prologue I found a charming close.
Mephisto is talking about God: "I like to see the Old Man when I'm
bored,/ and have a care to be most civil./ It's really kind of such a noble
lord/ to be so human, talking to the devil.") The record is of slow,
reflective music—violins, a cello, a piano. There is a feeling of water, sea,
and fishermen; I am sinking unresisting into that sea, my dark brown
body into the dark brown sea alongside long dark nets, lead weights

stretching them, deforming squares into rhomboids. Everywhere the brown fishes pass in review, aimless, meandering. The whole is a brown study, sand color to sepia to a brown-black, a little light filtering through. I am that totality. I am the many fishermen—a coarseness of hands, a stubble of unkempt beards, eyes brooding in crinkled eyesockets; I am the nets—the frayed twine and the patches of new cord, tiny knots tight; the pulling and stretching of the inexorable sea; I am the sea—the sepia sea, the scrotum-tightening sea; I am the fishes, indolent, inquisitive. I am everything wrapped in a sepia feeling and it is sad, so sad, so indescribably sad...

"Go with it," says the psychiatrist.

"Sad, sad," I murmur. "So bereft." The feeling is squeezed, intensified, an emotional plasma in a fantastic magnetic field and I am weeping, weeping ... It is all the Ash Wednesdays and all abandoned children and wing-crippled birds and deserted lovers... forlorn, forlorn—the word tolls despair, the end of the world. Sobs are clawing at my chest and throat, wild sobs tearing my guts ... "Oh, doctor, doctor," I seek comfort and a reprieve. I need time, time to work and not to die "before my hand has gleaned my teeming brain." To die is such a waste, such a pity, such an injustice: "It isn't fair," I burst out. "It just isn't fair." It's not a human cry but the ululation of a dog in pain. I regain a little control, and repeat dully, helplessly: "It just isn't fair."

Suddenly it is over. I open my eyes, there is the room. The episode has lasted seconds, minutes, I cannot tell. LSD plays havoc with the sense of time. I light a cigarette. I am wet with perspiration. I tell Dr. Watts how I feel and he says: "Let's go for a walk."

It is early afternoon. I have been under the drug five hours. I feel its influence waning, a great but not unpleasant lassitude. Things—trees, colors, faces, textures—have a clarity, a sweet freshness. The psychiatrist produces two gorgeous sun-ripened peaches from a paper bag, and we sit on the stoop, eating them.

We amble along Central Park. He plucks a leaf and holds it to the light; the minute tracery of the veins has an incredible distinctness. The bark of a sycamore is velvety to the touch, dappled browns and grays shading into a sensuous tapestry. A stone wall has tiny shells embedded in it from forgotten geological eons, and the tips of my fingers explore them as a blind man touches a face. Casually the doctor asks: "Have you ever wept like that before?" "Oh, yes," I say. "Once when I was seven or eight in a Catholic retreat. In my young teens, fresh in America, frustrated at being beaten by other kids. Again, when my father died."

Our dialogue is amiable but serious. He doesn't push and his questions seem random but he won't be sidetracked. When I digress, he gives me a little leeway, then quietly reins me in. His questioning is skillful, the words adroit in never leading, but always searching. He does introduce a distinction between needs and claims. You love someone dearly, a common example, and you think the intensity of your love will make the other person reciprocate... but we all know that is not so. Your *need* to have your love returned is legitimate, but your *claim* to be loved is spurious. I find the concept valid but irrelevant. He concentrates on three phrases I've used: Faustian feeling, eternal scholar, it isn't fair. He emphasizes that these are my own expressions—no input from him—and my interpretations: Faust is ambitious, knowledge and scholarship are the roads to pleasure and happiness, and justice or "fairness" is somehow related to these two attitudes.

We talk a lot as we amble and sit, sit and amble, for three hours. There are long pauses. I am the talkative one, and I finesse obvious resistances. We manage to see nebulous connections among my feelings by the time we return to the office and Anne comes for me. (Watts won't let patients go home alone; bemused by their experiences, they often pay no attention to traffic.) During the following days, ideas, feelings, reminiscences churn, clarify, jell into a semblance of wholeness.

My identity, my psychic structure, seems to regard knowledge as the *summum bonum*, gained best through the printed page. Books have the greatest amount of oxygen, but articles, news items, labels on cans—all written words contribute. To a lesser extent so do dialogue, relationships, the minutiae of manual craftsmanship. To seek knowledge is the scholar's pleasure; to use it for power is the Faustian ingredient. That entails recognition by the world around me, and such was the case throughout my childhood, youth, and maturity. My need was satisfied, and this need for recognition insensibly became a claim to recognition. When reality intervened, I found life unfair.

Beginning with my trial (at age thirty-five), I had boxed myself into an insoluble position: I wanted to change society drastically; yet, unconsciously, I also wanted the Establishment to welcome my activities. I remembered Edith's amusement at my anger over the trial: I was out to eliminate the good life of judge and prosecutor and was surprised when they were ruthless in defending it.

I said all this to Dr. Watts at our third session. I also remarked that neither Eve's nor Edith's rejections had made themselves felt in my ruminations, not even obliquely. He said, "That's true. Why do you think that is?" Perhaps, I said, once their rejection was seen as part of deeper problems, its importance faded. I asked what he thought about my interpretation of my feelings. Speaking as an observer, he said, my analysis made sense. He thought it likely that, given a stronger dosage, my unconscious might have something to say about it.

He gave me the LSD, and I ended up with a stunning experience. The session started mildly enough. He put on a record of an African chant, with a rhythmic drum and soft voices. I respond directly, no images, the drum beat in my loins, the voices an enveloping feeling of femininity. There is no eroticism; the sexuality is abstract, a lingam–yoni rarefied cult. Then I am off, a fish streaking up from ocean depths, a blade of grass breaking ground, a rotating, roaring column of fire, a jet-driven rocket up, up, up, as if I'm leaving earth forever, but... but simultaneously deep in the pit of my stomach a sense of hunger holding me down, a broad pectoral muscle holding me to the ground, tenacious. I am both soaring and restrained, the two feelings fused in a sense of enormous strength, of creative power, of making babies, houses, books, societies... anything!

All along, I've been pouring out my feelings in an unimpeded stream of words and the voice of the psychiatrist, aloof and serene, is saying: "This is you, these are your feelings..." Of course they are, I feel like saying as I open my eyes, and my conscious mind is happy. This feeling of self-confidence is what I had lost and here I have it. Dr. Watts does not challenge or disagree with my conclusion; on the contrary, he re-iterates that we are dealing with my whole being. I respond by playing the devil's advocate: how do we know I am not kidding myself? "Take my word for it," he says, "the unconscious does not operate that way. Moreover there is the corroboration of your dreams."

It is almost noon and Dr. Watts suggests we try another record before going out. I lie down again and think about the role of my dreams. LSD affects dreams in several ways: thy seem to be more numerous, they are more vivid, and they are more lasting. It is much easier to write them down as Dr. Watts has requested. We discuss them. Some are obvious, others more oblique. Here are two examples. I am covering a shed with cedar siding, one-by-six tongue-and-groove. I fit the boards carefully and the job goes on and on, which seems peculiar since the shed is a small one. But I am not concerned: I know the job will end and I work contentedly.

An oblique dream follows. A voice is insisting that I am lusting after my daughter. I deny it. The voice says: every father feels lust for his daughter; what makes you think you're different? You wouldn't be aware of it, your censor wouldn't let you. This makes sense and I try to explore my feelings, visualize my daughter. She is eighteen, long-legged, curvaceous, with red hair. I can see how she would be sexually attractive—but not to me. I'm glad she's lovely and I wish her well. The opposing voice insists I make myself a chastity belt with two strips of brown wrapping paper and some safety pins. I put one strip around me like a belt, the other under my crotch and pinned... an ersatz loin cloth. I awaken feeling the silliness of the paper diaper, an absurd solution to a nonexistent problem.

In one way or another, my dreams restore my self-confidence. Either in a positive way—I'm getting my work done—or, negatively, by showing that the obstacles are not real. Feeling at peace, I close my eyes, hear the slight whir of the tape recorder, and I am off, immersed in colors that are a medley of soft pastels. Suddenly, I find myself hissing, a very soft, sibilant *sssssssssssss*, which shades into a sharper *zzzzzzzzzzzzzz*. There are no images, just a murky darkness and a sense of mystery. The hissing gets stronger, my teeth begin to chatter; as the chattering increases, my breathing gets faster, deeper. There is no mistaking what the hissing is, it's a wind, and I am that wind, rising in violence as if on a Beaufort scale, moving up, Force 1, Force 2, Force 3, and I feel certain it is going to be a hurricane, Force 12.

Another powerful feeling grips me: I am the rigging of a sailing ship—the masts, the yards, halyards, and stays, all the cordage straining, the sails furled... a loose end snapping, the ship scudding before the wind with bare poles, creaking, shaking. The murky darkness is clearly a night of storm. I am the whole, the totality, wind and night and ship— a battered, tormented world of poles and ropes driven to the uttermost limits of resilience. I am the force and the forced, the driven and the driving, the lash and the endurance.

The tempest grows. Force 10, Force 11; the eye of the hurricane expands and I am gasping. Air, air, I need air. I must have oxygen... I feel on the verge of nothingness, of annihilation. "Ride it!" I hear myself saying. "What did you say?" says the doctor. "Ride it!" I half shout, fiercely. I feel my shoulders hunching as if to use my fists, muscles tightening, and from my gut the repeated cry: "Ride it! Ride it!" The hurricane is merciless, but I am unafraid, inviolate. I gulp; air rushes into my lungs. I open my eyes, sit up. "Phew," I say, and we go out to walk and talk, each of us quietly rejoicing.

* * *

From my notes, in a week, I wrote up my experience—forty pages. I sent them to *Esquire* magazine. A month later, an editor wrote that he liked the article but that it is too long: would I cut it in half? I know cutting won't work; I would have to rewrite a shorter version and doubted it could have the same impact. I said to hell with it, feeling cocky. A Churchillian quip about Field Marshal Viscount Montgomery of El Alamein seemed to fit my mood—allowing for the difference in stature between a minnow and a marlin. Churchill said of Montgomery: "In defeat, indomitable; in victory, insufferable."

—8—

Fare Politica

The 1950s had been hard years for the American left, isolated as it was from mainstream Eisenhower America. But the upheavals of the 1960s galvanized the left. The decade began with the disaster of the Bay of Pigs, followed by the terrifying thirteen days of the missile crisis. Then, in the space of five years, the country saw the assassination of a president followed by that of his brother, a would-be president. And finally, there was the murder of a great leader of the black people. All this was played out against the background of the ever-expanding Vietnam War, a period that climaxed with President Johnson refusing to run again. Rarely has so much drama been packed into so few years.

By a quirk of fate, my personal life was comparatively tranquil. The two years 1959 and 1960, starting with Prometheus Paperbacks and ending with JFK's election, were pivotal in rekindling my interest in the Cold War. Not that it had ever really waned; rather, it had been put on a back burner. Through my work on *Inside the Khrushchev Era*, I got a flavor of Khrushchev as an outspoken, gregarious type who reminded me of many American politicians; indeed, when he did arrive in the United States, I was not disappointed. His temperament put the American Establishment in a tizzy: he wanted to meet as many people as possible; the Establishment wanted, as far as it was able, to restrict the number. The result was a constant seesaw, which caused much amusement among people in the know. Every time Khrushchev made a speech or said anything, the Establishment would produce a commentator, an academician, or an expert of some kind to weaken or refute whatever Khrushchev had said.

It is difficult to assess Khrushchev's overall impact on the general population, but clearly he improved on acquaintance. We tend to forget that scattered throughout the American people there are many groups and individuals who are not fond of the profit system. In any case, the lessening of tension was all to the good, and I even began to think that some thawing might take place in the glacial relationship between the two superpowers.

We are talking politics. Political activity is a highly important function, half art, half profession—as much a part of the humanities as is the law. The master politicians of our times, in my opinion, were Franklin Roosevelt and Palmiro Togliatti. Togliatti was cofounder and general secretary of the Italian Communist Party (PCI) and the initiator of Eurocommmunism. He used a phrase, *fare politica*, which meant anything from local politics to the strategic stratosphere of a Bismark. (One of Togliatti's private jokes was that he survived Stalinism because "I stayed out of politics. I was the expert on literature." He continued the private joke when asked about setting up a new government: "I did a little editing, adding a word or two." He had inserted the word "Constituent" before the word "Convention," which meant that instead of the Convention taking place under the old Constitution, the Convention itself was going to make a new Constitution. *La Constituente* is Togliatti's legacy to modern Italy.) *Fare politica* implies counterintelligence—finding out what the opposition is up to—by paying attention both to set speeches and to slips of the tongue. Some things are so big that they cannot be hidden, but need to be explained away. I have in mind specifically the NATO maneuvers of June 1955 and of February 1960, which I was writing about in my book with Victor Perlo, *Dollars and the Sense of Disarmament*. The 1955 maneuver was called *Carte Blanche*; the 1960 maneuvers, somewhat smaller, were known as *Winterhelfen* and were specifically designed to find out as much as possible about nuclear weapons. In both cases it became clear that military installations could not be separated from civilian targets, due to the speed of modern warplanes. Most important was the fact that no one would dream of waging nuclear war because the devastation would be so enormous. (Of course, that does not include the ineffable Dr. Kissinger, whose reaction was: we must learn to make clean bombs, and teach the Russians how to make them.)

June 1960 was the twenty-fifth anniversary of my graduation from Williams College. Usually at reunion gatherings time is spent reminiscing and joking. But on this occasion, partly because I was there, partly because a couple of our classmates were history professors, and partly because Dick Helms was then a high official of the CIA, there was a lot of talk and discussion about nuclear war. With NATO's nuclear maneuvers fresh in my mind, I declared that nuclear war was unthinkable. I argued that the real military power of the United States did not depend on nuclear weapons but on the skills, freedom, and independence of its citizens. A huge nation such as ours need not fear anyone if its house were in order.

It is customary at a twenty-fifth reunion that the president of the class give the main speech. Dick Helms spoke for the class of '35. I was surprised and pleased that the tone of Dick's speech followed my line of argument. It was not that I had convinced him, but rather that he was thinking along similar lines. After Dick finished, he walked down the center aisle. When he saw me, he gave me a wide grin, leaned over, put his hand on my arm, and said: "Check out?" And I said: "Check out."

John F. Kennedy was about to be nominated, and he was bound to have his own ideas if only because of his comparative youth. It was my opinion that he would have a hard time getting elected and that a few hundred thousand votes might make the difference. Most people on the left were not inclined to vote for Kennedy: though they hated Nixon, they didn't trust JFK's father, Joseph P. Kennedy. If JFK could send a signal that he had an open mind on the issue of disarmament, that alone might swing a lot of left votes. I read that Arthur Schlesinger, Jr., was involved in JFK's campaign, so I wrote him a note. I got back a courteous letter saying that newspapers had exaggerated his contribution to the campaign and that the man to see was Professor Archibald Cox (who would become the Watergate Special Prosecutor in the 1970s), that Arthur had spoken to him and that Cox was expecting my call. I called Cox, made an appointment, and went to Boston with the galleys of *Dollars and Sense of Disarmament.*

Cox agreed that it would be a very tight race. He wasn't sure I was right about the left's disaffection but was willing to consider my judgment that a signal from JFK would be useful. "Of course," said Cox, "it could also stimulate the opposition." I demurred: I thought the main issue nationwide was Catholicism and further that those who thought JFK too liberal had long opposed him. "Finally," Cox said, "my inclination is to do nothing. But I promise that the Senator will receive your suggestion, look over these galleys, and we'll be in touch." Five weeks later, I got a telegram from Cox saying, "My original opinion stands." All this confirmed for me an inner core of meaning: namely, that men of good will should be seeking solutions to the devil's trap—thermonuclear war.

* * *

Khrushchev's visit had whetted my appetite to see what was going on in the Soviet Union and Eastern Europe. Several of my books had been translated in various countries—Hungary, Romania, a Slovak television adaptation of *The Survivor*—and I had a lot of royalties which had to be spent over there. In September 1960 I spent two weeks in Moscow and another week in Eastern Europe.

Even in such a short period of time I was impressed by the widespread affection for American people—not for the government, but for the country, our literature, our humor, and our way of life. I was surprised at the number of Russians in influential positions who had studied for a degree in the United States. This was less the case in the other socialist countries.

I found that in Romania one of the members of the Politburo, Andrei, was reading my translation of *The Open Marxism of Antonio Gramsci*. In Moscow I was surprised how cramped the living space was. The translator of my book, the widow of the noted Soviet composer Dmitri Kabelevsky, had a kitchen, a bedroom, and a living/dining room, the largest of which was about ten square foot. It was on this trip that I saw the dying Gerhart Eisler and asked him what he had learned in his long life. He whispered, "I learned how hard it is to build socialism."

Because of the great interest in America I told many stories about my experiences over the past couple of years. For example, I told them about Helms's speech. I told them about George F. Kennan and how he had begun to change his mind about American–Soviet relations. Walter Lippman had also been more conciliatory towards the Soviet Union. The support of other comrades in the various countries I had visited would contribute greatly to my self-confidence.

*　*　*

One pleasant surprise in the countries I visited was the number of people who received *Monthly Review*, which was running at the time a series of three articles (September, October, November 1960) by the editors on "A Theory for American Foreign Policy." (I had carried the September and October issues with me to Moscow, and I read the November issue in Bucharest. This coincidence was useful because I was able to discuss the material with like-minded people in all the countries I visited.) To my surprise I found myself in disagreement with Leo Huberman and Paul Sweezy, the editors of *Monthly Review*. While they were far better grounded in Marxism than I was, our orientation was generally similar when it came to analyzing events or trends. Our disagreement, when it surfaced, though, turned out to be sharp and insoluble.

The first two articles and half the third were devoted to an examination of U.S. diplomatic defeats. These defeats in the United Nations and around the world had few repercussions among the American people. The editors and I agreed, for example, that what Syngman Rhee, the strong man of South Korea, did had very little influence on American domestic affairs. If foreign problems did not fill the television screen, few people paid any attention. The power of the media and of the system as a whole obscured these diplomatic failures. An exception was during the Korean War when the Chinese Red Army routed General MacArthur in a long-drawn-out and disastrous defeat, which could not be kept from the television screens.

(I have often speculated that if the Establishment were a small enough body, say a Council of Seven, they might, when faced with disaster, all have a simultaneous heart attack and give the population a chance to set the house in order. But when the power of the Establishment is actually the sum total of thousands of individuals, no such simple solution offers itself. What can be expected is a swift rallying around a reasonable explanation: in the case of the Korean rout, for example, it could all be blamed on General MacArthur.)

The string of American diplomatic defeats and setbacks in the Third World was very real and undoubtedly caused much amusement among the foreign offices of the world, but had very little impact on the economy. In fact during this period, American investments and profits in the Third World increased considerably.

The editors of *Monthly Review* had a much wider acquaintance than I, so it was a surprise to read: "the American ruling class is not only unwilling to face the implications of fundamentally altering its foreign policy; it is not even capable of understanding why its present policy is failing… the implications of this analysis are unfortunately all too clear: the United States is going to plunge along its present disastrous international course, suffering defeat after defeat, *even after these defeats have begun to inflict increasingly direct and serious losses on the giant corporations that dominate American life*" (the stress is that of the editors).

I interpreted this to mean that the editors of *Monthly Review* believed that the mind-set of American corporations was so rigid that they were incapable of change. I strongly disagreed. While there were thousands of shortsighted corporate men, there were also many of high intelligence able to analysis the economy as a whole. I did not believe such people would allow the economy to self-destruct without trying to do something about it.

From its inception, I have almost always been attuned to the thinking of *MR*. Its editors have become my friends and I have written articles for the magazine. Our sharp difference of opinion over the theory of American foreign policy was most unusual. The editors of *Monthly Review* wrote:

> Where will it all end?
> One possibility is economic collapse.
> Present-day monopoly capitalism is essentially an international system. It needs a big "free world" to live in. If its living space progressively contracts, and if its present structural characteristics were to remain unchanged, a crisis comparable in scope and severity to that which overtook the capitalist world in the early 1930's would be the logical outcome.
> Such a crisis, needless to say, would create an entirely new situation, about which there is no need to speculate here. Suffice it to say that the breaking of the spell of capitalist prosperity in their own right and not simply as support for this or that ruling class faction. If and when that day arrives we may begin to emerge from the nightmare world in which we are now condemned to live.

I did not believe that the ruling class was a monolith. I wrote in the January 1961 issue of *MR*:

> I think defeats are giving rise to a reconsideration of that [foreign] policy, to a division of opinion within ruling circles, and to the creation of a climate of opinion in the ruling class where such a change can take place, because, as stressed above, such a change is *objectively possible in their own* capitalist self-interest.
> ...Anti-Communism has been the main weapon of thought control in America, the main weapon for smashing left unions and bringing the rest into line, the main weapon to prevent a resurgence of political action. There is another obstacle, not mentioned by *MR*, which I think is also important, and that is the fear of the American ruling class that disarmament will release Soviet funds which can be used to increase Soviet influence in underdeveloped countries. All these reasons, including the economic reasons, are weighty and may perhaps turn out to be decisive, but this is not proven theoretically. I think, rather, that the weight of theory is on the side of the possibility of change.
> My own judgment is that there is an ever-developing split in the ruling class on the question of change in foreign policy.

The significance of this exchange is that it expressed my dissatisfaction with the existing analysis of the Cold War.

* * *

The prevailing view among the left and moderates at this time was that there should be "peaceful coexistence," which implied low-level competition among the superpowers for the allegiance of Third World nations. It might be said, "You win one, you lose one, but no war." (I seem to recall an article to this effect by Professor Hans Morgenthau in the *New Republic*.) That formulation always left me a little uneasy; it sounded more like competition than coexistence. Even the slogan "peaceful coexistence" sounded a little tired. Many books had been written on the subject, but very few new ideas developed. I thought there should be a sense of urgency because of the global environment, which was steadily deteriorating.

——9——

Assassination and Beyond

I was becoming increasingly interested in ecology. This interest was further developed by my acquaintanceship with Barry Commoner, who had moved with his family to Brooklyn and lived nearby. I had already read a good deal of his work. I would have lunch with Barry from time to time; at these meetings he would suggest books and articles of interest. I remember in particular an article in the *New Yorker* on supertankers, some of which were so poorly designed (by computer) that they failed to float. Their sheer bulk when fully laden, and their size and behavior in the water, made them vulnerable to the destrctive power of violent storms. Once damaged and at the mercy of the sea, they would break up and send rivers of oil into the ocean, causing incalculable damage to marine wildlife and destroying the food chain.

The environment was being increasingly polluted. In my view the problem could only be dealt with on a cooperative national and international basis. (Some years later I wrote *The Wounded Earth*, an environmental survey for young adults.) It was clear that a policy stronger than the current one of peaceful coexistence was needed.

Among the many factors impelling me to write, the response I had received from Archibald Cox ranked high. It showed that the new, young president was directly accessible on many subjects that were important to me. I felf strongly that the environment was such a subject and that in due course, when it became coupled with major issues of foreign policy, it would be recognized as crucial.

In truth, I became a bit euphoric, as if my new manuscript was already in the hands of JFK. The working title reflected my optimism: *A Text for President X*. I circulated mimeographs of the manuscript among thoughtful people such as Carey McWilliams of the *Nation*, John Kenneth Galbraith (a friend of Paul Sweezy), and Professor Frederick Schuman. Among the suggestions and corrections I received, a new title emerged: *Peaceful Co-Revolution*.

The opening chapter was titled "The Population Explosion," as the most effective way of drawing in the reader. Many population trends are both dramatic and encourage a sense of despair. For example, what happens to a town of 50,000 people in Latin America which doubles its size in twelve years? What is the effect on its schools, hospitals, jobs? When Chapter 1 was finished we made thirty mimeograph copies and laid them out on a long table. I reflected that the piles looked impressive. I was pleased with my work to date. As I picked up a bundle and skimmed through it, I felt I had made a solid connection between foreign policy in the abstract and what was happening to people in towns and villages around the globe. It seeemed to me a wise decision to have approached diplomacy through the environment.

* * *

My feeling of euphoria about the book suddenly seemed ridiculous when the radio announced that the young president had been shot. It would be a long time before the mimeograph machine would be used again.

In the hours following the assassination the news had a steadying effect: the man who shot the president had been caught, his name was Lee Harvey Oswald, he worked as a clerk in the Texas Book Depository, and he seemed clearly deranged. But, with so many news investigators on the trail, discrepancies began to appear which were, to say the least, puzzling. I will not rehearse these here, as they have been so well documented over the years. Suffice to say that question of whether Oswald could have been on the sixth floor of the Texas Book Depository at the time of the shooting kept me running up and down our office building stairs, stopwatch in hand, to the great amusement of my staff. Thoughts and suppositions about the case filled my mind for some long while.

The Oswald case quickly became one of the great unsolved mysteries of my generation. In Great Britain, a book appeared titled, *Who Killed Kennedy?* This was followed, in America, by a manuscript on the case by Joachim Joesten, questioning some of the earlier assumptions. I got hold of a copy of this manuscript; while it was very speculative, it nevertheless seemed to me worthwhile. Marzani & Munsell duly published it as *Oswald: Assassin or Fall Guy?* It was the first book published on the assassination. After the release of the Warren Commission report, Joesten wrote a short analysis of the Commission's work. This we published as *The Gaps in the Warren Report*. (The second edition of *Oswald: Assassin or Fall Guy?* included this material.)

I will add minor footnote to history. At a small dinner-party reunion of our class around this time, Dick Helms was asked to say a few words. Since he was at that time deputy director of the CIA, he couldn't say much. What he did say was that "I want you know we're all honorable men." Considering this was the time the CIA was exploring ways of assassinating Castro, it might be considered that Helms was stretching unacceptably the meaning of his chosen adjective. Perhaps, however, he was using the word "honorable" to indicate that there were no rogue elephants inside the CIA—that is, people acting on their own.

* * *

I eventually returned to the work of completing *Peaceful Co-Revolution*; to the long table where Chapter 1 had been accumulating dust. I developed my arguments chapter by chapter; the piles on the table grew. Finally, after several weeks of hard work, mimeographed copied of the finished manuscript took up the entire length of that long table. The time had come to circulate it to a broader audience. Some I knew wouldn't read it—Arthur Schlesinger, Jr., Walt Rostow, George Ball, McGeorge Bundy. Others I knew would read it and give me feedback: Cedric Belfrage, Jack McManus, Tabitha Petran. Copies also went to Marxist academicians, such as Professor Dirk Struik of MIT. Finally, the manuscripts went to friends, such as my doctor, Percy Brazil, and Joel Rothman, who had printed the *UE Steward*. The bulk of the manuscripts, though, were sent to people across the country who shared my interests; these individuals included Bill Glazer, legislative representative for Harry Bridges of the Longshoreman's Union, and Al Pezzati, treasurer of the Mine, Mill and Smelter Union. As with the first draft, I enclosed a note with the manuscript, urging the reader to send comments. I thought of it as a poll on the central idea: that the United States should accept land reform, and that revolutionaries should accept the middle class.

Within a few days, the responses started coming in. Only one person said I was crazy. No one shared my optimism, however, with the possible exceptions of Brazil and Rothman. A particularly thoughtful response came from Staughton Lynd: feasible, but improbable, was his verdict in a nutshell. Frederick Schuman wrote: "A great contribution. God bless you, Carl." Cedric Belfrage was very positive and, good editor that he was, practically rewrote the manuscript.

Overall I was encouraged by the feedback. Most people thought I had a good idea that could never be carried through. In light of the comments and criticism, I did further work, strengthening the manuscript.

* * *

My work was becoming increasingly intertwined with personal affairs. Indeed, I was getting married. Ever since the missile crisis brought Charlotte and me together, it was abundantly clear that we were well matched. Still, our first four years constituted a rather zany courtship. At the beginning, it was all business. Charlotte worked on many projects at Marzani & Munsell, the most notable being *A Quarter Century of Un-Americana*. Working with her I grew to appreciate her delightful wit. I remember on one occasion we found a dead mouse, which Charlotte immortalized:

> TO A BABY MOUSE FOUND
> DEAD IN THE TOP LEFT-
> HAND DRAWER OF MARZANI &
> MUNSELL, PUBLISHERS:
>
> Sad inelegant death
> of a wee little mouse,
> To have breathed your last breath
> in a left-wing book house.
> Had you not run amok
> on a radical tandem,
> You might have, with luck,
> died at Knopf—or at Random!

Charlotte, now in her mid-thirties, wanted children. I liked the idea; however, I was fifty-four and could barely support myself on the what I made at Marzani & Munsell. It was clear that if Charlotte and I married, I would have to find a better source of income. We decided that I should ask her father for her hand in marriage.

Abraham L. Pomerantz was one of the stars of the New York Bar. Although he charged huge fees in the corporate world, he was notorious for declaring in court that he was a socialist. He had recently been asked to serve on the Advisory Committee to the Supreme Court. When I appeared at his office, he knew something was up and said to his secretary, "No phone calls." His duly gave his blessing, adding, "Well, eighteen years is not too big a difference" (Charlotte and I had never given it any thought). The wedding date was set for November 12, 1966.

Well before that time, however, in March and April, we had started looking for a place to live. I had learned that to be rent-free in

Manhattan, you must remodel two brownstones. The first thing was to settle on a neighborhood, to avoid looking for brownstones over the entire metropolitan area. We could not afford real estate in Greenwich Village. However, north of the Village, in the twenty-block stretch from 14th Street to 34th Street, the area known as Chelsea, the situation was more promising. It had mixed working-class and professional residents, good public schools, an artistic community and busy streets (which police will always tell you makes a neighborhood safer). So we went looking for two brownstones. We ended up with four.

—10—

Oh No,
Not a Landlord!

We arranged the purchase of four contiguous, dilapidated brown stones built aa hundred years ago, all on the verge of being condemned by the city (of the five stories in each house, there was only one functioning toilet). We rehabilitated these buildings and created thirty-seven modern, fireproof apartments, including one with a big backyard for us. The role of landlord did not fit people's image of Carl Marzani. I did not think of myself as a landlord, of course. I was just building my own home. Nevertheless, I could not blink away the other thirty-six apartments which made possible our own.

Buying old brownstones and renovating them was a fairly simple business. I had already done it twice successfully. The first step was to pay 10 percent of the selling price to the previous owner—in our case, this was $18,000, which used up the bulk of our savings (Charlotte had about $12,000 in stocks from her grandparents and I had been accumulating rents from the property on Fire Island). Having managed the down payment, the key to success was to obtain a construction loan from a bank. This would be paid out as the work progressed and turn into a regular mortgage when the construction work was finished. The big hitch was that the bank insisted that at least one house be empty of tenants. Organizing this could take many months and hold up the work; it was here that my left instincts came in useful.

The houses were SROs, single-room occupancies. Leaks in the roof meant there were few tenants on the top floor. I had what I hoped was a workable idea. We bought the houses on a Friday; on the Saturday I called a meeting of all the tenants to put to them what I hoped was a mutually beneficial solution. The reaction that followed was typically

Manhattan: what was my game, and how was I planning to take advantage of them? The moment I said that I would collect no more rents, they thought there was a catch. I went to great lengths to explain that I needed to begin renovations immediately and I was therefore willing to forego the rents in order to empty the first building. My proposition was that if people would move out of the first house into one of the others, they could live rent free—and we would eventually find them new apartments. Slowly it all pulled together and on the Sunday the first house was emptied.

On Monday, a wrecking crew came in—four brawny men with their own truck. For $1,000 they gutted the first house except for the brick walls and the floor beams. As it turned out, a lot of the beams were rotten, but their replacement was inexpensive. A couple of blocks away, a 20-foot-wide brownstone (like ours) was being torn down, and I bought all their beams for $3 each. Then, with the assistance of two strong young men working a jackhammer, we replaced all the defective beams. By mid-June, when the bank came to inspect, it looked like a lot of work had been done. We got a big loan without any difficulty—$400,000—and I immediately hired a working crew. I put in fourteen-hour days and by Christmas Charlotte and I had an apartment on the ground floor of the first house. We had no heat or electricity, but we had plenty of heaters and we could take all the electricity we wanted from the next house.

As renovation proceeded, we were preparing for our marriage. Charlotte's brother Daniel and his wife Sally came from Massachusetts to be our witnesses at City Hall. In the afternoon, before a small gathering of family and friends, Angus Cameron read a secular wedding ceremony which he had written. (My dear unworldly mother confided in me later that she was disappointed that we did not have a priest, but was glad that at least we had a rabbi! I later teased Angus that he had just been promoted to Chief Rabbi of Scotland.) That night Charlotte's parents threw a wonderful reception at the National Democratic Club.

* * *

The national drama of the Vietnam War continued to unfold. I was in Washington in the summer of 1965 when there was a rumor that President Johnson had decided to send 165,000 troops to Vietnam. The "rumor" was of course a calculated leak, a way of breaking the news gently to the American public. There was no question about what was happening: the country was shifting from guerrilla warfare to conventional warfare, replete with artillery, tanks, and so on.

Marzani & Munsell had fought against the involvement in Vietnam from the beginning. We had launched a series of pamphlets titled *The Unspeakable War*, which were brought up to date every three or four months. They consisted almost entirely of the best photographs available. Among them was the famous one of a destroyed village, of which an air force major said: "We had to destroy the village in order to save it." At this time I was "commuting" between the Marzani & Munsell offices on 23rd Street and Sixth Avenue and the house renovation at 21st Street and Eighth Avenue. I became aware that I couldn't sustain a family with the pittance I made from running the publishing company. We continued to publish until December 1967, when fate intervened and our office was destroyed by fire.

Renovation constantly creates problems which demand solutions, so I was kept busy, but I was mindful that *Peaceful Co-Revolution* needed my attention. I had shown it to Angus Cameron, who thought it was definitely worth publishing. As a senior editor at Knopf he had sufficient authority to publish it; given his relationship with me, however, he wanted Mr. Knopf to read it. Months went by and Knopf still hadn't read it. Angus needled him once or twice, but he could not be too pushy. Finally, after nine months, Knopf informed Angus that he had passed the manuscript to a knowledgeable friend who thought the book had some interesting ideas but was not strong enough to warrant publication. I was deeply disappointed, yet could not fault Angus for proceeding as he had.

Then the gods seemed to smile: I was handed a second chance with another major publisher. This was due to a chance meeting with Hyram Hayden, senior editor at Harcourt Brace. I knew of Hayden as editor of the *Key Reporter*, a publication of the Phi Beta Kappa Society, and as one who had had editorialized and written in defense of civil liberties, but we had never met. It happened that in the summer of 1968 Charlotte's parents had taken a house on Martha's Vineyard. Charlotte and I took our little girl Gabrielle, who had been born in 1967, to visit her grandparents. As the ferry from the mainland was unloading, I found myself next to Hayden, a tall, somewhat lugubrious fellow whose smile turned him into a cheerful Goth. When I introduced myself he seemed delighted to meet me. He had come to help out at the local newspaper, *The Vineyard Gazette*, and suggested I stop by the office.

At lunch the following day I mentioned my manuscript of *Peaceful Co-Revolution* and my bad luck with Knopf. He said he'd like to see it. At lunch a week later Hayden told me that, while he found the manuscript very interesting, he could do very little about publishing it. He explained his relationship with Harcourt Brace: he could pick any ten manuscripts to be published provided there was one bestseller in the bunch. Hayden said that without that one bestseller the arrangement wouldn't last long. "It's perfectly obvious", he said, " that *Peaceful Co-Revolution* is not a potential bestseller and I cannot sacrifice one of my ten spots. However, I have talked it up, particularly with our new partner, Jovanovich, and he's reading it."

I later received a note from Hayden indicating Jovanovich liked the book and that I would probably hear from him. I therefore fully expected to meet Jovanovich, in preparation for which I proceeded to buy his just-published memoir *And Now, Barrabas*. As it turned out it was a waste of money, which I regret to this day, for I never heard from him (Hayden, for his part, had his hands full, starting a new publishing firm, Atheneum, together with Pat Knopf and Simon Besse.)

This personal setback would have hit me harder had I not been so overwhelmed by news of the resignation of President Johnson. The president announced that he would not be a candidate in 1968 because he was going to devote all his time to ending the war. He did not say that the war was lost, but his own actions indicated that this was so. What was notable was how the Establishment handled the resignation: they played down its importance.

Personal events of the time also served to mitigate my upset regarding the fate of my manuscript. Two wonderful moments stood out: the birth of our son Daniel Avram Marzani on February 19, 1969, and the completion of our living space in the spring. The renovation was finished; our family was complete. Marzani & Munsell had closed down but I had a way of earning a living: running a complex of four renovated houses with thirty-seven apartments was a a full-time job. I had help with the day-to-day problems in the person of John Lewis, a wonderful superintendent, who had an apartment in the building.

This idyllic situation was short-lived, however, for our little boy suffered a serious bout of asthma. We were advised that the climate of Puerto Rico might be beneficial, so we went down for a visit. We had hardly arrived at the hotel when we learned that my first wife, Edith, had died suddenly of a heart attack. We hurried back for the funeral. I was faced with the daunting task of speaking at Edith's service. I had to reconcile the feelings of Edith's conservative family and the fact of her radical life. How was I going to make a statement that would satisfy everyone? The solution I came up with was to "blame" Edith's Communism on the liberal upbringing in her home. I began my address by saying that although Nooney (the nickname of Edith's father) was a conservative, the family had been brought up with a sense of social responsibility. For example, Nooney was very involved with the Boy Scouts; Bobsey (her mother) belonged to several organizations concerned with settlement houses. There was a definite belief in the family that one should help. When the Depression broke, Nooney voted for FDR and Bobsey voted for Norman Thomas. Given that background, it was not altogether surprising that Edith joined the Communist Party. I considered my remarks at Edith's funeral a good example of *fare politica*.

—11—

Eurocommunism

When President Johnson announced that he would not be a candi
date for a second term, it was taken for granted that the end of
the Vietnam War was near. We had not, however, counted on the belli-
cosity of Henry Kissinger and his sense of imperial "honor." There had
to be peace with honor, and in the process the fighting would have to
continue. As Kissinger suggested various deals, and they were discussed,
the fighting went on, and the casualties kept piling up—twenty thousand
more dead to the Wall on the White House lawn. At the end, when the
Nobel Peace Prize was awarded jointly to Kissinger and his opposite
number in Vietnam, Le Duc Tho, Kissinger sleazily accepted it while
Vietnam contemptuously rejected it.

In practical family terms, my main concern at the time was Danny's
asthma. It turned out that the winter months in Puerto Rico were of
great benefit to him. So, given my building syndrome, we bought a
shack—a house by courtesy only. Mostly wood, ramshackle, with trees
growing inside and out, it looked more like the product of an earth-
quake. However, it did have a fine location, overlooking the Bay of
Guanica. I went to work with a will and in three months made it habitable. Money was scarce, so we rented our apartment in New York for the
winter months and the house in Puerto Rico for the summer.

The election of Nixon and the appointment of his henchmen boded
ill for civil liberties, and ushered in a period that came to be known as
"friendly fascism." I thought it would be wise to write a pamphlet about
it. The title of the pamphlet was *The Threat of American Neo-Fascism: A
Prudential Inquiry*. I outlined what Nixon could do (some of my suggestions he was already doing), but the thrust of my pamphlet was that if

the American people stayed alert, the danger of fascism could be contained. I had hoped that it would be published by Carey McWilliams as a special issue of the *Nation*; he did this from time to time and it had a great impact. We came close. The publishing committee was four people: two of them were in favor of publishing it and two were not. Carey wanted to do it, but one of the people who did not want it was the publisher, so that was the end of that.

As if to bolster my ego, however, I had a phone call from a writer, Vivian Gornick, who wished to interview me for her book, *The Romance of American Communism*. She had compiled a list of interesting people on the left who were getting along in years. It turned out that there was a movement of historians, sociologists, columnists, and journalists who were interested in what Communists did on a day-by-day basis, as compared to the people who wrote the big studies covering foreign policy, Soviet–American relations, and so on—what might be called the big guns of history. Of course oral history has its drawbacks and faults; however, the daily life of Communists is equally as interesting as all the big events in Soviet foreign policy. Some people did not want to be identified, so she gave everyone a pseudonym: mine was Eric Lanzetti. Working on the book helped to distract from Kissinger's various ploys to end the war, all of them involving more and more American casualties.

At about this time I began writing about George Orwell. For a very brief time he and I had been at the same front of the Spanish Civil War at the same time, although we had never met, so many veterans of the Brigade wanted me to write a pamphlet to counter the inaccurate account in Orwell's *Homage to Catalonia*. The worst slander in it was considered to be that the Republican premier Juan Negrin was Moscow's man. This of course was absolutely untrue, but it fed into the propaganda of the British and French appeasers. (Years later, in an article looking back on the "Spanish War" and in various letters, Orwell took back the charges about Negrin and other opinions on the Civil War. He wrote that the basic reason for the defeat was shortage of guns and artillery. Of course, these articles did not get the attention as *Homage to Catalonia*.) I started to do a little research and got intrigued by Orwell.

I spent years researching and writing about Orwell, and the manuscript grew to be so big that it was no longer a pamphlet. It still remains unpublished, and my work on George Orwell remains an aside in my writing.

* * *

In this period, a new concept had seized the headlines: Eurocommunism. There had been a national vote in Italy in which the right to divorce had been central. It had been assumed by those aligned with the Establishment that women would be against divorce. The Communists, though, ran on the opposite platform—and it turned out they knew women better than did the Establishment did. The Communist vote was enormous, about a third of the total. That made for a lot of news, and there arose a new emphasis on the term "Eurocommunism."

Eurocommunism represented a less rigid position than Soviet Communism. Such a position had in fact been taken in Italy since Togliatti returned at the end of the Second World War. Togliatti kept looking for ways to agree, rather than disagree, with other political parties. For example, at a time when the North Atlantic Treaty Organization was being regarded as an enemy by the left, Togliatti said: "But NATO says it is defensive, and we Communists are in favor of defensive actions, so there is no reason why we shouldn't join NATO," and added that if elected, they would not oppose Italy's membership. This can be seen as another instance of Togliatti's *fare politica*. The right-wingers didn't like his approach, but there was nothing they could do about it.

Eurocommunism, as its name implies, was the adaptation of European Communist parties to the impact of Stalin and of Khrushchev. The Italian Communist Party, based on the tenets of Antonio Gramsci, was the largest in Europe. Both Togliatti and Berlinguer, the general secretaries were skilled in *fare politica*. For this reason the Soviet Union accepted Italian Eurocommunism, while rejecting the French and Spanish varieties. In a sense, though, this is a distinction without significance, because at international gatherings the Italians were given full time and so could lay out Eurocommunism for everybody. The idea, the word, and the various activities practised by the Italians achieved national publicity.

Irwin Glickes of Basic Books was interested in Eurocommunism and suggested I write a book on the subject. He paid me an advance and in 1977 I set to work. I spent almost a year covering Italy, from Sicily to the Alps. Everywhere I went, my visit had been facilitated by friends, although once in a while there was a hitch. Because of the notoriety of Eurocommunism, there were quite a few sociologists and professors of all kinds roaming around Italy to study the subject, and once in a while, I'd be taken for one of them. I went to an early morning meeting of top organizers for Fiat. Somebody said: "What is this professor doing here?" To which my sponsor said: "It happens that this man introduced Gramsci to the American public!" The other apologized. I should have a sign around my neck, he said, and we all laughed in good spirits.

My main objective as I went around was to examine the organizational innovations of the Communist Party itself. For example, in elections the Communist Party backed candidates who were not Communists. I talked to one of them, Luigi Spaventa, who was a professor of economics, very well known in the social sciences. I knew Spaventa was a candidate and asked if he was a Communist. "Oh no," he said, "I'm not even a Marxist." Well, why did you run for election on a Communist ticket? "Because," said Spaventa, "Communists are the only serious people in Italy, and when they say they'll do something, they do it." He was free to vote as he pleased, but was asked to abstain if he opposed party policy. I did ask what brand of economics he favored; he smiled and said, "Keynes." I was a little startled and he laughed: "There are a lot of different kinds of Keynesians. Let's say I'm a very Left Keynesian."

Perhaps the most important new contribution of Italian Eurocommunism was its acceptance and defense of religion as a force for social good. Such a change cannot occur in a vaccuum. The person who made all the difference was Pope John XXIII, the greatest pope of our time, whose encyclical *Pacem in Terris* became the rallying point of all opposition to the Cold War. They were an extraordinary pair, Pope John XXIII and Palmiro Togliatti, founder and general secretary of the Communist Party. Although both had risen within two tough organizations, they were in the deepest sense "good" men, where goodness means searching for brotherhood and sisterhood. People were very aware of this: when they died (within a year of each other: John XXIII in 1963, Togliatti in 1964), over a million Romans turned out into the strees to mourn them. As one reporter quipped, there were as many Communists mourning for Pope John as there were Catholics mourning for the Communist leader.

Their successors, Pope Paul VI and Enrico Berlinguer, continued the process of *rapprochement*. The process was a living thing: thousands of little meetings, encounters, and accidental conversations, in a general atmosphere of floating friendship and goodwill. This warm *rapprochement* germinated many ideas and activities, one of which was to have worldwide repercussions: the entry of the Italian Communist Party into government. Nowhere was the shock greater than in the Central Intelligence Agency. It is impossible to exaggerate the importance of this crisis to the CIA. If the Communist Party of Italy entered the government as a junior partner of the conservative ruling Christian Democrats, the

CIA's entire house of cards would come tumbling down. Not only was Italy a major nation, and a very sophisticated one, but a lot of other nations might have followed the Italians.

Yet, from the standpoint of Italian national interests, including the Communist Party in government made a lot of sense. It was the old *fare politica*, with a vengeance. Elder statesmen of the ruling Christian Democratic Party, such as the conservative premier Aldo Moro, had been concerned that, if it continued, the prevalent widespread corruption, with its huge payments (the president of the Republic had been bribed by the Lockheed Corporation after all), would stultify all government. There was no use singling out any one instance of corruption; in an astute political move, Moro calculated that bringing in the Communists would keep the government honest. Over time, of course, a number of Communists would themselves become corrupt, though they were comparatively few in numbers. The primary actors were as follows: Premier Aldo Moro would become president of the Italian Republic; Benigno Zaccanini, now general secretary of the Christian Democrats, would become premier; and Flaminio Piccoli, a half-liberal, would become general secretary. The entry of Communists into the government as junior partners was not only an effective scheme, it also met a very strong desire in the nation—one-third had voted Communist. Politically brilliant, the scheme seemed irresistible. Yet within two months the political situation was completely reversed in a miasma of treachery, lies, and murder.

On March 16, 1978, Aldo Moro was kidnapped by the Red Brigades and on May 9 he was murdered. The Red Brigades were an anti-communist ultra-leftist outfit which had reputedly been infiltrated by the Italian Intelligence Service, itself practically owned by the Central Intelligence Agency. In less than three months, they had completely reversed Italian politics. Moro was dead, Zaccanini was voted out, and Piccoli switched sides, becoming a half-reactionary and general secretary of the old gang of Christian Democrats.

The CIA policy was ruthless and paid no consideration to Italian national interests. It was not an isolated case. In October and November 1994, the *New York Times* exposed that the CIA had bribed and practically bought the leadership of the Japanese Conservative Party. In both cases, conservatives were bribed in order to prevent Communists from making any headway. The lies continue to this day. In my mind, the responsibility of the CIA was plain. The ultra-left Red Brigades were to do the dirty work, but the planning was plain. When the CIA struck, it struck hard.

* * *

At the time of Aldo Moro's death as I was finishing the manuscript of *The Promise of Eurocommunism.* I delivered the manuscript to Irwin Glickes, who later called me in to tell me that he was sorry but they were not going to publish it, saying: "It seems as if it's written from the inside." I had thought that that was why he had hired me, but I did not say it because, of course, I knew what he meant. His publishing firm, Basic Books, was conservative, and while he was prepared to publish a book friendly to Eurocommunism, he was not prepared to publish one that championed it. We parted friends. Larry Hill at Topical Books published the book. In the process, I made two wonderful friends: Don Davidson, the editor, and Arthur Hamparian, production man, who have since been instrumental in publishing my memoirs. I owe them a considerable debt of gratitude.

——12——
Beating the Odds

From time to time over the decades, there have been worldwide gatherings of the International Brigades. While my service in Spain had certainly been brief, the Veterans of the Abraham Lincoln Brigade have been kind enough to consider me an honorary member. The City of Barcelona had set aside a portion of one of its parks for some kind of memorial to the Brigades. In 1988 Charlotte and I decided this was a good excuse for a trip to Europe.

It would have been a good idea except that as we left Rome on the way to visit friends in Florence, I had a heart attack in the town of Perugia, halfway to Florence. I was lucky that it happened in Perugia. Ten years earlier I had made a close friend there, Dr. Germano Marri, a surgeon who was then a top Communist. I described him in *The Promise of Eurocommunism* as "a lithe man in his early forties, with a handsome, thoughtful face. As Communst president of the *giunta* (the executive committee) of the region of Umbria, his job was comparable to that of an American state governor, requiring political and administrative skills. I asked him if he regretted giving up his profession of surgeon and he said no, his present work was exciting and rewarding."

With the combined clout of an ex-surgeon and a present political leader, I was treated royally throughout the period of my slow recovery. I was very fond of Perugia: one of my uncles or relatives had been Justice of the Peace there. It had weightier credentials, of course. In centuries past, Perugia was crest of the Etruscan expansion, still represented by a great city door. Perhaps more important, Perugia was the battle city of the papacy. Due to a quirk of geography, one side of the city is even with the surrounding terrain, whereas the other drops fifty or sixty feet straight down. A system of inner stairways and corridors leads downward. Whenever a war was brewing, the Pope would leave Rome and go to live in Perugia.

Although I was preoccupied with my condition, I was not unaware of the outside world. There was a distinct feeling that the Cold War was petering out, particularly because Mikhail Gorbachev and Ronald Reagan had seemingly become very friendly. The aristocrat from the steppes and the vulgarian from Hollywood truly liked each other. Equally important, a shift on the Cold War was taking place within the Establishment. Some of the original planners were aghast at what had happened. George F. Kennan, as much as anyone the initiator of the Cold War, said recently that he had read his own plan with "horrified amusement." He had been regretting his policies for years. Perhaps more important is the fact that more active and influential members of the Establishment had begun to move. Significant in this regard was an op-ed article in the *New York Times* by Governor Averill Harriman which implicitly predicted the consequences of opening a discussion on the policies of the Cold War.

The condition of my health increasingly dominated my thoughts. Just before I left Perugia, one of the doctors examined a discolored patch on top of my head and said that I ought to have it looked at, that it might be a kind of skin cancer. On my return, I had a checkup at Sloane Kettering Memorial Hospital, and it was just as well. It was confirmed that I had melanoma, a skin cancer which, if it invades the body, can only be treated surgically. The hospital was very impressive and for a fleeting moment I thought that I was living better than an ancient king. Wy should I be against a capitalist system that could provide such facilities? I started to laugh. Here I was, approaching eighty, highly educated, and still susceptible to the power of appearances. What is the reality? Charlotte and I, as one couple, paid Blue Cross Blue Shield $12,000 a year. Further, all these facilities had been made possible by charitable donation. Somebody had $10 or $20 million, so he or she gave a couple of million to the Memorial Hospital, deciding by their gift that it should be a heart hospital or a lung hospital or whatever, irrespective of community needs.

In June 1988, I was operated on for six hours by two teams of surgeons, on the head and on the neck and chest. The operation left me some mobility, enough to read but not to dance. By good fortune I received an advance copy of *The Grand Failure: The Birth and Death of Communism in the Twentieth Century*, by Zbigniew Brzezinski, former national security advisor to President Carter. The book was a blessed irritant, a useful distraction. As far as predictions go, Zbig didn't do too badly: he won one and lost one, predicting the breakup of the Soviet Union over the issue of separatism but not foreseeing the ruthlessness that would culminate the following year in China's Tiananmen Square.

In talking with the doctors after my operation, it came out that one half of all people with my condition usually die within three years. When I heard of it, my mind said well then, 50 percent live. And I said to the surgeons that if they kept me alive, I would write my memoirs.

I had always had a kind of a yen to know why I had always found myself on the left, so I started my memoirs to find out. My health held out for the first four volumes. Then, about halfway through the fifth volume, I was hit by double pneumonia and other infirmities. It meant I was no longer able to sit at the computer and type. Fortunately, a wonderful woman came to my rescue. I would shape the paragraphs in my head; she would check them and edit as she typed them into the computer. In this way, this final volume was finished. It is only fitting, therefore, that among the last words of these chapters should be these: Thank you, Jennifer Dent.

* * *

I have run the course, and learned very little. I did cure one misapprehension: my sense of justice is no finer, loftier, more ever-present, than anyone else's. Because I seemed always to be ending up on the left, I thought maybe that was the basic reason. But many, many experiences have shown that I get madder at injustice no quicker, no more deeply, and no more lastingly than anyone else. I think the real reason that I found myself on the left so often is because I happened to be there, on the spot, when the injustice or the evil was done. For example, I was in Prague at the time of Munich. It's very hard, looking at people's stricken faces, not to realize that something terrible has been done. Munich and its aftermath would dominate the first half of the century. For me, jail dominated the second half.

The political path of every human being develops personally, but there are factors which affect a lot of people. Most important is something which I would call the "mood of the nation"—the sum total of events and news, real and distorted, that impact on people every day. I do have two suggestions for people who find themselves on the left. One, try not to fall in love with someone who has the same interpretation of Marxism as you have: you'll spend all your time arguing. The other is to learn a trade, not necessarily a highly skilled one, but one that is always in demand, such as a construction carpenter or a plumber's helper. In times of financial difficulty, one can almost always find a few hours' work which will help hold together body and soul.

As certain as there is no God in heaven, there will be times of reckoning for the people of the United States. The great gift that the United States of America gave the world was the truth that that poverty is not genetic. People came to America and made their life anew. Yet we cannot blink away the fact that 5 percent of the world's population consumes 50 percent of the world's resources. How the reckoning will be resolved is history's secret.

PART II

Prison Notebooks

I feel like Lazarus—resurrected from oblivion. In 1986, at the age of seventy-four, I am reading a book I wrote in jail in 1949. It was then confiscated by the government. For decades, they said the manuscript could not be found, despite prodding by my then congressman, Koch. Thirty-seven years later, a copy has been retrieved from the FBI files, thanks to the Freedom of Information Act. The copy was made from a microfilm and was devilish hard to read—in parts the writing had to be reconstructed word by word.

The account has been left as it was in 1949 except for minor corrections. It is a testament to the way President Truman initiated the anti-Communist hysteria that opened the door to McCarthyism and remains alive to dominate the Reagan era. The events related in the book show how the Truman administration engineered a postwar witch hunt. A crucial fact was left out of the account at that time. This must now be placed on record. I was indicted in 1947 and charged with having lied to the government in 1942 about having been a member of the Communist Party in 1940 in order to infiltrate the key U.S. intelligence agency, later known as the Office of Strategic Services. In fact this was not the case. The OSS was fully aware of my political past *before* I was hired. *All* my superiors knew. I was unable to state this in the book because the other individuals (most of whom were postwar officials or professors) would have been vulnerable to attacks by McCarthy. That the OSS knew of my political past is evidence of the malice and malevolence of the prosecution. Until recently, I had no means with which to back this story up. However, now I do, in the person of Professor Edward S. Mason of Harvard University, who was the OSS representative on the intelligence arm of the Joint Chiefs of Staff. Responsible only to General Donovan, he had to give his approval to my employment.

While working on my memoirs, I wrote an account of how I came to be hired (included in Book 4 of these *Memoirs*). The concluding statements went like this:

> There was absolutely no question in my mind at the time, and there isn't now, that all the people involved in hiring me were *au courant* [with my past] ... Després consciously avoided the imprimateur of FBI clearance by getting Baxter and Mason to agree to a check by G-2 and ONI. [Emile Després was the man who hired me; Phinney Baxter and Edward Mason were Després' superiors.]

At the age of seventy-four, I do not fully trust my memory. I sent the account to Professor Mason on March 15, 1986, asking him to confirm or correct my statements. He replied on March 20: "With respect to your employment at OSS, I think you have stated all the relevant facts."

I attempted to smuggle the manuscript out of prison because previous experiences had convinced me that the prison authorities would not let me take it out. The smuggling failed and I was punished with seven months in isolation plus the loss of five months' "good time." I was released in July instead of January 1951.

For the record, I was a member of the British Communist Party in 1937–1938, and of the American Communist Party from August 1939 to August 1941, when I left by mutual agreement.

Preface

This preface is being written in a federal prison, November 1950. During 22 months in jail I have written this book, laboriously, night after night, and these opening pages are intended to place the book in perspective. It is the first example of a type of writing common in old Europe, but hitherto little known in the United States—jail memoirs of political prisoners. The point can be sharpened by answering the question: Why was this book written?

Physically, I wrote because I had time—in jail, time is not in short supply. But if this condition is useful, it is not sufficient, for writing is hard work and strong motivations are essential. One such motive is self-defense. In five months I shall be free on conditional release, popularly known as "good time." I will have nine months of probation. It can be revoked at any time and the revocation is not subject to appeal. Having seen at close range the unscrupulous conniving of federal officials, I do not trust them an inch. They may well try to put me behind bars again on some pretext. The publication of this book may at least give them pause.

Another set of motives is narrowly psychological. Writing relieves the frustration of being helpless and idle in a time of grave crisis. It is, in a way, a therapeutic measure. I am doing something, and so I can read with less anger and despair the daily ominous headlines of spreading witch hunts and regimentation of thought in our country, the wanton laceration of the fabric of American democracy.

Aside from what could be called a therapeutic purpose, there is a desire for self-analysis, what Catholic ground rules term "an examination of conscience," a kind of moral and intellectual inventory. I passed my thirty-eighth birthday in jail. Twenty-seven years of my life were spent in formal education, four were taken by the war, five by the government on this case—trial, appeals and imprisonment. I haven't had much time to sit down and take a look at myself. Why am I in jail? Is it worth it?

* * *

The most powerful impetus to writing, however, is political; to turn into a political asset what has been in essence a political defeat. The real, though unacknowledged, reason for my prosecution was the fact that I produced a labor documentary film, *Deadline for Action*, which exposed

Truman's foreign and domestic policy as early as 1946. It had a not inconsiderable effect. But if jail was intended to silence me, I intended to make of it an amplifier for my speech. I wanted to use my enforced leisure as a weapon against my jailers.

A man often becomes a symbol *malgré lui.* I did not seek imprisonment, nor the attendant publicity. I had, and have, no desire, no inclination, for martyrdom. Temperamentally, I am not a rebel. I rarely resisted the authority of parents or teachers. My childhood was secure, my school life serene, my college years tranquil, my jobs successful. In a broader sense, I am not anti-social. I like to be within a community rather than apart from it; I like society rather than resent it. I have stressed all this because part of the current Big Lie is that people on the left are neurotic destroyers of society. Nothing could be more false, for the exact reverse is the truth. It is in fact the left that seeks to rid society of its disintegrating pressures: racial hatreds, religious intolerance, sexism, chauvinism, exploitation, discrimination, ignorance, superstition, poverty, unemployment and war.

I do not believe I am too atypical of my generation. Were I not a jailbird, I could be a government administrator, a film writer, a university teacher, a small businessman—all of which have been my occupations in the last ten years. I have a family with two small children, I own my own home complete with mortgage, I like a steady job and a movie once a week. The government, by the very act of singling me out, has given me an importance which my achievements did not warrant. It is an ironic justice that the government's prosecution, which sought to stifle me, has instead strengthened my resolution, sharpened my purpose, and increased my range. Jail adds resonance and penetration to words.

It is my opinion that the Truman administration is unwittingly preparing the way for an American-type neofascism. President Truman thinks he is defending the Democratic Party from accusations of leftism, but his courthouse politics may have terrible consequences. One of the factors in past fascist successes is the breaking down of constitutional and legal safeguards on civil liberties. My case falls squarely within this area. I was prosecuted by the government after five years of service to that government during a long war. The indictment in 1947 charged that in 1942 and in 1944 I had denied being a member of the Communist Party in 1940.

Whether I was in fact, or was not, a member of the Communist Party in 1940 I will not state. No one has any right to ask such questions in

America. Particularly at this time, I have no desire to say anything which might help the FBI and harm fine, decent people in the United States, some of whom are my friends. Of the two counts on which I am serving sentence, I am totally innocent: innocent legally and innocent morally. Obviously, this is only my say-so. To clarify the issues involved, therefore, I suggest that for the purposes of this book let us assume that I was a member of the Communist Party. Then let's see what follows.

There was *no* allegation or suggestion or imputation, in any way, shape or form that I had *acted* to harm the government or the people of the United States. There was *no* reflection on my work, *no* denigration of my professional integrity. On the contrary, it was admitted by the government that I had served with efficiency and devotion well beyond the call of duty. The *only* charge was false statements, and false statements *only* on the subject of Communist Party membership. When were those statements made? In 1942. Why? To participate in the war effort— for a man admitting to Communism could not be hired by statute no matter how much he might be needed or wanted. The "crime" was of exactly the same nature and seriousness as a youth misrepresenting his age in order to enlist.

What should be the punishment for such a "crime"? In a similar case of false statements, that of James K. Glynn in 1950, the punishment was a fine of $25. I was given *three years*! Three years is a stiff sentence; Ilse Koch, the Nazi woman who made lampshades out of the human skins of her prisoners, received four years.

But the sentence is not the fundamental issue. The fundamental issue is that the government is deliberately undermining constitutional safe-guards against the abuse of executive power. As I shall prove (to the hilt), the government prosecution knowingly used perjurers and psycho-paths in order to obtain a conviction; the government tampered with documents; the government, with a complaisant judge, subverted legal procedures. In short, the federal government knowingly committed against me the same specific crimes that I was accused of committing against it.

Domestically, the case was the opening gun of a campaign, federally led, which has terrorized the country. The destruction of civil liberties has taken place, and is taking place, on a scale unprecedented since the alien and sedition acts of 1901. Internationally, the case coincided with the Truman Doctrine, that open declaration of Cold War. Hot war abroad and cold fascism at home will be the inevitable results of the present administration policy which, in the person of Harry Truman, has been part instigator, part accomplice, part victim of the most unbridled reactionary drive in American history since the slaveholders' insurrection of 1861.

My imprisonment is an early domestic result of the Cold War and a step along its road. Not because of the particular importance of one Carl Marzani; I simply happened to be handy, and the fact of my person was in many ways an accident. But the policies that led to the prosecution were not accidental. They originate in the desperate attempt of American capitalism to maintain a world status quo by force of arms. The attempt may cause much suffering, but it is bound to fail.

To speak of the Cold War is to speak of American–Soviet relations. To attack the policy of Cold War is to be accused of being pro-Soviet. Well, I am pro-Soviet. I am also pro-English, pro-French, pro-Hindu, pro-Chinese, pro- any aspect of other countries which seems to me praiseworthy.

But as part of a political community, I am an American. I am American by choice and I'm proud of it. Of all the countries I have known, and I have known many, I like America best. I like its history, its traditions, its way of life. I like the rich, complex, and varied origins of its people. But I do not believe we in America have a monopoly on the Good, the True, and the Beautiful.

On the contrary; at the present moment, neo-fascism is a "clear and present" danger in our country. But there is no inevitability about it. This book is an affirmation that it will be defeated; that World War III will be avoided. I would not have spent the many nights in writing it had I believed for a moment that on leaving jail by one door, I should enter a concentration camp, or worse, by another. Yet fascism will not be defeated by wishful hopes—what is needed is a constant, skillful, courageous struggle. I hope these pages will help. Jail has contributed to my clarity and determination. To the degree I can pass these qualities on, my imprisonment will be fruitful.

* * *

In conclusion, it is customary to acknowledge obligations. As will be made clear, there is a group of people who have a lot coming to them, particularly Attorney-General Tom Clark, Mr. John M. Kelley, Judge Richmond B. Keech, Mr. Anthony J. Panuch. They put me in jail and therefore without them this book would never have been written. I devoutly hope that its effect will be such as to repay them in part for all they have done.

The obligations to my friends are more serious, for they are beyond repayment. I speak not only of my intimate friends, but also of those hundreds who have supported the defense in time and effort. Names are not mentioned for fear of the FBI... the watchdogs of freedom of speech in 1950 America. There are also the people I don't know—the thousands and thousands of working men and women throughout America whose hard-earned contributions made my defense possible and my family secure. To all, my grateful thanks.

To some friends whose activities are known to the FBI I can publicly express my thanks. To Hu Barton, one of the finest men and Americans I know, for his friendship, steadfast and serene. To Oliver and Betty Lundquist and to Paul Sweezy for their warm affection and their unbroken work on the defense committee.

To my charming fellow jailbird, Dr. Jacob Auslander of the Joint Anti-Fascist Refugee Committee, my thanks for his support as I wrote. We lived in adjoining cells and I can recommend him in all conscience as a good neighbor.

To my mother, my thanks. At first bewildered and frightened, she rallied courageously. She has borne her fears with that quiet stoicism which in ancient times was a birthright of Rome and is today an attribute of the working class. Mother can lay claim to both traditions.

Above all, my tribute to Edith, dear wife and comrade. Frail in body, ill in health, poor in money, overwhelmed with problems and two small children, she has never faltered. This native daughter of Manhattan can match any pioneering daughter of the Middle Border in unparaded fortitude. Her love and thoughtfulness, her gallantry and solidarity, have been my inner armory.

To her, and all the others, *salud!*

Danbury Jail
November, 1950

One

It is Christmas week 1949, and you're in jail. You're standing at the head of a long corridor, with barred windows overlooking the yard. At the end of the corridor is a room, and in that room your wife and children are waiting for a visit. A guard frisks you; you raise your arms and he feels your shirt, trousers, pockets. Nothing is allowed on pain of solitary confinement, but you've taken a chance and concealed two lemon drops.

You enter the room. There is your wife, her lovely face drawn and thin, her hair shot with gray, the result of illness and worry. She's heartbreakingly thin, incurably ill with a dreadful disease—multiple sclerosis. You force down your concern and bring up a smile; you give her the allotted kiss under the guard's eye, a chaste pecking as ritualistic as a genuflection. You silently turn to the children.

There's a squeal of "Daddy!" and Ricky, the older, throws her arms around you in a great hug. She's only six, gloriously healthy, with a stirring mop of wonderful copper hair. Only six, yet children sense things deeply, and you wonder. Is it only your imagination... or is there some extra meaning in the hug, a feeling of approval, or solidarity as it were? Has she been teased at school? In children's play, jail is "bad"; "bad people" go to jail, and though you know that many friends make a point of praising her daddy, still you wonder. Is her violent hug an affirmation against something on the outside? You'll never know, for she's too young to tell, though old enough to feel.

And there's Tony, the little one. All of two, elfin-faced, smiling shyly but happily, gurgling with odd noises. He's just learning to talk. You pick him up, with a little tickling, and he squeals delightedly. He's a squirming, delectable armful, eager for a roughhouse; but Ricky mustn't be neglected. No sense increasing jealousies. With both on your lap, when the guard isn't looking, you pop a lemon drop in each fledgling mouth, to everyone's intense satisfaction.

You visit under watchful eyes. The guard is not unpleasant or antagonistic, but he's there, a felt presence. Still, you visit. Your wife minimizes her troubles, she doesn't want to worry you. You minimize your problems, you don't want to worry her. Both of you know each is sparing the other, but you don't know how much and there's no way to break through. A wary, armed neutrality of benevolence. But it is good to see each other and you gaze at her—sweet, gallant, and uncomplaining, though you know money is scarce and worries heavy.

When they go, all too soon, your heart goes with them. She goes, leaning on a cane, walking with difficulty because of sclerosis, with a fast backward smile while the children are chattering happily.

Christmas week 1949. A home broken up, a woman in deep trouble, children under pressure. Why? Because there's a Cold War and the father is a political casualty—one of many. Christmas week 1949. All this occurred in a federal jail near the town of Danbury in the State of Connecticut, U.S.A.

In Arlington Cemetery, President Harry S. Truman said: "We have created here a government dedicated to the dignity and the freedom of man ... we must continue to safeguard at home the belief in ourselves and belief in freedom as the greatest force for human welfare." Brave words. Ringing words. Just—words.

Jail is quite an experience, one not easily communicable. Something there is in man that does not love a cell, but it isn't easy to express it. Though I had read considerably in prison literature, it wasn't too helpful in anticipating the actual conditions. As a child I read Silvio Pellico's *Le Mie Prigioni*, the classic account of an Italian patriot imprisoned by the Austrians. Later I read Oscar Wilde's experience in *De Profundis*. Then there was Jawaharlal Nehru's taste of imperial British jails in his *Autobiography*, Koestler's book on a Spanish prison, the impassioned letters of Sacco and Vanzetti from a Massachusetts cell. In our own immediate times there is the profoundly moving and inspiring testament of the Czech Communist Julius Fuchik in his *Notes from the Gallows*, written in the shadow of the Nazi executioner. None of these provided preparation.

American federal prisons (as contrasted to terrible state prisons) are physically superior to any other jails anybody has ever written about— the very latest in incarceration. Danbury has modern plumbing, clean kitchens, a fair hospital, a small library, some recreation and education. As for food, if meat is scanty, calories are plentiful and there is ice cream once a week. It's all very fine, but there are bars, there are locks, there are guards. Jail is jail, and the best psychological preparation I find is Thomas Mann's *The Magic Mountain*. For the sense of time is the essence of jail. Time dominates the prisoner, and Mann's probing inquiries reveal facet after facet, peel off layer after layer, of the psychological experiences of time which fit perfectly the prisoner's development. Time is the matrix of jail awareness.

The convict's jargon is focused on it. He has an illuminating phrase for passing of the hour. In jail, one builds time. Building time is an art, a ceaseless process of prudent socializing and wary introspection—like one's sense of political freedom or personal integrity. It is the result of many small acts, harmonized. A certain degree of channeled routine helps, making for "easy time"; but be careful: if the routine becomes monotonous it's "bad time," leading to "stir trouble"—that is, melancholia, depression, and despair. Sleeping is "building time," the best there is. "Good time" is card playing, if not done to excess, bull sessions and, above all, reading.

I had read steadily and solidly for fifteen hours a day for three months when I was alone in a cell in the Washington jail, until the supply of books became a logistical problem. The library allowance was two books *a week*; my consumption was three or four *a day*. Bridging the gap, or filling the pipeline, was not easy. I would get from a few friends their books when finished, and then, after reading them myself, exchange them in the few minutes before cells were locked upon return from dinner. Like a squirrel with his nuts, I'd gather six or seven books to operate my circulating library. Thus, strictly contrary to regulations, I operated a literary granary. The energy, time, and ingenuity spent on such a simple matter were considerable—about the same as that spent by Mr. McCloy in de-Nazifying Germany (and, judging from the results, somewhat more effective).

At Danbury, the book situation improved. There is a library of some four thousand volumes, helter-skelter in composition, but passable. I found a couple of works I especially wanted to read: Thomas Mann's *Joseph* series and Carl Sandburg's *Lincoln* in six fine, thick volumes. Both were a great treat.

In view of the nature of my imprisonment, the *Lincoln*, with its wonderful liberating insights, was a comment as well as a pleasure. It is a great job. An informed mind is at work when Sandburg writes; a sentient, attuned, deeply rooted American. He takes the details and sharpens the various aspects of Lincoln. It is an austere work of love, and a very moving one. Crucial among the strands of Lincoln's character that Sandburg stresses is the man's great capacity for learning both from books and from experience. Most of us get pretty set in our ideas by our thirties; thereafter ideas change with difficulty. But since the controls of society are almost entirely in considerably older hands, there is a wide cultural gap between knowledge and practice, which is itself the source of many difficulties. The awareness of this gap is a commonplace of modern sociology. There was no such gap in Lincoln. He never stopped growing, mentally and morally. Sandburg calls him a "learner," an epithet first self-applied by Lincoln. This, to me, is what gives Lincoln his towering stature and at the same time makes him the "parfitt" knight of democracy. For this man of the people, growing up with little advantage of a formal education, in a rude society where the struggle for a daily existence often was a concrete physical problem, achieved a measure of wisdom known to few. He lifted himself by his own bootstraps, symbolic of mankind's development. His life was a testament and an affirmation that man can rule himself—the very core of the democratic ideal.

Marx called Lincoln "the single-minded son of the American working class." Say rather, to avoid the urban connotations, the "agrarian toiling mass" and the description fits perfectly. Out of the rough, hard-bitten West he came, this great, compassionate wise man of democracy. Self-taught, self-trained, self-knowing: he was and is the living proof of the huge reservoirs of ability waiting to be utilized in the hundreds of millions of the earth's downtrodden. This is what makes Lincoln such a stirring figure for the left. I've never known a Communist or sympathizer who did not have both knowledge and love of Lincoln. It is a good test of leftism, the FBI will please note.

To me, Lincoln is the great American hero. In the city of Washington, his Memorial was a favorite place. On my way home I would often drive around it to glimpse his statue. Sometimes when traffic was light, I'd stop and visit for a few minutes. I put him in a film I made in 1946, *Deadline for Action*. The film, an exposé of American monopolies, is part of the reason I'm in jail. Its climax is an affirmation of faith in our democracy. It is a sequence based on the Lincoln Memorial. In the early morning the rising sun beams through the open columns, highlighting the statue of Lincoln, accenting the brooding humanity of his features. As we see a closeup of the face, wonderfully dear to us, we hear his immortal words: "that this nation, under God, shall have a new birth of freedom, and that the government of the people, by the people, and for the people shall not perish from the earth."

Here in jail as I write about it, I evoke another dear memory of the Lincoln Memorial, tied in with my daughter, Ricky. When I returned from army duty overseas, she was just two and talking—a witching age. I'd been away for a year and in reestablishing contact, I'd often take her out driving with me. We used to go to the Lincoln Memorial. I have no idea what went on in her head, but she loved the statue. "Stone Man" she would breathe, ecstatically, as I parked the car. Her little face glowed, excited, the red hair a banner to the breeze. I taught her the name, "Mr. Lincoln." She couldn't quite pronounce it: the first syllable came out a mingled "j" and liquid "l", like the double l in billiards. Mr. Ljinkon it was, and Mr. Ljinkon it has remained in our private vocabulary. In my pride and love for her I could only hope that these slim tendrils of interest and excitement might find purchase within her, to strengthen her grown-up mind and heart for the troublous times she will face.

I sit now and write, four short years later, and think of her already started, savoring to some extent the pain and heartache attendant on the struggle for human progress. I think, too, of her "Mr. Ljinkon" and what he would say to the Tom Clarks, the Rankins, the Mundts, and the Thomases. I find comfort in Lincoln as I read his biography, and my thanks go to Mr. Sandburg, who has made prison more bearable—made it easier to "build time."

* * *

A good way to pass time is to get to know people in this new environment. Unquestionably, jail is a broadening experience. Where else would you get free a meticulously thorough course in card cheating? Or in the art of mugging? Or learn "conning," the mellifluous patter of the confidence man where the tongue is quicker than the eye? Where else would you be in such clinical rapport with an old sex offender who had violated a little girl of five? Or with any number of thugs, forgers, embezzlers, burglars, robbers, and mayhem-makers of all kinds? Including some of the nicest people I know.

One of the nicest, who lingers in my memory, was a young prisoner who befriended me the first day in the Washington jail, when I was absolutely at a loss for help. I was in a single cell, one whole side open and barred, like a zoo cage, high on the fourth tier of a series of such cages. This young fellow came along—he couldn't have been more than twenty-two—with a cheerful swarthy face, tousled hair, and engaging grin. He looked like a young Paul Muni. He put his hand through the bars. "Hey, here's somethin."

The something was a pack of cigarettes—a real gesture of friendship. In jail cigarettes are scarce, in fact they serve as money, and when I was first locked up, all tobacco was taken from me. It is usually a week before you can buy some at the commissary. I was therefore grateful, but I hesitated. "G'wan," he urged. "Pay me back later, I don't want no interest."

I didn't understand this then, but did later. Cigarettes can be borrowed for a week or so with an interest rate for transients of one cigarette in five, or 20 percent a week, about 250 percent a year—bankers would love jail. As in the outside world, credit in jail depends on standing in the community. Standing in turn depends a good deal on publicity. Just like the outside world, I had not achieved as much space as a fine frilly murder; still, as I was the first casualty in the Cold War, the government had drawn up a pretty lurid indictment and the newspapers had played it up. At the time I didn't realize this, but I thanked my good Samaritan profusely.

"That's nuthin," he said gruffly. "I'll see ya later." He started to go and paused irresolutely. "Read aboutcha," he finally volunteered. "It's a futzin' shame." The reaction of this man was far from typical. Most inmates are very patriotic, the patrioteerism of the Hearst press and its equivalents. I had to be careful in making acquaintances to let others make the first move lest I be insulted and snubbed. But he got me off to a good start, and we got to be pretty friendly.

A week or so later the young Paul Muni came over all excited, his face glowing with happiness and joy. "Take a look," he chortled and shoved through the bars a crumpled telegram. It read: CONGRATULATIONS STOP BABY GIRL SIX POUNDS SEVEN OUNCES STOP ELAINE FINE LOVE MOTHER. "That's wonderful!" I said. "Congratulations poppa. Is it your first one?" "Yes sir," he said proudly, and then with a faraway, rhapsodic look he said most emphatically, "By Jesus, I'm gonna marry that girl when I get out!"

Another inmate was also friendly from the beginning, though he had some, to me, peculiar ideas. But he seemed to think we had a lot in common. He acted as a trusty and could move around with some freedom. The day after I was in, he came to visit. He threw his hand through the bars. "Shake," he said. "I read about you. I know how you feel. You're a man of principles. You're a damn fool, but you got principles. I know how it is, I got principles too." "That's good," I encouraged him. "Sure, I'll tell ya. I was in the army. Got to be sergeant. Then that futzin' Roosevelt died. Remember?" I did, I assured him. I was in the army too at the time.

"Well," he went on, "the army said we had to have a minute silence at attention, in his memory. And I said, not me, I wouldn't give that son-of-a-b—— the time, dead or alive. The commanding officer said he'd bust me, and I said go ahead. He did too, busted me to a private, but I wouldn't give him the satisfaction. Principle, see?"

Jail is full of characters. In Danbury, we even have a pirate, a man sentenced for piracy—he had stolen a boat. Another inmate was in for stealing a twin-engined airplane. He hadn't meant to steal it—he had given in to a transitory impulse. He was a farm boy from Vermont who at nineteen had gone into the army in the last days of the war and had trained as a pilot. Three years later and honorably discharged, he found himself unemployed at twenty-two and went bumming around the country. He was in Florida, and he passed by an airport where he saw this plane idling at the end of a runway, the cabin door open, the engine running. Somehow, the pilot had gone off for a few minutes. Looking at the plane, the young fellow was suddenly homesick, and, almost without thinking, vaulted over the fence, got into the plane and took off, flying north by visual landmarks. His family farm was close enough to a river so that he found it without difficulty and looked for a big meadow where he could set the plane down. He did a tricky landing, walked a couple of miles to his home, kissed his parents, ate a good meal, and went to sleep. In the morning, the FBI showed up at his door. An amazed farmer, who couldn't believe his eyes, had called the FBI. The young man got two years, a relatively mild sentence.

Another friendly soul was a youngster who came right out of Dickens—a real Fagin-trainee. He was a little runt, vicious, shrewd, sharp-tongued. He had been caught stealing sugar in the prison kitchen and was accused of stealing other missing stuff. He denied it angrily, though actually he had taken it. They seemed to disbelieve him, for later, telling me of the incident, he told me the truth and ended up saying, "I told 'em it wasn't me, but those motherfutzers wouldn't believe me." He brooded a moment and went on, seriously aggrieved: "God damn it, they don't take your word for anything around here."

One of the more acidly amusing incidents concerns a young Frenchman who was awaiting deportation for illegal entry. This is a common "crime." Danbury is full of Canadians who have been given a year for illegal entry and then deported. Most of these people are turned in by private citizens who want the $50 bounty given to informers. This young Frenchman was in the Washington jail. He was a charming fellow, with quite a resemblance to Maurice Chevalier. According to him, he had been in the Resistance movement in France and had been in French and German jails. He spoke as an expert, therefore, and thought American jails marvelous.

"*Merveilleux,*" he would say. "*Vraiment, vraiment incroyable.* This prison, it is marvelous. Like a hotel. A toilet in each cell; running water—even toilet paper. Very good?" He would look to me for agreement. "Is it not so?"

"Indeed, yes," I would say.

"And the food," he enthused. "Magnificent."

"You find it so?" I asked ironically.

"*Mais oui.* All the bread one can eat. And we have meat twice a week. In the Gestapo jail—no meat. Absolutely."

"Yes, I can see your point. It is certainly a better jail than the Germans'."

"Much, much better," said my Frenchman. "America, she is wonderful."

Finally one day, I thought he ought to know a few facts of life. I told him about my case and that I was in jail because of Communism. He flatly disbelieved me.

"*Non, monsieur*, not in America."

I told him, unfortunately, yes.

"*Mais non*," said he.

"But yes," said I.

"Even in France today," he argued, "this is not possible."

It was possible in America, I assured him.

"No, monsieur. In Vichy France, yes. Here, no."

I couldn't budge him. A few days later, there was an article by I. F. Stone on my case. I gave it to him to read. He was deeply troubled.

"But monsieur, it is like the Gestapo, no?"

I was tempted to say: like the Gestapo, yes. What I did say was that it could happen here if Americans didn't wake up. There were plenty of nasty people in government who were restrained by the Bill of Rights. Where the restraints were weakened, as in courts martial, cruelty and injustices abounded. We had several inmates who had been in military jails and had been transferred to Danbury as a way station to civilian life.

I was shocked to learn the kind of sentences meted out by courts martial. Seven years, twelve years, fifteen years, twenty years—the years were given out like confetti. Though the worse sentences were finally scaled down (say from twenty to fourteen, and seven to four), the sentences were still outrageous for the comparatively minor crimes. When news came of the release of top Nazi officials and generals, by "good time" given *retroactively*, the military prisoners were fit to be tied. The unfairness and the cynicism of the authorities nearly drove them crazy.

That some men go crazy in jail is neither news, nor surprising. Any abnormal tendencies or neuroses are fanned and fueled by prison conditions. For example, in the Washington cell block was an inmate awaiting sentence, an Italian in his late thirties: short, stocky, his hair clipped close. He was a "carnie," a veteran carnival man, barker, shill, concessionaire, and he was an amiable fellow with only one real problem—he had claustrophobia. In jail, that's tough.

During the day he was allowed out of his cell as a tier man, mopping, sweeping, doing odd jobs. At five o'clock he was locked up for the night in a single cell. His fears began to build. He kept himself in hand by chattering constantly, gossiping and talking with other inmates. It was against the rules but the guards let him alone beyond an occasional "Shut up, you!" The sound of his voice seemed to provide a refuge, but still his tensions mounted and by the time the lights went out at 9:30, his self-control had disintegrated. Clinging to sound, he'd start on an eight-hour jag of monologues, a kind of grotesque filibuster that was both fascinating and infuriating.

He was completely uneducated, but he was sharp, had a fine sense of humor and a flair for mimicry. Out of his colorful life would come hour-long dramatizations. Now he was a barker, now he was a priest. He would imitate a sergeant, a crooner, a fairy. He would be a judge, pious and sanctimonious, or the prosecutor, sharp and probing. Or maybe the rotund, hackneyed phrases of a defense attorney would come rolling out. As a Catholic he had a hodgepodge of liturgical Latin and a smattering of chants. *Pax vobiscum* and *Oremus* would sprinkle the air. He'd be a Father Confessor listening to a girl: "Oh you did, eh? And then what?" And he'd play the girl, in high falsetto with ribald details. There was a tendency in his acts to play a Charlie Chaplin type—fighting the cops, fighting the boss, fighting teachers. Somewhere he had picked up whole sections of Shakespeare so we would have quarter-hours of outraged fortunes, solid fleshes, and damned spots. Often he would give a running commentary to whatever part he was playing, or break into attempts at rational conversation. As the night went on, he became more incoherent, with spells of violent cursing, frightened and frightening.

He was effortless in his drama and he was good. When he started, the cell block echoed with laughter. His impudence toward the guards was pleasing to the convicts. He knew it and played up to it. But as nine became ten, and ten eleven, our laughter became strained, it ceased, it turned to grim silence and, finally, frustrated hate. He had a powerful, deep-seated voice and the incessant sound was torture. No one could sleep.

This went on for a week. I built up a powerful hatred, as did the rest of the block. I couldn't sleep at night; I couldn't sleep in the daytime. During the day there was a radio on, blaring all the time. There was a song about steers in the sky or something that drove me crazy; I couldn't get the refrain out of my head—Yeepi-a-yeay; yeepi-a-yeay. I tried stuffing my ears with toilet paper, but there was no evading the noise. Radio by day, carnie by night. Out of sheer exhaustion I would fall asleep during the day or night, but fitfully for an hour or so before a peak in noise would wake me up again. There was a nervous exhaustion as well as a physical fatigue which inflamed the tempers in the whole cell block. Moods were ugly, guards jittery.

During the night someone now and again would yell at him to shut up. It not only was useless, but, since it was a relief to him to hear others, any yelling would only incite him to greater efforts. This was so elementary and obvious to all, that when someone did yell, I was angrier at him than at the carnie. One night, when particularly exhausted, I suddenly found myself half sitting up very angry at someone yelling at the top of his lungs in a furious round of cursing. Suddenly I realized it was I who had done the yelling. For a space, I had cracked; the time was blank. It's a queer feeling, this sense of your mind having slipped.

In jail, of course, one's mind becomes even more a subject of interest than in the outside world. There were obscure corners in the labyrinth of my mind that proved refractory to introspection. My acts were clear enough, but they did not fit with what I thought I was thinking. For example, there was the case of the sex criminal. He was an old man, nearly seventy. He had lured two little girls of five to his room, sexually played with both and half-violated one. Luckily he wasn't a killer. We had seen the story in the newspapers and we knew he had pleaded guilty. He was awaiting sentence.

The old man was universally shunned. This is a rare phenomenon. In fact it was the only instance of ostracism I was to see in jail, where the broad catholicity of guilt and misery draws no line at the rapist, the murderer, the drug peddler. But the old man got the silent treatment, and it wasn't pleasant. At recreation time, while other inmates walked, talked, or sat on the floor playing cards, the old man sat in a corner with a book, alone. He was stringy and lean, with grizzled hair, drooly mouth, and somber, haunted eyes. Nobody talked to him; nobody noticed him.

For myself, I had a revulsion so strong that I couldn't stay in the shower room if he was there. My skin crawled with gooseflesh and I had a swift sense of nausea. With the feeling of disgust went a clamoring sense of anger. My reactions, like those of other people, were obviously due to deep-rooted social taboos. But in my case there was added sharpness because of my own female child. Inevitably, in the loneliness of prison, I idealized her. I remembered her sparkle and her affection, her sprightly loveliness and the charm of her nascent vocabulary. To think of a little child like Ricky at the old man's mercy, to think what it would do to a child's sense of security, was to provoke the sternest, most implacable feelings. Even the obvious fact of his mental illness was not too mitigating a factor!

And yet, there were countercurrents. I was not aware of them at the time, but in retrospect I think they were always there. In the dense jungle of my anger, dislike, and disgust there must have been tendrils of compassion. Looking back, I remember that while his body in the shower room made my gorge rise, at the same time it evoked a feeling of respect based on identification with a common human fundamental: the will to live. This the old man had.

He was, as I've said, seventy years old. Yet he had a firm grip on life. Not that he was well-preserved, far from it. He showed his age. His body was twisted, racked, grotesquely misshapen. Elbows, knees, shoulder blades were jagged peaks in a visible skeleton. The muscles had shrunk to thin cords. The hips were askew and the stomach like a hole in a catcher's mitt. His abdomen was corrugated with a hard round protrusion the size of a half melon. The scrotum was a tattered, withered remnant at a rummage sale.

There was about him the atmosphere of *Lower Depths*, a reminder of *The Man with the Hoe*, a whole range of evocative feelings about hard-worked men and women ground in the mill of never-ending toil, beaten and oppressed, caught in the hopeless squirrel cage of daily life. Hardly known to me at the time, my sympathy was played upon. More than sympathy was that curious element of pride I've mentioned. For this battered human being was still fighting, grimly and silently, for life. He willed to live. The shrunken corded muscles still had spring in them. Like a gnarled old tree, stubborn against the elements, the old man refused to die. Leathery, crinkled, and withered, he still had a self-evident powerful vitality. You had to hand it to him: brutish as he was, he was a champion of life.

All this I absorbed, unconsciously. Then one day by chance we were sent to court together, he for sentencing and I for a hearing on reconsideration of sentence. It turned out we had the same judge, the Honorable Mr. Keech. Toward me, His Honor was pitiless. But of him later. Then the old man came up. There was no possible defense; the court-assigned lawyer pointed out the man was sick, had a previous record, and should not be released until cured. He asked the judge not to give a long flat sentence but to make it as indeterminate one for the man to be held until cured.

The judge gave him nine to fifteen years. He prefaced the sentence with a scathing condemnation of the man's acts which bothered me. The facts were right, the emotion justified, but the undercurrent of unctuous sanctity peculiar to His Honor made me both uncomfortable and angry.

The old man came back to our corner. His face was blanched, the skin tight at the cheekbones. There was naked torment in his eyes, and through pressed lips I heard his mutter, "the bastard thinks he's Jesus Christ!" Just as I was standing there, I knew what he meant by the phrase. He meant, Does he think I have no contempt for myself? Doesn't he know that I hate myself—that my own guilt, remorse, helplessness drive me crazy? Who's he to judge me when I have judged myself a thousand times more bitterly, more pitilessly than he can ever know? What does he know of my daily personal private hell?

Though I couldn't stand his physical nearness, though I still couldn't control my feelings of disgust, I also knew that I had been just as sanctimonious as the judge—just as lacking in understanding and charity. I was ashamed. "Yeah," I said. "He sure does."

After this incident several weeks went by. A few times the old man asked me for a book, which I gave him. Beyond this he made no attempt to intrude and I kept out of his way. A day came when we were to transfer to other jails. I was going to Danbury, Connecticut; the old man was going to the mental institution at Springfield, Missouri. The first leg of the journey was a common one to the Lewisburg Penitentiary in Pennsylvania, made in a regular prison bus that comes in from Atlanta to Washington, then on to Lewisburg, Springfield, and Chillicothe, Ohio. The bus is fully equipped with barred windows, a small toilet, and a drinking water tank. There's a small cage in the back for an armed guard and a small cage in front for the driver. A lieutenant is in command. The morning of the departure, we transfers were assembled and the lieutenant spoke to us: "I'm going to handcuff you in pairs. You'll have a long ride and you'll have to go to the toilet together, sit together, get a drink of water together. So choose your partner now. You get a pack of cigarettes for each couple. I want no yelling, or singing—or whistling at the girls."

Inmates quickly paired up, but as I had no particular friend I ended up with the old man. During the long ride we were companionable though we seldom spoke. I found my original aversion greatly tempered by compassion. I dwell on this because my feelings for the old man are in sharp contrast to the feelings I have here at Danbury for another prisoner who is still here since he is serving a life sentence for treason. His name is Chandler. He worked for the Nazis during the war, broadcasting against the Allies much in the manner of Lord Haw-Haw, who was tried and hanged by the British after the war.

I first became aware of Chandler while still in quarantine (separated from the population for a few weeks of adjustment) through the books I was getting from the library. Many had marginal comments, bitterly anti-Semitic, anti-Roosevelt, anti-New Deal, anti-Soviet, anti-union, and anti-anything decent. Later I heard him expound to inmates who would listen the usual trash of the professional anti-Semite: *The Protocols of Zion*, the Jewish Conspiracy of International Money Lenders, Roosevelt was a Jew, and so on. This fascist degenerate, this "delicate ape" who had participated in a system that butchered six million innocent Jews, this slug considered himself a political martyr.

Chandler was a tall, lean, good-looking man in his early fifties, with a tanned muscular body kept in tip-top shape by daily sessions on the handball court. His body was not repulsive in the manner of the old pervert, but his mind was such a cesspool that it dominated my feelings. There was no compassion in me for him, only contempt, and I would never have sat with him on a prison bus as I had sat with the old man. Despite several overtures he made toward me, I refused to speak to him and steadily ignored him. It was not so much his treason—I am no flag-waver—as the cast of his mind. I could find some excuse for other traitors such as Axis Sally, who was in the Washington jail, or the Nazi broadcaster Bergman, who had been a clerk in the American embassy in Berlin. While I didn't condone Bergman's treason, some of the responsibility for his gullibility must rest with the Chamberlains, the Bennets, the Lavals, and all the rest of the "respectable" people who looked up to Hitler as the anti-Bolshevik savior.

It is an illuminating commentary on the current political atmosphere that many inmates and some guards considered Chandler a "political prisoner." One of the guards, by way of being friendly, said to me one day that after all my case and Chandler's were much alike. "Just shows you what kind of impression the newspapers give," I told him. "Just think about it a little bit. Chandler was a native-born American who hated democracy, went to Europe, and became a fascist; I'm a native-born European whose father hated fascism, came here, and became a democratic American citizen. Chandler joined the Nazi government and made war against the American Army; I was in the American Army making war on the Nazis. Chandler thinks he's a superior person hating the mass of people; I'm a democrat who believes in people. He preaches anti-semitism and I teach equality. He's in jail for acts against democracy; I'm in jail for wanting more democracy. Outside of those differences, the only thing the same is that the federal government was the prosecutor."

*　*　*

An incident happened in jail that reminded me of my first night in Barcelona during the Spanish Civil War. I was sleeping in a tiny room that just held my cot and a chair. I slept naked, between two sheets with a piece of rug for a blanket. Suddenly I was awakened by shrieking sirens. Air raid! My first air raid. I put on the light, swung my legs out, sat up, and reached for my pants on the chair. Just then the lights went out and in the pitch darkness the meaning of the howling sirens really struck home. Bombs were on the way. In fact, in my confused mind, the sirens were bombs. I was petrified, my body rigid except for my hands. And my hands—there, stretched out in the darkness, they were shaking, beyond control. Then I heard my teeth chattering insanely. My mind was very lucid, I could see and hear myself very clearly. There was great lucidity, anger, and contempt. I kept thinking what a rotten coward I was, and why didn't I stop; what a yellow stinker, put your pants on, stop shaking. In vain—I was scared stiff.

Similarly, in the Washington jail block, I woke up one night panic-stricken. My mind was clear and alert but I was terrified. It's a strange, eerie combination of fear and lucidity, for the clarity of the mind seems to heighten the terror. I had awakened, panic tight in me. Even as I realized where I was and the mind cleared, I knew that I was frightened, but I didn't know why. Dim bulbs outside threw barred shadows in the cell. I was alone, no intruder had wakened me. Then I heard it.

Sound came from the tier beneath me, such a sound as I'd never heard. It wasn't a moan, it wasn't a sob; it was more like a raspy whimper, an animal noise that suddenly rose abruptly and lashed out in an agonized scream. I had a sense of recognition and automatically registered the fact that a similar scream had awakened me. My reason told me it must be a human being; the noise had a disturbing animal quality about it, abandoned, unrestrained. It bounced off the steel plates—plates on the walls of the cells, on the tier platforms, on the stairways. It echoed in the huge, impersonal cellblock. "Maaaa…" I thought the scream said, distorted, incoherent. Once, twice, then chest–ripping sobs, whimpers, ululations, a dreadful cacophony.

To describe my feeling as one of terror or panic is misleading, for the words imply a swamped reason. My fear wasn't blind. It was alert, insidious, with an awareness that made for horror. What was overwhelmed was the sense of hearing. Sound waves breasted the eardrums with a physical violence that was tangible. My lungs were constricted, my stomach in convulsion; I had a sense of iciness in the legs, a desperate urge to retch, a throbbing pulse at the temples. On my back, the shoulders arching up, my head was bolt upright with neck muscles aching. It was a matter of seconds before I realized what was happening.

Below me was the row of death cells, four of them, and each held a man awaiting execution. During the day we would cast furtive glances at them, too abashed to stare yet with a curiosity not wholly morbid. Oscar Wilde, in *The Ballad of Reading Gaol*, writes of the man who was going to be hung and how the prisoners

> Forgot if we ourselves had done
> A great or little thing
> And watched with gaze of dull amaze
> The man who had to swing.

That was us; with dull amaze dimly comprehending—until this dreadful sound in the night. One of the men had broken down. His utter terror held us, and in the huge cell block there wasn't another sound but that of his despair. I could feel the silence of other awakened prisoners, tight in a fear like my own. There wasn't a peep from the guard, not even the rattle of keys that marked his slightest movement. There was awe in the cell block—as Wilde himself must have experienced:

> But there is no sleep when men must weep
> Who never yet have wept
> So we—the fool, the fraud, the knave,
> That endless vigil kept,
> And through each brain on hands of pain
> Another's terror crept.

Terror there was, yet something more—a queer kind of human solidarity, an attraction within the repulsion. In retrospect I can convey the feeling best by saying there was a solemn undertone of watching a somber, cosmic drama. Death walked the tiers that night, repulsive in its effects, for the doomed man was in his misery both degraded and degrading. He crawled and screamed and whimpered. He was more beast than man, and that was the fearful thing. For that there was an undercurrent of resentment, yet the awesome reality of his panic stirred our hearts to pity—hearts suffused by a shared relief that we were not the person in the cell.

I shall never forget that night, the obscenity of a personality in fragments. I was forced to think of death concretely, in relation to myself. I have faced the unexpected certainty of death a couple of times. Once, in Switzerland, my wife and I hitched a ride with a wild driver in an open car. On a narrow mountain road, high in the sky, he tried to pass one auto on a curve only to meet another one coming down. Our driver drove sharply off the road, literally into space. I pulled Edith tight against me, certain of the end, my mind saying over and over, "We shouldn't have trusted this bastard." Then, bang! The car hit a boulder squarely head on. The big rock zoomed off, the front of the car crumpled, the machine teetered on the edge... and held. No one was hurt except for a cut over my eye from a flying chip of stone. I recall no feeling of fear; the shock was an anaesthetic.

But death that you sit and wait for—that's something else again. The waiting that corrodes and breaks you down. That's what I thought about, for that is the possibility in our country. The death camps of a fascist America will be no different from those of Nazi Germany. The personnel for the camps is already trained—Heywood Paterson's *Scottsboro Boy*. To many readers this will sound melodramatic. Perhaps it is; I hope it is. But as I write this in a prison cell, a political prisoner, fascism in our country seems neither improbable nor melodramatic. I never would have believed in 1945 that I would be in jail in 1950. Yet here I am, and, looking back on the road we have traveled in five years, the Yankee Dachaus and Buchenwalds seem not impossible by 1955.

I thought that night, and have thought since, of Julius Fuchik, a Czech Communist imprisoned by the Gestapo in 1942 and tortured again and again, until he was executed in 1943. While in Pankratz prison in Prague, he wrote his thoughts and experiences on slips of paper, which were smuggled out, one by one, by a friendly Czech guard, A. Kolinsky. In 1948 his wife searched for the slips and had them published as "Notes from the Gallows". He writes:

> The clock in the tower of the prison strikes three ... I have regained consciousness ... it is hard to breathe for every spot of my body has a thousand pains ... I am dying.
>
> It took you a long time to come, Death ... This is my last will for you, father and mother, sisters, for you my Gusta [his wife], for you comrades, for all those whom I loved. If you think tears can clear away the sad dust of grief, weep for a while. But do not regret...
>
> In these hours, millions of men are fighting the last battle for freedom and hundreds of thousands die in the struggle. I am one of them ... I lived for joy; I am dying for joy ... I love you all friends. Be on guard.

Something in me responds. I am no hero—far from it. But deep within my mind and my heart I believe Fuchik is right; that he whose life is meaningful can face its loss with equanimity. The wretch who broke down had nothing to stiffen him; life is precious—and it was forfeit.

For me, too, life is precious. I know how much I miss in jail. Marriage and children and the heart-delighting wonder of their late infancy. Friendship, selfless and nonharassing. The racing excitement of new knowledge, the flavor of crackling discussion, the glint in a student's eye. The feeling of fellowship in struggle, demanding and inspiring.

All this and more I miss in jail; all this and more I would miss by death. Yet I know the good things in life follow from a decent social structure, which must be maintained, at any cost. Having had these good things has made jail more bearable; fighting for them makes the prospect of death not totally intolerable.

Two

M y twenty-four months in jail thus far have been spent in four prisons: Lorton Reformatory in Virginia and Lewisburg Penitentiary in Pennsylvania, each for a few weeks; Washington, D.C. for four months; and the rest at Danbury, Connecticut. Guards and officials seemed pretty much on the same level. In general, federal penology is improving, and guards (better known as "screws" and "hacks") are on the whole as decent as can be expected of people in that occupation. Officially, they are prohibited from touching inmates, though I think beatings are given. This, however, is strictly hearsay. The only time I saw force used was in the Washington jail on an inmate who had gone temporarily berserk. He was a powerful fellow, and ripping up his cot he had armed himself with a metal strip. A husky strong-arm squad came over. They connected hoses and through the bars drenched him with alternate streams of hot and cold water. When he was slightly subdued, they went after him in the cell. Tempers were high, the atmosphere one of great violence, and the self-control of the guards not all it should be. I was not surprised to read several months later that in a similar situation, an inmate was killed by a guard in the Washington jail. The guard, of course, was exonerated. In the case I saw, the guards-half carried him out to the "hole" (solitary confinement), and a perennial inmate said to me, "They'll give 'im a workin' over down there."

Whether they did or not I don't know. I'm sure, however, that beatings are rare in federal jails. In state prisons it's another matter. I've heard stories that made my hair curl, particularly of Southern jails. Conditions are incredibly revolting and shameful. One boy told me in detail how he tried to commit suicide. *Scottsboro Boy* shocks—but it is true. There is such a stench rising from the Jim Crow South that it should choke our pretentious hectoring of other nations' morals.

Federal prisons are not only of a much higher physical standard, but the personnel are greatly superior to those in state prisons. An extremely important factor is that they are sufficiently well paid that there is small temptation to chronic or alarming corruption. Here and there a guard will use prison facilities for private purposes; here and there minor kickbacks will come from contractors or dealers. But the infringements are not serious and do not involve inmates. I am speaking now only of those four institutions with which I have had contact. This lack of corruption in federal prisons is the more noteworthy in that it is in contrast with the corruption in the rest of the structure of justice. This corruption is, I am convinced, one of the underlying factors in the breeding of crime and the difficulties in rehabilitation of prisoners.

It is a truism to say that law is the essence of civilization. There can be no humanity without society, and laws are the embodiment of social relations. If laws do not function, society flies apart. Corruption is fatal to law. It dissolves and disintegrates the authority of the law and, inevitably, the society itself. The phenomenon is clear in the France of 1788, the Russia of 1916, the China of 1947. Conversely, the building of a new society means a new structure of laws. Every successful revolution immediately sets up a legal structure, sketchy at first, then more and more explicit and developed.

In the United States today corruption has not reached the disastrous proportions which make an upheaval both inevitable and necessary, but there is enough of it to give thoughtful people clear warning that our society is not healthy. Twenty years ago Lincoln Steffens formulated his warning analysis: the most serious corruption is that of Big Business; the most apparent that of the city machines. If interested, the reader will find excellent examples in Thurman Arnold's *Folklore of Capitalism*. I am speaking of jails, and corporation executives rarely see the inside of them, but I also have plenty of data on the corruption of justice at the city level. This corruption rests on three pillars: the police, the courts, and the legal profession.

The corruption of American police departments is notorious. There has recently been a flurry of newspaper publicity on the corrupt police of Washington and New York, and I know literally of hundreds of instances of shakedowns by detectives and policemen of those cities. The corruption is matter of fact and completely accepted. If I speak specifically of these two cities, it is only because they feed the inmate populations of the Danbury and Washington jails, where I got most of my information. But from what I gather, both from reading and talking, I doubt that there is a clean police department in any American city.

As to the courts, corruption is not as complete but it is nevertheless substantial. I know for a fact, though I have no legal evidence, that several trial judges in Washington, D.C. accept money in exchange for light sentences. It is difficult to prove connections between judges and the underworld, but sometimes the public gets a glimpse of it, as when Judge Aurelio of New York City called up the big-time operator Frank Costello and thanked him profusely for his aid. That same Aurelio pompously lectured on Americanism when he upheld the New York City Council's expulsion of Communist councilman Benjamin Davis. Or the public can draw its own inference from the assassination of Charles Dimaggio, the underworld political boss of Kansas City. The honorary pallbearers at his funeral included a police commissioner, two sheriffs and four judges.

Another judicial body that is generally corrupt is the parole board in various jurisdictions. The present federal parole board is not exempt from corruption. I am satisfied from what I've learned in prison that several of its present members have taken bribes. Furthermore, once the prisoner is out on parole, he often has to deal with corrupt parole officers who bleed him and blackmail him for money. This particularly petty and vicious practice is widespread and is a source of great bitterness.

The third element of corruption is the criminal lawyer's relation to the courts and the police. By training and social status, the criminal lawyer is generally closer to the judge, the prosecutor, and the higher police official than he is to his client. A certain amount of legitimate fixing develops, the bargaining for a light sentence in exchange for a plea of guilty. The trouble is that in this process the defense attorney comes to depend on the courts and the prosecutors for his success. Their goodwill means light sentences, and therefore he will rarely antagonize them. Moreover, the defense attorney sees his clients as a group. He will make deals sacrificing some friendless soul in exchange for a light sentence on the well-connected criminal. Conversely, the D.A. sees his convictions as a whole. He is looking for a statistical record of high convictions. In the process, not only are there great possibilities for corruption, but the achievement of justice becomes a by-product.

The entire system, with its attendant corruption, favors the hardened criminal. The first offender usually doesn't know the ropes. It is the hardened criminal who makes provision for money to be used for bribes and lawyers. The hardened criminal doesn't look for acquittal; he goes after a light sentence of six months or a year. That's why the "fix" is so easy in respect to judges and so hard to prove. The judge simply gives a light sentence and that's his end of the bargain. The hardened criminal counts on the light sentences as a professional hazard. The better his connections, the slighter the hazard. There are few "organization" men in jails, members of organized gangs. Inmates are mostly "freelancers" of crime. Their great ambition is a good "connection" when they get out. Just as in business.

I'm no expert on penology. I've noticed certain obvious influences on the criminal, such as the sensationalism of newspaper coverage on crime. The inmates read the stuff with avidity, discuss it, like to see their names mentioned, follow their friends' activities, and in general look to crime reporting as others look to their trade magazines and professional journals. It is difficult to generalize on crimes; there are many motivations, many individual quirks and characteristics. There are many patterns and subpatterns which I am not competent to analyze.

I have, however, one overriding impression: that is that the jail population is a cross-section of the society outside. It is striking how similar inmates are to the outside population. The chief motivation for crime does not seem to be economic need in a strict sense. In most other countries, and in most other times, sheer poverty is a prevalent motive. But this does not seem to be the case in the jails I have been in, though it is certainly a factor in the kind of upbringing most of the inmates have had.

Rather, what seem to me the dominant factors influencing crime are the false standards of success and happiness which are the norm in the outside world. The inmates, in their thinking and their standards, are conditioned by the same magazines, the same newspapers, the same radio programs, the same movies as the rest of the United States. The sexy glamour girls of ads and stories, the men of distinction, the glistening cars, the romantic hideouts—this is the mirage of a kind of life that is held up as the good, the true, and the beautiful. When the reality of a job at fifty or sixty dollars a week doesn't square with the mirage, they take their short cuts to wealth. In vain, of course. The real life of the criminal is one of cheap joints, unstable sex relations, untrustworthy friendships. The mirage of a slick highlife is as false in the life of crime as the mirage of a secure, decent home is false in the life of the sober, industrious worker.

Closely allied with a false monetary standard of success is the dullness of the daily life of the vast mass of the population. I do not mean by "dullness" that nothing happens. There are plenty of worries and ther is plenty of insecurity. But there is little creative continuity in adult lives, little joy of living, few possibilities of development. Society devours the personality at almost any level of work, rather than provide in its daily activities recognition of individual worth. In a twisted way this lack is seen in the vicarious living in other personalities—the film star, the great athlete, the demagogic politician. It is reflected even more bitterly in the pleasure criminals get seeing their names in the newspapers. At least they have "arrived," they have broken through anonymity—they are "somebody."

The inmates are not aware of the nature of their frustration. Out of several hundred prisoners I have known, only one was articulate and explicit on the subject. This was O'Brien, the man with "principles" who wouldn't give a minute's silence to FDR. He told me quite frankly, "I was going to be a math teacher," the result, I knew, of a college education he had previously mentioned. "I found I'd get forty or fifty bucks a week. What kind of a life is that? This way I have myself a good time while it lasts, then I go to jail for awhile. So what? It's worth it."

I am convinced that our society, with its stress on ruthless competition, its philosophy of *caveat emptor*, its daily denial of social values, provides an ethical culture that breeds crime as naturally as monopolies breed war. The inmates are not "bad" people in the sense of a special "criminal" mind. They accept the standards of the outside world, and it is significant that few of them feel any sense of guilt for what they've done. Their feeling is either a sense of bad luck or of stupidity in being caught. Their hope is to tie in with some "organization" on the outside. The ideal of every criminal is a sound little racket with good legal advice to keep them within the law. They are, to me, miniature caricatures of our corporation executives.

My relations with inmates were excellent. During the first stages of acquaintance I stayed away from politics so as not to offend "patriotic" susceptibilities, but soon I could say what I pleased with no trouble. I had an adequate command of obscenities for general amenities and quickly picked up enough prison jargon to be at home. I did not act, because I did not feel superior to others, and therefore my education was not resented. Once I was accepted, my political views were respected and often found agreement on specific issues. In all the jails, I got along fine.

My relations with guards were less cordial but not unpleasant. Most guards were decent, though there were inevitably some stinkers. A bad guard can make a prisoner suffer. He can ride a prisoner, provoke him, literally drive him into breaking rules. A prisoner has no formal defense against a guard; his word is valueless, he has no standing. The warfare between inmates and a bad guard becomes a vicious, merciless struggle. At Danbury in one case, a fire extinguisher was dropped on a guard from a two-story height. It missed him by inches, and the guard, for his protection, was moved out.

Generally the worst guards were those who assumed an attitude of moral superiority to the inmates. They were often the most ignorant as well. I remember particularly a captain of the guards at Lorton Reformatory. He was a cartoon stereotype of a Southern jailer, in body muscular and big-framed with a low-slung heavy belly overflowing the belt line; in mind narrow, prejudiced, ignorant, and barely literate; in spirit, a bully. This ill-mannered, loudmouthed oaf came to my cell one day with a letter in his hand,

"Hey yuh," he growled, "who's this heah Edith Marz——" he struggled with the name.

"My wife," I said.

"What kinda woman is she laik?" His tone said she was no better than etc. etc.

"What do you mean?" I asked, getting angry at his implications.

"Weal, she ain't no lady. Gotta dirty mind."

I didn't answer. I couldn't trust myself to speak.

"Yuh just tell her, she don watch her langwidge, she caint write no moah."

I took the letter through the bars and said nothing.

"Yuh heard me," he said, and, as I still kept silent, he stared at me a minute undecided whether to push the matter further. Finally he stomped away—luckily for me, for I couldn't take much more provocation.

Curious, I scanned the letter. In one place Edith had mentioned a discussion on jazz, referring to the fact that it had developed in New Orleans brothels and honky-tonks. "Brothel" was the only word in the entire letter that could be considered "indecent" by the clean mind of my Southern gentleman.

Another time at Danbury the day shift in the control room made an error in the work list and, as a result at midnight I was awakened to go to work, although it was my night off. I had been forcing myself to stay awake during the day following the night shift, so as to be able to sleep. As a result I had an hour's sleep in two days. Tired and angry, I griped about it with proper profane language, which is against regulations. The guard who had awakened me and would escort me to work was aware that a mistake had been made so, like a decent fellow, said nothing about the griping. But as we walked out of the dormitory a certain Lieutenant Cannon passed by and heard me. "You keep your mouth shut," he told me roughly. "It's my night off," I told him, "and I got a right to sleep." "You're in jail," he said to me, bullying, "and you've a right to nothing. So shut up or I'll put you in the hole." I could have smacked him, but I was constantly aware that Washington would be delighted with my breaking rules. It would justify them in refusing parole, lengthen my jail sentence by refusing good time and so on. So I held my peace.

Cannon was full of officious ideas. There were half a dozen of us on night shifts, and we used to put blankets on our windows to reduce the daylight as we slept during the day. For nine months there was no objection; suddenly one day Cannon ordered that henceforth no blankets be put up. No reason was given; there was none to give. Our sleep ceased to be restful.

These may seem like minor things, but jail is full of such and they mount up. One of the worst officials I had to deal with was a fellow named Gillikie in the Washington jail. He acted as a sort of parole officer, mail censor, etc. He was a mealy-mouthed, sallow-faced pip-squeak who dearly loved his authority. He was thoroughly hated by the inmates and I was warned about him within my first hour in jail.

I had trouble with him from the start, on my mail. I had entered jail unexpectedly because bail had been refused. I was in the midst of making a movie and a lot of needed information was in my head. I promptly wrote the data to my wife, giving the information so the work could continue. Two days after, the letter came back. It was returned for a tiny technical reason; I hadn't put my cell number on the back flap. Mildly irritated, I corrected it and sent it out. Two days later it came back. A note said crosses were not allowed. I use a tiny x to mark a period at the end of sentences. I went through the whole letter, laboriously erasing x's and substituting dots. I was pretty burned up by now because a week had gone by and the stuff was urgently needed at home. Also, the reasons were so petty that I suspected malice. I sent the letter out. The suspicion turned to certainty when the letter came back. Numbers had to be spelled out, no underlining allowed—why didn't I read the regulations. So ran the accompanying note. The fact of the matter was that no regulations were easily available to inmates. The officer of the cell block had a copy in his desk but inmates did not know he had them and he would only give them out upon request. A fine stupid circle. Later, upon protest, the regulations were posted. In any case, I grimly made the corrections and mailed the letter again. This time it did not come back; two days later a note informed me that it couldn't go out because it contained discussion of business, which was not allowed for ordinary mail. I had to make application to write a special letter.

Two weeks had elapsed since I had first written the letter. All along Gillkie knew that he wouldn't send it out. But he had sadistically played with me in a petty, childish, but infuriating game. I had kept his notes and proceeded to write a documented memo showing his attitude for my lawyer. My wife came to visit me and I spent the time telling her what was in the letter. I also told her of my memo. On the way out she saw Gillkie, told him what I was going to do—and he promptly gave her the letter. He was not only malicious, he was a coward. Even now, months later as I write about him, the recollection leaves a bad taste in the mouth.

By contrast I've had some good relations with guards and officials. Several were politically liberal and felt I was being treated shamefully by the government. I never sought, nor was offered, any special consideration by such people, except for expressions of sympathy, which were welcome and heartening. I obviously cannot mention their names or institutions, lest they be subjected do the tender mercies of the FBI, but if they should ever read this I want them to know their sympathy was appreciated. By and large everyone accepted the fact that I was a political prisoner.

* * *

My status created a problem in several jails. It was amusing in a way, if I could forget the fact that it was I who was involved. The government's official position was that I had committed a crime, and the various prison officials followed this approach in theory. In fact, however, in their dealings with me they acted on the premiss that I was a political prisoner. This was true at Lorton, at Washington jail, and at Danbury.

I had been at Lorton less than a week and was in quarantine when a guard came for me. The superintendent wanted to see me. I had learned enough to know that this was not regular routine, and I wondered what he wanted. I was brought up before three men: Superintendent Welch, his deputy, Faison and a Mr. Clammer, director of Washington, D.C. institutions. Welch was a small, shrewd old fellow, with twinkling tolerant eyes and humorous mouth. Faison looked like a quiet, cool customer, and Clammer was a plump politician type, somewhat flashily dressed. I sat down before them.

"How's jail?" asked Welch.

"Okay," said I.

"How's the food?"

"Okay." What did he expect me to say?

"How's quarantine?"

"Okay." I was reserved, nongiving. I trusted no one and wondered what they wanted.

Clammer leaned over chummily.

"You know," he said affably, "I was in Atlanta when we had Browder there."

Browder had been railroaded to jail on a flimsy passport charge at the time of the Nazi–Soviet Pact. He was then secretary of the Communist Party, U.S.A.

"So?" said I.

"He was a fine man," said Clammer. "A gentleman."

"So?" I repeated showing a complete lack of interest. Browder was nothing to me, and it was obvious Clammer was up to something. He wasn't throwing bouquets for nothing.

"Quiet and studious," pursued Clammer.

"Yes?"

"Yes," said Clammer and went on casually, "he didn't try to organize the place."

A great light broke in on me. They were afraid of agitation.

"Why should he?" said I.

The three of them visibly relaxed. They adopted pleasant smiles and looked on me with affection.

"I'm glad to hear you say that," said Clammer heartily.

I was getting bored.

"Look," I told them," I've only got one desire and one duty. That's to get out of here as quickly as I can. The government says I'm a criminal. Okay, treat me like everybody else. That's to say, at parole time, give me the same consideration. On my record, if no politics is involved, I should make it. I have no previous record, two small children, a job waiting for me. You promise me the parole board will behave decently and I will too."

Welch and Clammer looked at each other. The glance confirmed my belief that the parole board would not treat me as a routine case but that political considerations would apply.

"We cannot speak for the board," said Clammer.

"That's not strictly true," I said, "You have great influence on their decision and Mr. Clammer in particular knows on what basis the decisions are made. In effect I'm asking him to protest if there's any dirty work. Treat me like a criminal, that's all I ask."

I knew perfectly well Clammer would do no such thing. Even if he wanted to, he wouldn't buck a parole board on a Red issue. But I wanted them to face the fact. Partly for my own satisfaction, but more importantly because only by showing how hypocritical my imprisonment was would those people begin to think of what is going on in America today. In other words, I was agitating before them even as they were asking me not to agitate.

"All right," said Clammer finally, "I can promise that." He was lying and he knew it. My feeling for him was one of mild contempt. Welch, I noticed, hadn't said a word.

"Now Carl," Welch said, "we've got to find some work for you. What would you like?"

It happens I'm a fair carpenter and cabinetmaker. It's an old hobby of mine and I had already requested such work. Welch knew it; he was making conversation. However, I went through the motions. "I'm a pretty good woodworker," I told him. "I can handle machine tools and I like that kind of work. I don't like office work, filing and so on. I'd like to work with my hands."

"The pride of manual labor, eh?" said Welch with a tinge of sarcasm. I wasn't going to argue.

"If you wish to put it that way," I answered quietly.

"Mmm…" he mused, "We got a bull gang. We could put you on that."

"What's a bull gang?"

"Pick and shovel," he explained. The shrewd eyes were cold. This was the iron hand in the velvet glove. He was threatening, and the velvet was thin.

I looked straight at him.

"Okay," I said equally coldly. "I'll buy that."

He laughed suddenly.

"Now, now Carl, we don't want to fight. We need you elsewhere." He acted as if it had been a joke, but I knew better. The threat hadn't worked, so now he would try some pal stuff. I was fed up and disgusted.

"Look, this is your jail." I wasn't mad, but I wasn't friendly. "I've got to work wherever you say. I've got to do what you want. So what are we kidding about. You either give me a choice or you don't. *You* asked me what I wanted to do. I told you. My first choice is the carpenter shop, my second choice is the carpenter shop, my third choice is the carpenter shop. Now, you do as you please."

"You wouldn't like it," said Welch hurriedly. "We'll put you in the engineer's office."

Faison, the deputy, cut in casually.

"By the way," he said, "we photostat your letters, you know. For your protection and ours."

I looked straight at him. The phrase was meaningless, a lame excuse that didn't fool him and didn't fool me. Here was one more indication of political treatment while pretending I was a criminal. I already knew they were photostating my letters, the prison grapevine had informed me. I had therefore written my wife telling her specifically not to mention names in our letters, for the greater glory of the FBI. I told her my letters, incoming and outgoing, were being copied. Faison was telling me this when he knew I knew. I looked at the three of them. They didn't like what they were doing, but they were doing it. They weren't worth the trouble it would take me to be angry at them. I said nothing, and after a few meaningless phrases the episode was over.

In various forms, my politics kept cropping up. The problem of mail troubled the prison authorities. I had read the regulations carefully. I was prohibited from speaking of jail incidents, physical layout, or inmates. There were other prohibitions, but there was a specific provision that there should be no censorship of religious or political opinions. Naturally I wrote home a good deal on current political events. Partly this was because both Edith and I were interested in the subject, partly because there was so little else to write about, my own daily life being a forbidden subject. There was also an additional, important reason. Since we had no money, while I was in jail my family was supported by contributions of friends and well-wishers from all over the United States. As a way of thanking them and maintaining contact, excerpts from my letters were distributed to them. So for this purpose I made it a point to discuss major trends in economics and politics.

* * *

At Danbury the problem of my politics arose in still another context. While in quarantine I was interviewed as to choice of work. I asked for the carpenter shop. They put me in the machine shop. The result was I had nothing to do and was pretty bored. I began to explore other jobs, talking to people in them and finally found one that suited me perfectly. The job was the midnight shift as watchman in the refrigeration plant. During the night there were no officers on duty in the plant and the night watchman was completely alone. The job was simple—to record a few dial readings every half hour—and would be ideal for me: I could read and write. Also I would have a single cell with more privacy. While most inmates lived in big open dormitories, barrack style, there were two small dormitories for night workers with single cells so that officers could get men in and out at odd hours without disturbing the rest. Not only did these dormitories have more privacy, but, as they were small and with odd working hours, the discipline was less strict and the atmosphere more pleasant. Furthermore, I would have practically no contact with officers, since there was only one officer on duty in the night and I'd be asleep during the day. Finally, I would evade most of the prison routine and the feeling of regimentation. These last two advantages require a little more explanation.

The less an inmate has to do with guards or officials the better for him, particularly if he's at all independent and self-reliant. The only way to get along with guards is by an ingratiating "yessing" role, flattering them, laughing at their jokes and comments, and so on. The best guards fall victim to this atmosphere even when they think they don't like it. The aloof prisoner has a psychological black mark against him. Not the morose prisoner, who won't talk to anyone, but the independent prisoner who will mingle with the inmates but not the guards. Even when inmates ingratiate themselves in the guards' favor, they are not safe. Some small incident may turn the guard against them, and, as I've said before, a guard can make a prisoner miserable. The best way to stay out of trouble was to stay away from them. The night job meant a minimum of contact.

As to the feeling of regimentation, although Danbury is not as rigidly regimented as some other places, notably Alcatraz where all movements are by the numbers and by whistles, there was still a definite routine. Whistles blow at six, you get up. Whistles blow at seven, you go to breakfast. Whistles blow at eight, you go to work. Once at work there is no moving around without a pass. Whistles at eleven-thirty, knock off work; whistles at twelve, lunch; whistles at one, work; and so on. At mealtimes you go in order, dormitory by dormitory. You sit at long tables, five on each side, and you wait for a guard to check your trays

and give you a signal to go, five at a time. There are specific hours for
hospital sick call, for library, and so on.

By working at night, I had a degree of independence. I quit work at
quarter to seven and if I felt like it I could have breakfast with the
kitchen staff. I went into the dining room on my own, had breakfast, got
up when I was finished, and walked out or sat for a few minutes talking
if wanted to. There was no control. I could skip breakfast and go to
sleep. I could get up for lunch or not, go to the hospital when I felt like
it, to the library likewise. I could skip dinner since I got coffee and
sandwiches at night. I avoided most of the whistles and, much more than
the majority, followed my moods from day to day. Although I fell into a
routine of my own, I could break it. For example, I wrote this book in
longhand at night. After I had half written it, I began typing it, and
rearranged my sleeping so I would get two hours a day in one of the
radio classrooms where I could type. Ordinarily, such an arrangement
couldn't be made because people would be at work. This considerable
freedom flowed from the nature of the night job and was an important
item for mental health, as well as of value in doing things.

As it happened, the man who had the job before me didn't want it. For
him the job had drawbacks. He didn't like to read, so the night was long
and boring. He had a touch of asthma and some nights ammonia fumes
leaked in the plant and it was unpleasant. But it was perfect for me.

Three

Night was my freedom. A Cinderella in reverse, at the stroke of
midnight I escaped to the world of fantasy, books, and recollec-
tions. The refrigeration plant was my kingdom, a pleasant realm of tame,
purring machinery. Here was an array of compressors and pumps, con-
densors and coils, pipes, valves, dials, switches, and relays—an intricate,
ordered system that began with electric current and ended with frozen
slabs of water. In a fifty-foot room I had a stable of fifty horses, sans food
and sans manure, harnessed and controlled, from heavy-duty driving
motors of compressors to delicate mercury switches. Tirelessly and
equably they worked, hour after hour, day after day, month after month.

I love machines. I have little patience with those who blame American
"materialism" on machinery, rather than on the social system which

doesn't know how to use machines for man's freedom rather than man's exploitation. But as for the modern piece of machinery in itself—it is a lovely thing. I was amused one weekend to read a spirited defense of the machine by, of all people, Brooks Atkinson, dramatic critic of the *New York Times*. He waxes lyrical over a printing press:

> It is daring in conception, ingenious in design and perfect for what it is intended to do, which is to give fast and wide expression to information and opinion. Although it is made of steel, it is a thoroughly human enterprise. A human being imagined it; a great many human beings have made the drawings and moldings to build it. Human beings operate it and keep it in repair. There is nothing soulless about it; it is charged with human energy and spirit. It is a tool that expresses part of the human spirit, like the piano, brush, crayon and scalpel.

So it is with my plant. It is the heir of centuries of work of a thousand thousand scientists, the labor of a million million producers. I go around it and I'm happy. My hands are busy and I'm pleased. It is a form of inverted snobbishness, I suppose, that makes me proud that my hands are as useful as my head. On my time off, two evenings a week I work in the radio shop building myself a set; three evenings a week I build furniture. Time passes.

In the plant I have a lot of time to myself, alone. There's a small table and chair and there I read and write. There's a straight path between the machines, some forty foot long, which is my quarterdeck. Up and down I pace out my time, thinking, smoking, dreaming. Often the dawn comes as a surprise. There's a courtyard with a barred, huge sally port that gives on the outdoors. In summer I walk in the courtyard from time to time. I can see the garages, the silo of the prison farm, the scrubby woods stretching out to a lake. It's the outside world, cool and lovely in the moonlight, with the peepers strumming in the spring nights, the birds chirping in the summer dawns. In the corner of the yard is the power house, with a tall stack. Next to it, soaring much higher, is a water tower. It has a cluster of red lights on it, for airplanes, barely visible on a foggy night. A plume of smoke rises constantly from the power house, hardly noticeable in the dark, slowly visible as the dawn comes up. Then the white smoke takes on the shadings of the sky, delicate pastels, lovely, frail, evocative. There are mornings of sunlight and mornings of snow, mornings of wind and mornings of rain. Sometimes the rain is light and fresh and the dawn is perceptible; sometimes the rain is murky and oppressive; then there is the dawn unseen in the slate-grey sky, a slattern old at birth.

Throughout the year, throughout the nights, my solitude is precious. I'm at home to my memories. I think often of my father, dead these fifteen years. I remember him sometime as in the photograph in Mother's room. He stands, hands in pockets, smiling somewhat ironically. His clothes are neat, a hint of a dandy about him, what with the cocky handkerchief in the breast pocket and the fashionable bow tie warring with his Adam's apple. A slight middle-aged paunch is sternly suppressed by his belt. Most often I remember him in the pose made familiar during my growing years—seated at a table with paper and pencil, adding, subtracting, budgeting, squeezing out a pair of shoes or a length of dress material from wages sometimes as low as fifteen dollars a week.

There are two fathers: pre- and post-American. The pre-American father of my childhood I remember as an unworried sort of man, often laughing, though even then his humor was laced with irony. Life seemed rich and secure then. After he came to America, the laughter subsided. Life was pitched in a lower key; there was an indefinable sadness, not oppressive but pervasive. His remarks, particularly on politics and international events, were now sardonic—the irony was gone. He had always been a gentle man, but he became more so and more withdrawn into himself. In retrospect I see him and I know that Dante's bitter bread of exile is no figure of speech. Uprooted, without the close friends, the speech, the customs of his previous life, he lived only to support his family, to give his children freedom and education. He never regretted leaving Italy for he could never accept Fascism, but he paid heavily that his children might have a democratic upbringing. I think of him often now, a man of integrity and meticulous honesty, whose inner stature becomes clearer and dearer to me as I grow older.

I begin to realize now what a difficult decision self-exile is, for it may be that I too will have to make that decision. My father was thirty-three when he left Italy; I'm now thirty-eight. If the present trend continues in America, open fascism is in the cards, and men like myself, already marked, will have to escape not only for our sakes but for the sake of our children. It is not an easy decision, and I hope it will not have to be made, yet it is a tragic reminder of the state of affairs in our "Fair Deal" country that such possibilities have to be considered. In such circumstances I think of my father. I don't think he would be displeased to find me in jail. Unhappy yes, but not displeased.

Of Edith, my wife, I think. I could not even begin to enumerate the memories, episodes of fifteen years together. I think of the children:

Tony gurgling delightedly; Ricky more complex and impish. I have a candid photo of the family. Edith is tickling them and they are all laughing happily. Scenes of home life crowd my mind. Of them all, one is my favorite. It occurred shortly before my imprisonment.

It is evening in our living room and I'm in an armchair, reading. On the sofa Edith is telling Ricky her pre-bed story. Ricky has picked an illustration from the Bible and wants the story of the picture. I pay no attention but at one point Edith's words begin to impinge on my consciousness.

"...and so," Edith is saying, "they ran away to Egypt."

"Why?" says Ricky.

"Because of King Herod."

"Why?"

"Because he's a bad king."

"Why?"

"Because he hurt children."

"Why?"

"Because he was a bad king."

A pause. My attention has left the book and I'm listening. Ricky's voice goes on.

"Are there bad kings now, mummy?"

"Sure," says Edith.

"Where?"

"In Greece. The King of Greece is very bad." I look up amused at the political seminar.

"Why?" Ricky's whys are practically automatic.

"He hurts his people."

"Why?"

"Because he's a bad king."

"Why don't people do something?"

"Oh, they will."

"What?"

"Someday they'll throw him out of Greece."

"Then what?"

"Why, he'll come to America."

"Then what?"

Edith has noticed I'm listening. She smiles at me fondly, a mischievous gleam in her eye.

"That's easy. Daddy will get up and make a speech against him."

Ricky looks over and sees me grinning. She scrambles off the sofa.

"Daddy!" she yips and scampers over, her copper hair a-bannering. She throws herself at me.

"Will you, Daddy? Will you?"

"I certainly will," say I, in my most heroic tone.

"Then what?"

I grin at Edith,

"I'll probably go to jail."

"Oh," says Ricky suddenly thoughtful. This is a sobering end to a wild story. There's a longish pause and she comes up with a solution.

"I'll get you out," says Ricky.

"Will you sweet?"

"Huh, huh," she nods vigorously, her hair dancing. "All my friends together."

I give her a quick hug. Over the beloved head my eyes meet Edith's. She smiles gravely, her glance steadfast and unafraid. I see her ill, emaciated face and a surge of love and pride goes through me. A well-known line, modified, passes through my mind, "I thank whatever gods there be, for her unconquerable soul."

At night, in jail, I do not dwell too long on such reminiscences. From a sense of pleasure one is apt to slide into a demoralizing loneliness and longing. So I move on to other people, other events. One sequence of memories recurs as I think of the long road that led to jail. I refer to the memories of my teachers, the men and women whose teachings are very relevant to my present condition. The schoolteachers of my youth, most of them sound Republicans, are more responsible for my beliefs than any other single group of people. Not only for my beliefs, but in a large part for the specific decisions which molded my life to fit the pattern of a Trumanized conviction and imprisonment. As I look back on the path I've traveled, again and again at important crossroads there stands a teacher.

One of the three or four most important events in my life was participation in the Spanish Civil War. I went to Spain as a sidetrip on the route to Oxford University on a fellowship from Williams College. The teacher at this particular crossroad was Tyler Dennett, President of Williams. Tyler Dennett was a great educator and a great democrat. There is a poignant story of democracy betrayed in the life of Dennett which would make a thoughtful novel. Dennett was a staunch conservative in his politics, but his deep-rooted Americanism made him very progressive in educational matters. He set out to give Williams College the finest liberal faculty in the country, and to give it a student body based on merit rather than wealth. He wished to attract the best of American youth, even if poor. I should say, rather, *especially* if poor. For, with great insight into the dynamics of society, Dennett knew that in the final analysis the strength of our democracy lay not in its wealth but in its people and its leaders. In a time of change, men were needed who had not only training, but imagination. He was well aware that ability knows no social or economic caste but is to be found throughout the body of the population. A democracy is stronger than an oligarchy because its seedbed of leadership is wider; the more democratic the society—the more reality there is to freedom of opportunity, the careers open to talent—the more certain it will be that the society will find the leadership to match its needs. This is one of the great lessons of the Lincoln legend, and Dennett was explicit about it.

He wanted to make of Williams an instrument of democratic leadership. It was a daring and noble vision. His goal entailed a shake-up in the existing faculty and a great emphasis on scholarship funds. In the process he ran afoul of reactionary trustees, who maneuvered him out of office. Dennett retired to his home on Lake George. I don't think he ever got over the cruel and ruthless liquidation of his hopes. He died while I was in jail so I couldn't even send a message of sympathy to his wife. Dennett was a fine man and true; I think of him with respect and affection.

If Williams College in general and Dennett in particular were the main signpost on the road to Spain, another signpost, a previous crossroad, was also put up by a teacher. I went to Williams College as a direct result of Professor Jordan, teacher of mathematics in Scranton's Central High School. Professor Jordan was what is known as a "character," a white-haired, portly, courteous man of sixty-odd, well preserved, who moved with stately, energy-preserving steps. He had a cherubic countenance, finicky enunciation and a deceptively low voice, masking a formidable and truly demoniacal temper. This terrorized not only the student body but the faculty as well, since most of the teachers had once been his students. He was held in fearsome awe—and greatly beloved. I remember him well: he could easily have been ridiculous but he never stepped beyond the sublime. He was a fine man and a great teacher, a wise, deeply moral man. I admired him greatly.

Throughout high school I was determined to become a scientist. Mathematics fascinated me and I took to them as the proverbial duck to water. Day in and day out I rolled up what is probably still the highest record in the school, an average of 97 percent over the four years.

Imagine my surprise therefore when Professor Jordan, in his Johnsonian manner, threw cold water on my ideas. I should be a writer, he insisted. I should go to a liberal arts college; in fact, I should go to Williams College. Such was his strength and influence that after some rearguard skirmishes I gave in: Williams it was—perhaps to that school's regret.

I have been very fortunate in my teachers. The few unworthy ones have faded from memory. There hasn't been a school where I haven't found one, and sometimes several, real teachers, dedicated men and women of the highest mental and moral caliber. I should perhaps say ethical rather than moral, for morality has a connotation of churchly maxim and sterilized impulses. The good teachers were wonderfully alive. They had standards of right and wrong and they taught them. They all had in common a splendid democratic approach to me as an immigrant which was deeply moving. They gave of their time and energy, often out of school hours, to help me acclimate myself, making me at home in a new society, improving my speech, fitting my manners to prevailing customs. Their thoughtfulness was due in part to the fact that I was eager to learn and thus made a satisfying student. Primarily, however, their interest was the expression of the fundamental decency and democratic outlook of our teachers. Most of them I remember with gratitude, many with affection, and a few with something like love.

As I write this, my wife sends notice that over a hundred college professors from various universities have signed a petition for a presidential pardon for me. Of those, some thirty teachers were from Williams College. The news touches me, for I know that probably all the Williams teachers are opposed to my views, yet it is clear that they consider my sentence unjustified.

I am very much the product of the American school system. This is something for the FBI to worry about. I was engaged in formal study until the age of twenty-seven and the best in American education has been my privilege. Here in jail I am fulfilling my training—my presence here proof of the loyalty to the teachings of my youth. At present Williams College would hardly agree with this estimate. As a subversive jailbird, I'm probably their least prized alumnus. One can only hope that developments in our country will be such to make them reverse this imputed judgment.

I owe Williams College a great deal—not, incidentally, in the field of radical ideas, for education at Williams is of a remarkably sheltered nature. At the age of twenty-four I was appallingly naive, in spite of the fact that both in high school and college I had a reputation for radicalism. It was quite undeserved and due primarily to my constant anti-fascism. In fact my contacts with the left were exiguous. Norman Thomas came up once a year to give a sermon in the chapel. His socialism left me unmoved. I had seen enough of class warfare in the mining regions to know that sweetness and light have little weight with employers. On the other hand, when William Z. Foster came up for a lecture, I was alienated by him as well. This was the heyday of Communist sectarianism and he practically insulted us students. I resented his assumption that we were all tools of the capitalist class and also his obviously contemptuous attitude. John Strachey came to lecture and there was a flurry of excitement. He was ordered deported as a subversive the night he was supposed to lecture. He finally got a couple of days' postponement and the hall was jammed with the whole student body. It was a most disappointing lecture, innocuous intellectually and very condescending. On later occasions I found condescension to be a quality of Strachey, a quality I never thought warranted by his mind. A man like Palme-Dutt in England towers over him. The fact that as minister of defence in the British Labour government he is supposed to be one of the smarter Labour men is only a reflection on the rest.

There was only one, live, genuine, AI Communist around Williams. His name was Spitzer and he lived in North Adams, five miles away. He was a farmer's son and was home recovering his health after having spent time organizing the marble workers in Vermont. He used to come to guest lectures and was a great favorite of the students because at question times he would give the lecturers, men like the vice-president of Chase National Bank and such, a very hot time. He was lean, aggressive, sarcastic and smart. He was the only Communist I ever saw at close range until I went to Spain, and though I would have liked to know him I couldn't penetrate his disdain. Spitzer wouldn't even talk to me. In those sectarian days, Williams students were obviously much too bourgeois to be spared a few words from a tough Communist organizer. Once or twice he missed the last bus to North Adams and I offered him my bed while I slept on a couch. He took the bed, exchanging a minimum of words. He never thanked me; he never even gave me a pamphlet. I thought him very rude. I've often wondered what became of him. But there was one thing about Spitzer: everybody respected him, faculty and students both. He was infuriating, but he was a man.

There was a subsidiary reason why I was considered radical in college. I did a little writing, mostly short stories, for various campus publications. The short stories shocked the community; "raw" was a favorite epithet for them. Actually I wasn't trying to be sensational, only writing of the people I know, the miners, the immigrants, the neighbors of working-class districts. In the cultured, refined atmosphere of a remote New England college these people and their actions were strident. It didn't seem possible that life was like this; I must be exaggerating; I must be a radical.

But life was like that. Unconsciously, my feeling of identity with the working class, its problems, its attitudes, went very deep. I resented fiercely the drudgery, fear of unemployment, exploitation of the people I knew. I resented their ignorance, the superstitions fostered by the Church, the warping of people and particularly of children. Inevitably this attitude was reflected in my writing. But I wasn't conscious of it, and I wasn't writing in protest; this was life as I had known it and it was pretty grim. What seemed radicalism to the outsider was only the articulate expression of working-class feelings. From my point of view, the two are the same.

The character of my writing was in part responsible for the fellowship to Oxford. I was sent to England to be tamed. Miller, Professor of Philosophy, was explicit about it. He told me that the general opinion was that I had talent, but that my view of life was rather "one-sided." Oxford, as he put it, would 'broaden" me and "mellow" me. If anyone had accused these professors of corrupting a possible working-class leader, the accusation would have been bitterly resented. Yet objectively, this was what was going on. I am very grateful to Williams College, and my gratitude is the stronger because my conscience is at ease. Far from being a corrupting influence, the fellowship to Oxford turned out to be a means of working-class development. Ironically, the results were the reverse of what had been anticipated. I was "broadened" all right, but in the wrong direction—to the left. For I went abroad just as the Spanish Civil War broke out, and because of my curiosity and my anti-fascist feelings I ended up in Spain.

Spain was a training ground *sui generis*. Its teachings were harsh but clear cut; my development was incredibly rapid and very solid. In Spain political arguments and ideas were the very essence of daily life. Socialism, anarchism, monarchism, Communism, republicanism—any and all political concepts ever developed were here seen in action. Newspapers devoted long articles to criticisms and expositions of various parties. There was the freest clash of ideas, and, more important, these ideas were carried out and their results seen in practice. Through a series of accidents I ended up with the foremost anarchist column in Catalonia, the Durruti Column. I saw their theories translated into actions, and I was completely cured of any anarchist tendencies I might have had. In Spain daily events were seminars of politics and economics. From this time dates my interest in Marxism.

While the world went on its way to Munich, I studied Marxism. My first lectures on the subject in Oxford were a series by university professors. Professor Harrod on the labour theory of value, Collingwood on historical materialism, someone else on dialectical materialism, and so on. The lectures were held in the dining halls of various colleges, impressive chambers of echoing stone and solid oak, hoary with tradition. In these arch-conservative, almost feudal, surroundings I heard Oxford dons in mellifluous tones tackle Marxism. To my initial surprise they praised Marx. Professor Harrod opened the series. He was a young, good-looking, brisk man in his thirties. He began the lecture by saying he had no antipathy towards Marx. On the contrary he considered him one of the towering minds of the nineteenth century. He might go so far as to say that Marx was probably a genius, and he had a lot of respect for him. In fact in his (Harrod's) family, the name of Marx was as accepted and respected as that of Darwin. As a historian and philosopher Marx was superb. As an economist however—ah, there unfortunately Marx missed the boat. He had never heard of marginal utility, the foundation stone of modern economics. From there on, the lecture was a merciless, and biased, criticism—an annihilation of Marxism done in the most aloof and detached way imaginable.

A week later was Collingwood on history. Collingwood, too, had no feelings of animosity against Marx. In fact he (Marx) was quite a great man. He might go so far as to say he (Marx) was a genius. Marx's analysis of capitalism was penetrating, his ability to foresee economic developments, booms and depressions, falling rate of interest, and so on was astounding. Unquestionably, Marx was a great economist. As a historian, unfortunately, he was naive. His theory of the class struggle was greatly oversimplified, the economic motivation in history is by no means adequate as an explanation, the role of leadership of the individual is grossly disregarded, and so on and so on—the whole lecture a devastating attack on Marxism in the most urbane manner possible.

The philosophy professor also liked Marx. Marx was unquestionably a great economist and historian, but as a philosopher, ah, there unfortunately Marx was only a bright amateur, etc. This went on through government, sociology, religion, each professor seemingly a soulmate of Marx, except...

I do not know whether the approach was worked out in concert or whether they all arrived at the same line of argument by that process of intellectual osmosis so prevalent in England. It was a very shrewd approach. It did not tell the students that Marx was forbidden fruit and thereby stimulate the appetite; rather they made Marx *vieux jeu*, something pretty good in his day but now hopelessly antiquated. It wasn't Marx's fault of course; actually the old boy was pretty good, but he couldn't help it that he missed some of the important developments in the social sciences. After all, considering that a hundred years had passed, he had done pretty well within the limitations of his times. It just happened that those limitations were fatal to Marxism. It was a very smooth performance. Contrasted to the American universities' attempt to stifle Marxism by silence and suppression, the English were more subtle and more effective. They injected enough of the disease to draw its virulence, a kind of anti-Marxist vaccination.

On me the vaccination didn't take. I was just old enough and trained enough to be stimulated by their inconsistency. I went and read Marx. I was delighted. I found his history magnificent, his philosophy absorbing. I had trouble with the economics, particularly certain sections of *Das Kapital*, though no more so than I find with most contemporary writers on marginal utility. All in all, I thought Marx was tremendous, Engels likewise. From them I moved to Lenin, from Lenin to Stalin. I was impressed by what I read. These men thought deeply and seriously about modern problems and modern conditions. The value and efficacy of the Marxist method was shown in their application of it. The reader may discount my opinion, but here is what Professor Laski said about Marxism:

> no tool at the command of the social philosopher surpasses Marxism either in its power to explain the movement of ideas or its authority to predict their practical outcome. On the nature and function of the state, on legal institutions, on capitalist habits, on historiography, on the development of philosophical systems, Marxism holds the field against any of its rivals. On the breakdown of capitalist democracy, the decline of bourgeois culture, the rise of fascism, the role of non-revolutionary socialism it has insights not possessed by any alternative method of analysis.

A most attractive characteristic of Marxist leaders is that they were all teachers. Marx and Engels were indefatigable in lecturing and organizing study groups. Lenin had a favorite saying that the first job of a Communist is "patiently to explain." Under Stalin, the Soviet Union has literally been a nation in a classroom. All observers, friendly and critical, agree to this feature of Soviet life. There is in all those Marxist thinkers a great and abiding faith in the power of reason and the unlimited value of education. In fact, to find any parallel approach we must go back to the French *encyclopédistes*. And to find a parallel to the Soviet government's emphasis on education we must go back to that group of revolutionaries who founded the American Republic. The Founding Fathers looked to education as the very core of our national development and our democratic birthright.

It is a mark of the corruption of our contemporary society that this birthright is being challenged. For the first time in American history influential people are suggesting that too much education may be harmful, that college graduates have difficulty finding work, that our society cannot absorb the trained people. The answer seems simple enough: change the society. Another flank attack is to suggest that standards ought to be raised, meaning by that not that better teachers be trained or more able people attracted to the teaching profession, but rather that students be excluded from schools by higher entrance qualifications. The more thoughtful educators are becoming concerned over this attack of education. Writes Professor Perry Miller, "Restricting the body of knowledge to a small group deadens the philosophic spirit of a people and leads to spiritual poverty." Just so. It also leads to a decline of science, industrial progress, economic development and political democracy.

The current attitude of our society to education is seen in its attitude towards teachers. Teachers are the molders of our society. It is in the schools that the ideas and premises of democracy are made explicit. If there is any profession that can claim pride of place in a democracy, teaching is surely the one. Teachers should be the best defenders of democracy, and our schools citadels of freedom. Unfortunately this is not the case in the United States. From kindergarten to graduate schools teachers are poorly paid, their contributions minimized. In many areas their pay is insufficient for a decent living standard let alone that degree of cultural life that their work needs and warrants. Our society gives fabulous rewards to the hucksters; it treats our teachers shabbily. In the popular mind the teacher is a subject of amusement, the butt of jokes and snide remarks.

An illuminating episode occurred while I was in jail. When the head of the Chinese People's Government, Mao Tse-tung, went to Moscow to negotiate a treaty, he greeted Stalin as "teacher and friend." This caused great hilarity in our press, in comments, cartoons and editorials. It seemed very funny to them that a grown up, presumably tough,

Communist leader should use such words. The hilarity of our press is understandable. After all, can anyone imagine Attlee or Churchill greeting Truman as a "teacher"? Or the Shah of Iran? I suppose the appropriate salute from Europe's political leaders to Harry Truman would be "paymaster and drill sergeant," or, more politely, "banker and strategist." Unless Mr. Truman, nostalgic for the vernacular of the Pendergast machine, might prefer the elegant simplicity of "Hello boss." This is not a crack at Truman as a person. The point is that even FDR would not be considered a "teacher" by foreign statesmen. The concept simply does not apply to the relations between capitalist states. Capitalist leaders do not teach other nations; they outsmart them. The ethics are those of the marketplace, not of the schoolroom. The great contemporary statesman is Winston Churchill, crowned Man of Mid-Century by Henry Luce. In the half-century that produced Einstein, Lenin and Freud, Henry Luce chooses Churchill! One would think that the spiritual influence of Clare Booth Luce might have inclined him towards Gandhi at least. But no, Winston's the man. Let's look at him.

Mr. Churchill is a colorful figure. He smokes long cigars, wears siren suits at formal international banquets and drinks wine for breakfast. He paints watercolors and lays bricks. He is a fine orator, a skilled debater and a successful writer, though his prose is somewhat turgid. Admittedly he is a brilliant man, a courageous man, a tenacious man. Admittedly he has a gift for leadership. But obviously these attributes are neither unique nor necessarily praiseworthy. Goebbels was brilliant, Goering colorful, Himmler tenacious; Hess obviously had courage and Hitler a talent for leadership.

What makes Winston the Man of Mid-Century? He stood firm against the Nazi onslaught in England's darkest hour, as the saying goes. All honor to him, but it was the British Labour leaders who forced Chamberlain to resign and demanded Churchill. Attlee, Bevin, Morrison, Cripps, they too stood firm, had courage, are colorful, brilliant, etc. To Churchill's credit he has made it a recurrent theme in his memoirs that he was only a spokesman for a united British nation. At the time of Dunkirk when he told the cabinet that of course they would carry on, the cabinet exploded in enthusiastic support. Adds Churchill, "There is no doubt that had I at this juncture faltered at all in the leading of the nation, I should have been hurled out of office."

What, then, makes Winston the Man of Mid-Century? Why, says Luce, he's the twentieth-century Saint George slaying the dragon of Communism. Well, so was Hitler. Ah, but Churchill does it as a defender of democracy. To which I can only reply by paraphrasing a well-known saying: "God deliver democracy from her friends; she can take care of her enemies." This defender of the democratic faith has a long and unsavory history. He was either a member or a supporter of the British government that let loose the Black and Tans in Ireland, that massacred Hindus at Amritsar, jailed Nehru for years and years, led intervention in Russia where they shot Communists out of hand, the most notorious example being the execution of twenty-six commissars in Baku. (Incidentally, Hitler gave the same orders to the Nazis in 1941—Communists to be shot out of hand.) From the earliest days of Fascism, Churchill supported and defended Mussolini; for over a year he defended Franco in spite of such atrocities as the massacre of Badajoz. During the war Churchill put anti-monarchist Greek soldiers in concentration camps in Egypt, and in Athens in 1944 turned British guns on unarmed demonstrators to the intense disgust of FDR. This great lover of freedom whose heart bleeds for Hungarian feudal landowners and Polish noble anti-Semites has never, to my knowledge, raised his voice against the de facto slavery in the Union of South Africa where racism of a most virulent kind is rampant. A white minority of two millions rule a Negro majority of eight million with a ruthlessness and viciousness that make American Southern reaction seem namby-pamby by comparison.

The British know Churchill. British trade unions have no use for him. They haven't forgotten that he was the organizer of the defeat of the General Strike in 1926. They haven't forgotten that as Chancellor of the Exchequer in 1924 he set the economic policy of the gold standard wanted by big business, which resulted in vast unemployment and downward pressure on wages, even before the American collapse in 1929. As Minister Nye Bevan said recently in parliament, in miners' homes the name of Churchill was "execrated."

Mr. Luce's effrontery and propagandistic intent become obvious when one measures Churchill against other world figures of the past half-century. I've already mentioned Einstein, Lenin, Freud. I could name twenty others whose achievements cut Winnie to size. But these three are a good example of men in different fields whose impact on present human events is already greater than Churchill's and will become progressively more so in the future. I picked them because among them they cover the waterfront of human life.

Human activities can be categorized in an infinite number of ways. A well-known convenient classification is that of a university catalogue, with its series of physical sciences, social sciences, arts, and so on. All these can be subsumed under three headings which exhaust the range of human activities. These are: man's relations with nature, man's relations with other men, and man's relations with himself. Each of my nominations for mid-century hero corresponds to one of these three areas.

Professor Einstein is the greatest practitioner in our times of mankind's mastery over nature. He is reaching close to ultimate mastery in the sense of having perhaps achieved a unitary theory covering all manifestations of matter—the goal which is the culmination of several centuries of titanic scientific activity. Einstein will be remembered as long as the human race shall live. Churchill's name will be lumped together with a hundred thousand others, with Holofernes and Tutankhamun, Saladin and Kublai Khan, Ulysses and Hamilcar, Akbar and Montezuma, King Alfred and Charlemagne, Cavour and Bismarck, Clemenceau and Pershing—statesmen, warriors and politicians during those first few millennia which posterity will know dimly as the bloody dawn of recorded history. Their names will be known to specialists and antiquarians, just as today only specialists know the names of Greek tribal chiefs or the names of Roman consuls.

On the narrowest basis, Luce's criterion fits Einstein more snugly than Churchill—namely, as the man who has most influenced the mid-century. Einstein's work on the equivalence of matter and energy is the theoretical basis of atomic development, and his letter to Roosevelt urging atomic work was the immediate stimulus for the Manhattan Project. The influence of atomic power in post-war world affairs has been incalculably greater than any Churchillian contribution. Its influence for the future is beyond imagination at this time.

While in a sense Einstein's influence on our century is derivative, Lenin's is direct and self-evident. To compare Lenin and Churchill is to compare genius with talent. Lenin was the founder of the Soviet Union. This fact alone, in its influence on our times, completely overshadows Churchill's career. But Lenin did more. He developed the form of organization known as the Communist Party and developed Marxism in the era of imperialism. Lenin's teachings applied by Communist parties everywhere are changing the face of the earth. The Chinese Revolution is only the latest of Lenin's legacies. Lenin was as great a genius in understanding society as Einstein is in understanding nature. To read Lenin, whether his books or his brief impromptu speeches, is to see a profoundly creative mind at work. He improvises political and social forms, he shapes strategy and tactics of social struggle, he illuminates with incisive clarity the problems of a new society—and he does all this with a profusion of ideas, a power of prediction and a seeming ease which are literally awe-inspiring and at the same time gratifying … for this is a Man at Work. It is the distinguishing mark of Lenin's genius that in an ostensibly chaotic welter of events, he recognizes in its earliest stages the possible patterns embedded in the chaos; that he unerringly pinpoints what is valid, useful, permanent. The power of his mind on one hand and his great sensitivity to the moods of the masses on the other enabled him to find the limits of the possible, thereby giving him the power to shape developments, to make the possible probable and the probable inevitable.

Compared to Lenin, Churchill—whether as a historian, a statesman, or a thinker—is shown up for what he is: a talented, but profoundly imitative man. It is Churchill's good fortune and talent that he imitates great men—the Cromwells, the Pitts and the Disraelis. But imitation in a convulsive world can easily lead to disaster. Churchill may already have crossed the line at Fulton, Missouri.

I have also mentioned Freud as a candidate for Man of Mid-Century not so much for the specific content of his theories as for his method and approach. Freud is the father of a scientific approach to man's personality. He is as much an innovator as Copernicus in astronomy. Ultimately, the science of man's mind may turn out to be the most important contribution of the twentieth century. The science of psychiatry, in the proper setting of the findings of the behaviorist school, anthropology and with due importance given to the social framework, may one day be as important to mankind as politics and economics are to our generation. For our times, he is the least important of the three men I've suggested; even so, his stature dwarfs Churchill.

These three men have one thing in common. They are great teachers; they loved to teach, and they recognize the importance of teaching. If I had to pick the one who has most influenced our century, I would choose Lenin. Lenin, in a peculiar sense, is the man of the present. Einstein is in a sense the culmination of the past; Freud is the glimmering of the future. But Lenin deals with the problems which are essentially of the twentieth century—the creation of a society which can fully utilize the Einsteins and set the stage for the development of the Freuds. As in the past twenty-five years, the next quarter-century will be dominated by Lenin's teachings—as section after section of mankind will be guided to victory and reconstruction.

As for Churchill, Luce's Man of Mid-Century, when the present flood of propaganda subsides, he will be remembered as the great leader of a great nation in a great crisis. At least I hope he will be. I hope that he will be recalled with admiration as the resolute fighter of Dunkirk, the man of clarion words and trumpeting deeds, rather than as the architect of the Third World War—the incendiary instigator of future Hiroshimas. As of today, 1950, Luce can have him.

Four

J ail is made for reflection. I ruminated over my trial and the events that led to it, the war-time years during which I served my country, all unsuspecting of the ultimate reward for it. My trial was an outrage— but that's a prejudiced opinion. I was amused to find indirect agreement from a most reactionary source, Mr. J. Parnell Thomas, ex-congressman, ex-chairman of the un-American Activities Committee, and, at the time of this writing, jailbird.

Thomas had been a member of the House Un-American Activities Committee from the pre-war days of Martin Dies, when he argued that the New Deal "was not far different from the socialism of Hitler, that of Mussolini, and the Communism of Stalin," although he explained, "This does not mean that I am opposed to progress or liberal causes." He was fuzzy on political science but expert on petty thievery. He had collected kickbacks from the salaries of his staff—as little as $1.50 a week from his secretary. He was a bully, and to look imposing as chief inquisitor he always sat on two telephone books to offset his short stature.

By one of those coincidences which would not pass muster in a novel, Thomas was in jail with three of his victims: Ring Lardner, Jr. and Lester Cole of the Hollywood Ten and Dr. Jacob Auslander of the Joint Anti-Fascist Committee (this was an organization set up after the defeat of the Spanish Republic to aid the anti-Franco refugees in France, Mexico and elsewhere. Ring, Lester and Jake had refused to answer questions by Thomas and the HUAC staff and were in jail for contempt of Congress. It was self-evident that their contempt of Thomas was fully justified.

In jail, Thomas got himself a deflated ego. He lost the arrogance and dictatorial manner that marked his investigations. Stripzped to bedrock, he was not a very complicated character, an average kind of insurance salesman, with a certain shrewdness and a certain friendliness which are the hallmark of the politician. He wasn't stupid, but he wasn't overly bright and I was tickled when inmates would come to me and say "How did he get to be a Congressman?" Most people have a glorified notion of the abilities of the average Congressman.

I got to know Thomas. It took a little finesse because he was wary at first, but we ended up talking. I had no feelings of hatred or contempt for him; in fact I had hardly any feelings at all. He had become a harmless nonentity. He was one of the minor tools reaction uses, like my judge and prosecutor, and there's no sense wasting emotional energy on them when they become useless to reaction. But I was interested in seeing his mind at work.

"I don't understand your case," I said to him, "you didn't do anything other Congressmen don't do."

"That's right," he said eagerly.

"Somebody had it in for you ... I mean, to single you out ... pick on you..."

"Sure," he said. "Just like you."

"Oh? How so?"

"Well," he said knowingly, "the government just used you as a scapegoat."

"But why?"

"Sure," he said, "the government was being pushed on the Red issue..."

"By you," I said pointedly.

"Oh sure," he acknowledged with a dismissing wave of his hand. The gesture implied that he had no hard feelings. Politics is politics. "See, Truman had to show people he was just as anti-Red as anybody. He had to pick on somebody and it happened to be you."

"Kind of tough on me," I said.

Again the dismissing gesture. "Just the way things break."

There was more to my prosecution than mending a section of a political fence. The explanation ignored the Truman foreign policy which required an anti-Red hysteria for its acceptance. But Thomas had a point. What interested me was his complete aplomb over the fact that naturally scapegoats are needed and if it happens to be you, why it's too bad. Politics is politics, scapegoats are a necessary adjunct, and if they can't defend themselves the sky is the limit. This is the kind of Americanism which seems perfectly natural to the man who was for so long the arbiter of Americanism. The reader may find its cynicism repulsive, but Mr. Thomas found it only realistic.

Personally I found it shocking, even though I'm not politically naive. I know that our governments, local, state and federal, are shot through with corruption. Tammany Hall and Harding's cabinet are only the most blatant examples of what goes on all the time. Steffens's *Autobiography* is an excellent book to cure any illusions on our political life. Yet in spite of my knowledge, there remains ingrained in all of us a feeling that at least the federal government is not as bad as a Hague or Pendergast machine. To meet an attitude such as Thomas's, which takes for granted congressional corruption and executive disregard of justice, is still something of a shock. The amorality is so deep-seated, so unselfconscious, that it has a certain wry charm. At the same time, when I thought of my own attitudes, my own conception of Americanism, Thomas and what he represents were somewhat sickening.

In my case the ward-healer's ethics of federal government was the more revolting because to prosecute me they used my work for the government. In proper focus, the government put me in jail as a result of my war work. This is not an exaggeration. Since my indictment and trial cannot be understood without the background of the war years, I'll describe some of the significant events.

When Pearl Harbor occurred, I was teaching economics at New York University. I had been teaching there two years, after months of unemployment. My wife and I had left Oxford in 1938, had spent a year travelling around the world, through Europe, the Near East, India, Southeast Asia, China and Japan, and arrived in New York in 1939. I tried to find work, any kind of work, but couldn't. My degrees didn't help: degrees were cheap. Finally I went on relief and then on WPA for a year. This the reader should remember is not a tale of depression years; this was 1939, a time of recovery. In 1940 I became an assistant instructor in economics and in 1941 an instructor.

During this time, we lived on the Lower East Side of New York, a slum area well suited to the WPA wages and later to my NYU salary. (I made two dollars a week more than on WPA.) In the Lower East Side political and civic activities were widespread. My wife participated fully, and I to a lesser extent. I spoke and lectured in Settlement Houses, for the East Side Tenants League, the National Negro Congress, the International Workers Order, and so on. For several months I was secretary of the East Side Defense Council. At this time my wife was a member of the Communist Party, and I was keenly interested, not only as a citizen, but as a political scientist. Ever since Spain I had studied the Communist Party as an organizational structure, just as I would study the American Corporation, the German Cartel, or the Catholic Church. These institutional structures are of primary importance in modern life. In fact, it is impossible to understand what goes on without some idea of these and similar organizations.

After Pearl Harbor I went to Washington to see about doing something to help in the war. I went around to several agencies and finally joined a newly formed intelligence agency under General Donovan which later became known as the Office of Strategic Services, the OSS. I entered government service on March 4, 1942. It was my thirtieth birthday.

An interesting incident took place. New York University tried to keep me on the faculty. The head of my department hinted at promotion; I had a talk with a vice-chancellor, in which he tried to have me stay. I couldn't see it, the country was at war and I was naive enough to think in terms of duty; I was surprised at the mentality of these high university officials. The official in fact flatly stated that if I went, there would be no place for me on the faculty after the war—this is spite of public hoopla about leaves of absence and so on. Later on when I was indicted the head of my department was heard to express his views on my "lack of patriotism."

In Washington, almost from the start I had problems over my politics. First I had to show I wasn't a fascist; then I had to deal with my reputation as a radical, which kind friends and former teachers had spread around. To meet the fascist charge I went to see Professor Salvemini of Harvard University, the outstanding anti-Mussolini fighter in America. The Professor had known me some fifteen years, had visited me in England, and was aware of my radical sympathies. So when I asked him for a reference, he worried whether I was a Communist. He was very friendly but he was very firm.

"Carl," he said in so many words, "whether you are a Communist or not makes no personal difference to me, or to our friendship. Furthermore, your beliefs are none of my business. But if I give you a letter, I am in effect sponsoring you, so I want to know what I am doing. I want you to tell me, on your word of honor, are you at present a member of the Communist Party?" I told him I wasn't and he said he would write the letter. I couldn't resist teasing him. "But professor, how do you know I'm telling the truth? Communists are supposed to lie, cheat, do anything to achieve their ends; why do you trust me?" With a dismissing wave of his hand, he sputtered: "Don't be stupid. We are both honorable men." His letter began: "Carl Marzani is not only a young man of exceptional ability but he is also wholly reliable from the moral point of view. Anyone who trusts him can be sure he has put his trust in the right place."

Washington was a madhouse with many difficulties in housekeeping. Yet there was a great feeling of high purpose, a release of one's energies that was stimulating and rewarding. It is by no means the least bitter commentary on our civilization that only in war do we seem able to fully utilize our human and material resources.

I was a part of the Economics Division of the OSS, which was under the guidance of Dr. Edward Mason, a brilliant Harvard economist. During the war he served on the Intelligence Sub-committee of the Joint Chiefs of Staff; after the war he became Dean of the Graduate School of Business Administration at Harvard. The Economics Division was probably the best organization of its kind in Washington, with many first-rate economists, including my section chief, H.C. Barton, Jr. The work of the Division was almost exclusively military intelligence, such as estimates of Order of Battle, capabilities of German transport, estimates of casualties. We often had jobs dumped on us from other agencies which were unable or unwilling to do them. One of these jobs supplied one of the minor highlights of my trial, so it's worth detailing.

I had been in the Division two weeks when a hush-hush job came in which we accepted. I found myself assigned to the HQ Commanding General, Army Air Forces in charge of a small OSS contingent of three economists and a Far Eastern expert. The job—picking the targets for Doolittle Raid on Tokyo. For one who had just started in the government this was very exciting indeed. This episode of target selection is full of memories and ramifications. In Japan before the war I had been detained by the Japanese as a suspected spy. It was in the spring of 1939; my wife and I were nearing the end of a round-the-world hitch-hike. We had come from Shanghai to Nagasaki (a lovely town then) at the southern end of Kyushu island and had gone north by train to take the Shimonoseki ferry to the main island of Honshu.

Our camera got us in trouble. It was a German camera, a Contax III with a 1.5 lens, a very expensive and very professional affair which was clearly out of place with our obvious poverty. When we landed in Japan we had been given maps with restricted areas where photographing was prohibited and I had scrupulously followed instructions. In fact when I was stopped I had only taken seven pictures—a fish market, a woman

and child, and so on. Once when the train had stopped in the country-
side, I had taken a couple of shots of factories. At the ferry slip there is
a long underpass, quite dark except for a neon sign that said in English
and in Japanese characters "This way to Shimonoseki." I took a picture
of it, someone got suspicious, and when we landed at Shimonoseki the
secret police were waiting for us. They allowed my wife to go to a hotel
and detained me. I was cross-examined exhaustively for two days, my
passport scrutinized, my story cross-checked for discrepancies. It was
very exhausting. They suspected me of being a spy, and when the pictures I had taken were developed they were sure of it. For, with that
kind of grim coincidence which sends innocent men to the electric chair,
I had unwittingly taken pictures of one of the most strategic and important industrial spots of Japan. I had photographed the steel mills of
Yawata, the Pittsburgh of Japan. Forty percent of all their steel was
produced there, concentrated in a small peninsula a couple of miles wide
and about six or seven miles long, impossible to mistake from the air and
impossible to camouflage. The ideal target.

For two days they pounded at me. Why did I have the camera? Why
such an expensive camera for a poor student? Who had paid for it?
Above all, why had I photographed the steel mills? To all their questions
I had reasonable answers, except to the last one. There was no answer. I
hadn't intended to photograph steel mills, or Yawata. I had seen factories and on an impulse had snapped them. But it was no use telling them
it was the result of a meaningless impulse. Not only would they not
believe me, but in my refusal to answer they would see the proof of my
guilt. Such is the police mind, the world over. I had to give them a
reason that would make sense to them and yet show that I had taken the
pictures with no ulterior motives. I had an idea.

"There's a reason," I said, "but I'm afraid to tell you."

They pounced on it eagerly, wanted to know what it was.

"No," I said, "I'm afraid you wouldn't understand."

Not at all, they assured me, they would understand perfectly.

"Well," I said reluctantly, "it's like this. Americans are crazy about
factories. It stirs their emotions, you know, gets them excited." No, they
didn't know. They were puzzled and wary. I warmed to my theme.

"It fires their imagination. To Americans factories are like ... like a
church almost. They have great beauty—you understand." No, they
didn't.

"It's ... well, it's art, really ... that's it. It's like an artistic impact. It's
just a national peculiarity. For example, in Japan you love flowers, right?"

The examiner nodded, forgetting he wasn't supposed to understand English and not waiting for the interpreter to translate. I had him.

"You love flowers. The lines, the color, the texture of flowers has meaning for you, traditions, associations. You've built up a complex art of flower arrangement. Right?" He nodded again.

But no other nation has such an art. That is so, isn't it?" It was so.

"Well, what flowers do to you, factories do to an American. They excite our esthetic sense. We love them, just like you love flowers."

They were obviously and clearly puzzled. The examiner who had nodded was on my side. He expanded the interpreter's words, argued volubly and vigorously. Incidentally, the widespread belief in Oriental impassivity is pure poppycock, like so many beliefs about peoples we don't know. I have seen Burmese, Chinese and Japanese as animated and full of gestures as the most abandoned Provençal or Neapolitan. Their gamblers are as feverish as ours and my examiner's nervous conversation would out-Winchell Winchell. The officials were uneasy, but my examiner was in there pitching. I must have struck some deep resonant chord within him (I'll bet he was a great flower arranger) and my impromptu esthetics were just enough within their picture of America to make sense. America is thought of as a mechanized land of gadgets, something like the sets for Charlie Chaplin's *Modern Times*, so it was possible I was telling the truth. Obviously a mechanized society must develop some reactions to machines. If I wasn't a spy it certainly made sense. If it made sense, perhaps I wasn't a spy.

Eventually, to keep the record clean there was a trial, I was fined ten dollars, my camera restored and the prosecuting attorney with a big grin shook hands. What might have been a serious business ended up as a charming memory. I have always been convinced that the chief reason for the friendly outcome was that I did not behave with the usual arrogance of the white man in the East. I didn't threaten to call the U.S. Navy, I didn't even try to call the American Embassy. It was their country, they had a right to be suspicious; so long as they behaved decently, it was up to me to be likewise. My behavior revealed my attitude and they reacted instantly. Edith and I have traveled in some of the most isolated parts of Burma, Siam, Indochina, and China; by adhering to this simple and fundamental point of view, we've never had trouble of any kind. On the contrary we were overwhelmed by friendliness and hospitality. I've always believed our attitude to be the truly American one; that same attitude carried over into foreign policy would pay bigger dividends than the current one of atomic diplomacy.

With this story as a background I felt a little ashamed when I was faced with selecting targets in Japan, for Yawata was obviously high on any priority list. When I distributed various sites amongst our group, I retained Yawata, Tokyo and Osaka for myself.

Air Force HQ was in the Maritime Commission Building, and there our group was welcomed by a captain commanding the Target Section, the unit which should normally be picking the targets. The captain, in civilian life a professor at Yale, was very hush-hush. He showed me a "flimsy" (a strip of onion-skin) marked *top secret* alerting his unit on a 24-hour basis. He had, and therefore we had, three days to pick two hundred targets in ten leading Japanese cities. The most important targets, the captain said. I asked him on what basis and he looked puzzled. I explained that to decide on what is more important or less important, one has to answer the question "important to what?" The captain clearly considered such attitude academic. Never mind the abstract stuff, pick the targets. I found to my dismay that the Air Force had paid almost no attention to the key question in strategic bombing, namely "What do you bomb?"

This was 1942 and I was pretty starry-eyed over the Air Force. I got my first glimpse of brass-hat thinking and I haven't got over it yet. For the American Air Force had committed itself to strategic bombing without doing any basic theoretical work on its application. This, incidentally, was true not only of the Americans but of all other proponents of strategic bombing in other countries. The question is worth a little discussion because it has its contemporary lessons.

The grandiose strategists of victory through air power are very offhand. Strategic bombing, they say, annihilates the enemy's economy and his will to resist. Short and simple. But the "economy" is neither short nor simple. It is a huge complex of factories, mines, roads, railways comprising hundreds of thousands of units. It cannot be annihilated in one raid, not even a raid with a few atom bombs. Any raid, whether of a hundred planes or a thousand planes, must have specific targets. How do you decide what to bomb?

The military mind has a number of reflexes and it immediately dishes one out. Simple, they say: destroy the enemy's counterweapon, his fighter airplanes. But the answer isn't simple at all. The fighter plane industry is the end product of a number of other industries. There is mining; iron ore and coal for steel, bauxite for aluminum. There is electric power, transportation, components plants like ball bearings—dozens of industries on the back of the airplane industry. Which do you bomb?

Or take the airplane industry alone. It is itself a big complex: engine plants, frame factories, sub-assemblies like carburetors, tall controls, undercarriages, instruments, items such as tires, weapons, small motors of all kinds. Which do you bomb?

All kinds of considerations are important. Suppose you bomb engine plants but the enemy has excess capacity—you've done no vital harm. Unless you study the problem you don't know what the key bottleneck may be. It may be blast furnaces; it may be mines. In the case of Germany it turned out to be ball bearings, but you'd never know it without thorough study. At one time it looked as if the abrasives (grinding wheels and compounds) were more important; that is, the tools to make the planes might have been the bottleneck.

Again, to show how wide the ramifications go, it may be that to stop the fighter planes, it isn't the airplane industry you should bomb at all, but the petroleum industry, wells, refineries and so on. Or maybe you should bomb the pilot-training schools.

Then there is the question of recuperation. Some factories can be repaired more quickly than others. A bridge can be repaired more quickly than a tunnel or a dam; a railway embankment more quickly than a marshalling yard, and so on. There is the question of how quickly are the effects of the bombing to be felt. Take a fighter air force. It is echeloned in depth. There are the front line squadrons, the reserve squadrons. There are warehouses at repair centers with engineers and spare parts. If you bomb engine plants it may be a year before lack of engines is felt on the battlefield. On the other hand, if you bomb an assembly plant, the effects may be felt within a month. However, the assembly plant can be repaired in two weeks while the engine plant may take six months to be back in production.

All these considerations, and hundreds like them, must be weighed. I had never seen any literature on the subject, but I assumed that the Air Force had studied the matter thoroughly, and they had certain tests which could be applied to select targets. I was dead wrong. In 1942, *the air forces hadn't even begun to ask the questions*, let alone find the answers. It took us and the British nearly a year to build up the necessary organization in England to make strategic bombing significant.

There is in all bombing one basic fact that must be known. It is a trivial, self-evident, obvious fact, so much so that it is completely taken for granted; a very trivial fact, but paramount—namely, where is the plant located? Not only the city, but where in the city? You've got to know within a mile or so or you might as well stay home. There is no sense bombing Manhattan if the plants you want are in Brooklyn. Nor is area bombing the answer— that is, plastering the city indiscriminately and hoping that chance will take some bombs in the right places. For every raid you are paying a price in casualties and lost planes. Take a concrete example. A city like Los Angeles covers, say, a thousand square miles. A factory covers one square mile. Bombing blind, the chances are a thousand to one for any one bomber. Yet the chances of the bomber being shot down are perhaps one in ten, or one in twenty. These odds are dreadful. Unless target information is extremely accurate, strategic bombing doesn't pay.

I've gone into the problem of strategic bombing because it has relevance today. Precise knowledge of plant location is essential and we have very little information of that sort on the Soviet Union. During the war we did our best to find the location of Soviet airplane plants with little success. Atom bomb or no atom bomb, we lack the essential knowledge of the location of many key factories in the USSR. This is the reason incidentally for the tremendous secrecy in the Soviet Union, the limitations on travel for diplomats and correspondents, and so on. Also it is the background of various spy trials. When Vogeler was arrested in Hungary he insisted he was not guilty of espionage. But his boss, Mfr. Behn of the American Telephone and Telegraph Co., let the cat out of the bag when he explained to newspapermen that ordinary economic and industrial information which in the United States is freely available is considered secret in the USSR and the Eastern European countries. The fact is that "ordinary" information such as plant capacity and location are of the highest order of military importance for strategic bombing—as Mr. Vogeler and the State Department know perfectly well. If we in the U.S. feared strategic bombing as much as the Soviets did, we would not be so self-complacent about "ordinary" information.

In 1942 when I found out that the air forces hadn't any doctrine on the subject I decided to do the best I could by guesswork. As previously mentioned, I had taken Tokyo, Osaka and Yawata. The captain gave me a list of 3,000 targets in the Tokyo area and I settled down to what I thought would be several hours' work. Each target had a folder and I picked up the aircraft plants first. There was accurate information on them because they had been set up by American engineers. We had a street map with their exact location, their capacity, and so on. I put the folder aside as highly probable targets. I figured to work the 3,000 targets down to a couple of hundred and then pick the fifty most impressive sounding. I went on to the folder on arsenals. It was very skimpy, a sheet with a list of arsenals, and opposite an address plus a latitude and longitude. This seemed strange—no other information. I skimmed through the other folders and was dumbfounded. Folder after folder contained nothing but the same address that was on my typewritten list, plus a latitude and a longitude, which actually was the same for all of Tokyo. Some folders had a certain amount of information, but I guessed that out of the 30,00 targets listed, some 2,700 or 2,800 had nothing but an address. I felt kind of weak—on what basis could I pick any targets at all?

Even as I digested the distasteful discovery, the captain came over, pompous and self-assured. "By the way," he said, "there's one plant here that's a must. The So-and-So Instrument Company." He pointed it out on the list and it was already underlined. "It was specifically mentioned in a broadcast as having been praised by the Emperor for its great contribution to Pearl Harbor." He paused impressively and ended, breathless in adoration, "General Arnold has sworn to get them!" That was very commendable of the general, I thought, and who was I to dispute his desires? Yet there was no folder on the Instrument Company either, nothing to indicate its size or importance; just an address plus the latitude and longitude of Tokyo. It didn't seem very smart to choose a target on such a basis, but General Arnold was General Arnold and I put the company down. Then something happened that shouldn't happen to a dog.

As I've mentioned, we had on our OSS team a Far Eastern expert, a scholar who spoke and read Japanese and who knew Japan intimately. He circulated among us economists, answering questions, translating, and so on. He was a quiet, sweet fellow, with a thin face and that kind of intellectual intensity one sees in specialists who are complete absorbed in their subjects. (His name was Charley Fahr—I haven't seen him since.) He came by me and I chatted with him, about my problems, about the instrument company that had no information, about Arnold and so on. He smiled sympathetically, looked at the name and address and suddenly stiffened like a dog at point. I can still see him and I remember distinctly what he said because it struck me as so funnily melodramatic. He said, "No, no, it couldn't be!"

Writing now, many years later, I reconstruct the conversation as something like this.

"What can't be?" said I.

"That address," said he. "That can't be a factory. It's in the heart of Tokyo's financial district. Like saying 11 Wall Street, New York City. It's just the front office of the company. No sense bombing that."

He scanned the list rapidly.

"See, here's another... and another... and here..."

In the list of three hundred some two hundred companies had addresses in a small section of Tokyo. The story was obvious. It was like reading Standard Oil Co., 40 Wall Street, and expecting to find an oil refinery there. I called the captain and asked where he had gotten the address.

"I don't know," he said. The list was here when I came, two months ago. I couldn't tell you."

"Well," said Fahr, "I can tell you. They came from a telephone book."

"Could be," said the captain, "we have a lot of telephone books here."

"What a mess," I said. "Well, one thing is sure. We can't put down this Instrument Co."

"But we've got to," said the captain. "General Arnold's orders."

"You're not serious?"

"Of course I'm serious. It's an order."

"Nonsense, we can't."

"We must."

It was like a musical comedy, only it wasn't funny.

"Look," I told him, "don't you understand? The factory isn't there. It just isn't there. We can't put down something that isn't there, can we?"

Fantastic as it may seem, he wouldn't give in. We had quite a set-to and I finally became rude and told him Arnold wasn't my boss and he knew what he could do with his order. The captain retreated storming and sulky. I wanted the others to use no targets which didn't have at least one independent confirmation. When I applied this standard to Tokyo, I was flabbergasted. Out of 3,000 names, not more than fifty were surely in the area, and of those not more than half a dozen were important targets. All my worries about choice and economic criteria and what not were irrelevant. I felt a little silly for my stewing.

The three most important targets were aircraft plants on the outskirts of Tokyo. As I said, since American engineers had set them up, we knew exactly where they were and their importance. There were a few plants whose location was certain, though we didn't know what they were producing. For example, the Otis Elevator Company had a subsidiary in Tokyo. The manager, an American, was back home and had been interviewed. He stated that he had important machine tools in the plant and it was undoubtedly producing war material, though just what, he didn't know. I put Otis down. In this manner by scraping and stretching I put down on a map of Tokyo fifteen targets of which I was sure of their location and reasonably sure of their importance. I put the map away and went to work on Osaka.

The next day one of the enlisted men in the section spoke to me. "I thought you'd like to know," he said, "the captain has added targets to your map." I went to the drawer and took the map out. Sure enough there were an added thirty-five targets, including the instrument company, put down at random. Fifty targets was the order, and fifty targets were on the map. Captains don't argue with generals. I was angry of course, but even more I was shocked. A plane with its trained crew costs over a half a million dollars, plus the lives of the men and the scarcity of crews. To send such a plane over a target which, like the instrument company, *didn't exist* was not only stupid, but in a real sense treason.

Reactionaries talk loosely of treason, accusing Hiss, Coplon and so on. This was real treason—namely, knowingly aiding the enemy. If the reader thinks I'm exaggerating, let him consider this: suppose an enemy agent was in the captain's position, what would be the easiest way to sabotage the intended attack? Why, to send the planes over a nonexistent target. That was precisely what the captain was doing. The only way a saboteur could have improved on the captain was by destroying my map and making all fifty targets phony, instead of thirty-five.

I was so angry I couldn't trust myself to say anything. I made a new map, dividing the targets into two groups, one written in red, the other blue. I initialed each target and then listed them at the bottom with a brief description. I added a note that went something like this: "Eight targets marked in red have been verified from trustworthy sources. Their location and importance are certain. Seven targets marked in blue are probably important. They should however be considered targets of opportunity. Signed Carl Marzani Economics Division." I tore up the first map and took the new map to the captain. "Captain," I said, "I've made a new map with fifteen targets and initialed them. I've destroyed the other map. You can add anything you like to this; just sign your name to it." I walked away. He didn't, of course, add any targets. Because of this incident the map had my signature on it. Ordinarily such documents are unsigned; the first map was completely anonymous. But this signed map was, and is, in the files and the signature was to have great significance at the trial. That is why I've gone into the incident in such detail.

To return to my work in the OSS. A few months later my section chief, H.C. Barton, Jr., set up a new division for reports and analysis that came to be known as the Presentation Division, Office of Strategic Services (later, State Department). The division was to achieve quite a reputation. Just the other day, the *New York Times* mentioned the Division in an editorial as the creator of the United Nations flag. Hu Barton at that time was thirty-one years old, the youngest chief of division in the government, I believe. He was a career man, and, though a liberal in his views, did not mix in politics. Before the war he had been in the Research Division of the Federal Reserve Board, where he had made a fine reputation. Barton happened to have a distinguished family background going back to Revolutionary days in New England. More important, he had a first-class mind, great energy and an uncommon flair for leadership. Combined with a lively imagination and willingness to experiment, he had a rigorous training in economics and statistics. The war was made to order for his abilities.

Out of his decade of government experiences, Barton had arrived at a theory: namely, that one of the pressing needs for high government and military leaders was some improved method of intellectual communication—the passing of ideas and information from one mind to another more quickly than by writing or talking. Men like Roosevelt, Marshall, Stimson, and so on are fantastically pressed for time. They are under great pressure to make decisions and haven't time to absorb the torrent of information involved. No matter how much they delegate authority, and rely on advisers, there is an irreducible amount they have to know. As events pile up, that work can become overwhelming. The result is longer and longer hours, which results in lower and lower vitality. Churchill, for example, in his memoirs tells of working very late at night and taking an hour's nap in the afternoon, to reduce his time asleep. Stalin was apparently on a regime of five or six hours of sleep at night. Whoever could ease the burden of absorbing information would make a real contribution to the war effort.

Barton's idea was to bring to bear all the modern techniques of visual communication available in the commercial world, such as movies, charts, models, and so on; and at the same time maintain a high degree of accuracy and objectivity. He envisaged mixed teams of experts, some on subject matter and others on communications, who would tackle a problem, digest and present the pros and cons quickly and accurately. The reality and urgency of this problem of conveying data to top leaders is seen in the fact that something like our kind of work was attempted in the case of both Churchill and the German high command. Churchill in the third volume of his history reproduces some charts which are extremely amateurish. As for the Germans, we captured some of their work after the war. It was of better quality than the British, but still vastly inferior to what our division produced. Not only was our work of a technically higher quality, but it was more explicit. While the British and the Germans were either using old ideas or feeling their way to new ones, we in the Presentation Division had developed both theory and practice to such an extent as to virtually create a new field of communications.

I firmly believe that the techniques we developed during the war are of great value in the modern world. In his charming and interesting book, *From Cave Paintings to Comic Strips*, Mr. L. Hogben traces the development of communication techniques and in a final chapter outlines some of the most recent experiments. In our division we went well beyond anything he shows. All the arguments he makes for widespread use of new techniques apply to our work. The complexity of our society and its problems is tremendous—whether we deal with corporation managements, international trade, a Five-Year Plan or an atomic control program. Not only has complexity increased but it has become more explicit—that is to say, we are more aware of our problems, study them more thoroughly, bring more experts to bear on them. This is all to the good, and indeed carries hope for the future; mankind is increasing the tools to control society. At the same time, however, the increase in "expertise" tends to atomize the problems; the process of studying is the process of isolating areas and studying details. As a result the ability to grasp a problem as a whole, and still to obtain a significant knowledge of its details, is often beyond the ability of anyone but the most gifted individual. It is in this vital area that the kind of work we did during the war is of great value.

Yet it isn't only the leading elements of society that should be well informed. Democracy's continued existence and development require that large sections of the population be capable of analysis and judgment. Cordell Hull bemoans the fact that people today pay less attention to government than they used to. He points out that in the old days when two people met on the road they talked politics; today they are apt to talk about movies. There are many reasons for this phenomenon, not the least important being that present-day problems tend to be very technical. The presentation techniques of analysis and information coupled with the use of mass media, particularly films and television, hold great promise. I had always hoped that the United Nations might pioneer in the field, and even began working towards that goal. Jail stopped that dream. But the time will come when the education of the world's masses will be the paramount duty of statesmanship. The wartime experience of the Presentation Division, now buried under the Cold War, will be of value in the long run.

The success of our division was extraordinary and gratifying. We received commendations from the highest officials, including Secretary of the Army, Henry L. Stimson and Secretary of the Navy, James V. Forrestal, as well as from many top military men. Here for example is one of 1943 from Major General I.M. Edwards, Assistant Chief of Staff, G-3:

> Dear General Donovan,
>
> I should like to have this opportunity to thank you and the personnel of the Presentation Division for the excellent work done on the film, "U.S. Army Manpower" ... This film is a clear presentation of the Army's need for men and taking only statistical details, your people conceived and executed a production that is very useful and instructive.
>
> I should like especially to commend Mr. Carl Marzani for his work on the project. His untiring and continuous supervision of every detail made the production possible.

There were several reasons for this success. The most basic was Barton's clarity of conception, the fact that he knew what he wanted and had the drive to get it organizationally. Because his ideas were rooted in governmental experience, his organizational forms were sound. He combined in his outfit the techniques of the artist and the social scientist, both equally important, but working under the control of a supervisor who played the role of consumer and tried to bridge the gap between research and policy.

Second there was General Donovan. He was quite a character. A deep conservative in politics, not to say reactionary, he had a receptive and open mind on almost anything else. Under a semblance of genial practicality he hid a great respect for ideas, an avidly inquisitive mind and a flair for innovation. He backed Barton completely, shielded the Division in its infancy from the ax of the Bureau of the Budget, and was proud of our outfit when it had proven itself.

The third element of success was a corollary to Donovan's attitude. Because of his backing we had plenty of money for equipment and ability to get men out of the armed forces assigned to our unit. Barton was able to collect an aggregation of talent that was outstanding even in wartime Washington. This high concentration of talent in one division was the third element of its success. The division included architects and designers such as Eero Saarinen, Joe Mielziner, Oliver Lundquist, and Don McLaughlin from Loewy's office, and Will Burtin, who was to be art editor of *Fortune* after the war. It included editors like David Zablodowsky of Viking Press and Modern Age Books, and Ed Barnhardt, professor of philosophy at Berkeley; it included film writers and directors such as Ian Hunter, Bob Russell, Garson Kanin; artists and illustrators such as John Cosgrove, Alice Provensen, Don Kingman—all top people in their field.

A fourth element of success was the caliber of the other divisions in the OSS, like the Economics Division, the Map Division and so on. It was from them that we obtained the various experts for our teams. The result was high-quality work and a fine reputation for accuracy and objectivity.

The fifth and last element, setting aside due modesty, was myself. I was with the Division from the beginning till nearly the end, for four years as a civilian and a soldier, both in the U.S. and overseas. For the greater part of the time I was the Deputy Chief of the Division. My own contribution to the work was scattered over many areas. I early recognized the validity and importance of Barton's ideas and helped to clarify them. I happened to have enough know-how in both the arts and the social sciences to be at home in either field and thus be of use in bringing them together. Finally, I had a sense of what is important in a problem. This last requires some explanation.

Part of the job of a high official, in any field, is to be able to look at a problem as a whole, without getting lost in details, and to perceive its key points. This ability is partly due to temperament and education, but a good deal of it is the result of experience. As officials rise in their profession they deal with larger problems, and, political influences aside, those with aptitude for analysis (or for picking good analysts and advisers) will rise higher still. This ability to analyze a problem and seize its main points is so important that the highest compliment Churchill could give Harry Hopkins was to call him "Lord Root of the Matter."

Barton had this ability and so did several of our section chiefs and project supervisors. I happened to have more than my fair share of it so that in my dealings with the highest officials I could talk their language, see problems through their eyes, and not infrequently make some contribution to the discussion. As a result, I was usually the representative of our Division vis-à-vis our customers, particularly the General Staff, and was responsible in the main for the production of the Division.

The work of our outfit was extremely varied. It ranged from reports on new weapons like rockets, radar, Dukws, for the Joint Chiefs of Staff, to analysis of General Staff procedures for General McNarney. We

designed and supervised the map room of the Joint Chiefs in the Public
Health Building, the physical setting of the Nuremburg trials, and the
San Francisco Conference of the United Nations. We made training films
on sabotage for OSS agents in the underground of Europe and Asia and
films like *War Department Report* for industrial workers. (This film is in
the Museum of Modern Art collection in New York.) The work might be
a big job like a long intricate study on strategic bombing with flow charts
by Joe Mielziner, or a small but important job like the present seal and
flag of the United Nations designed by Oliver Lundquist.

In carrying out my work I had two valuable assets. One was that the
talent and efficiency of the Division made us keep incredible deadlines
without loss of quality. This was a big plus since in war time is precious.
Second I was bureaucratically independent. Donovan's confidence in
Barton, and Barton's in me, meant a chain of command which gave me
a lot of elbow room within the agency. Furthermore the OSS was an
autonomous agency directly under the President and reporting only to
the Joint Chiefs of Staff. Therefore I was not under the bureaucratic
control of the Army, Navy, or Air Force. Even when I was an army
private, I could, and did, talk back to generals (I was in civilian clothes).
I did it courteously, but I did it, in the form of both criticisms and
suggestions. If I thought circumstances warranted and a shock treatment
was necessary I could dispense with courtesy. I will give an example.

Late in 1943 the War Department prepared a two-day conference for
the leaders in America—national leaders in industry, labor, press, radio
and Congress. This was to be a progress report on the war with emphasis on the need for greater effort. It was to be opened by Secretary
Stimson, chaired by Mr. Robert Patterson, with the participation of all
the big guns, Marshall, Arnold, Somervell etc. The preparation of the
conference was the responsibility of the Undersecretary of War, whose
assistant, Howard C. Petersen, was in charge. We were drawn into the
conference through the General Staff, preparing some charts for General
Marshall, and visuals for G-2.

A few days before the conference there was a dress rehearsal. It was
a dismal affair, overlong, dull, verbose, extremely boring and clearly a
failure. During a break in the proceedings I saw Petersen pacing the
corridor with his aide, Lt. Colonel Larry McPhail, of baseball fame. I
was at that time an army private, though in civilian clothes. I walked up
to the pacing pair and gave them the shock treatment.

"Excuse me, sir," I said, "but this thing stinks!"

McPhail froze me with a stare and I saw Petersen's glowering face become still more thunderous. I wasn't worried; they couldn't do anything to me.

"I know it's none of my business," I acknowledged, "but the fact is, it *is* a flop. It does stink." Suddenly Petersen grinned.

"So it does," he said. "Who are you?"

"My outfit made the G-2 charts," I told him. He shot me a keen glance and each of us knew what was in the other's mind.

"Mmm..." he growled, and then grudgingly, referring to the charts, "the only good thing in this mess. He made up his mind. "Can you fix this show?"

"We have complete authority?" I countered. He seemed to like my impudence, for he grinned.

"Under me?" he pleaded mockingly.

"Naturally," I grinned back. Then seriously, "We'll give you a good show," I promised.

"Go right ahead," he said.

We did. We worked day and night and turned out a first-class show. Never before or since has the War Department had a more successful reaction from press, radio, and magazines. From that time on I was always welcome in Petersen's office. Until the indictment.

Although we worked for nearly every war agency, our biggest customer was the Army. We had close relations with the Office of the Undersecretary and with the General Staff. Our closest relations were with the Office of the Deputy Chief of Staff, General McNarney. This was the result of one of our earliest jobs, the one in fact which firmly established our division. Back in 1942 General Marshall requested a top-secret presentation of the U.S. Army—its size, structure, deployment, activation schedules and so on, the works—to be shown to Admiral Leahy, who had just been appointed FDR's military adviser. Our contact on the job was Colonel Otto L. Nelson, Assistant to the Deputy Chief of Staff.

Colonel Nelson was one of the Army's leading organizational experts. He had written the orders reorganizing the Army into the familiar Army Ground Forces, Army Air Forces, and Army Services of Supply and Theater Commands, eliminating the old divisions. Nelson was exceptionally well trained for an army man. I believe he was, at the time, the only West Pointer ever to receive a PhD at Harvard on army time. After the war he wrote a definitive 900-page study of the General Staff. A roly-poly Nebraskan, decent, genial and without pretensions, he struck me as a good example of what an army officer of a democratic republic should be. He had great admiration for General Marshall, and through his eyes I too came to see and respect Marshall's great qualities as a soldier. Nelson seemed to me to be a liberal and I liked him from the start. I think the feeling was reciprocated. I did many jobs for him in the U.S.A. Then in 1945, while he was Deputy Theater Commander in the Mediterranean (with the rank of Major General), I went to Italy for three months at his request, and finally worked with him in the State Department after the war.

For the Leahy presentation we suggested a film. It had to be done in thirty days, four reels, an almost impossible task. In fact, Darryl Zanuck, at that time a colonel in the Signal Corps, flatly stated that it was impossible. But by using four production teams, each doing one reel, and working night and day, we made the deadline. In the last week I was up continuously for seven days and seven nights without any sleep at all. Then I collapsed, but the film was a success and I received a fine letter from General McNarney:

October 22, 1942

Dear Mr. Marzani,

I wish to express my sincere appreciation and thanks for your work in producing the film, "The United States Army."

You should be highly pleased and derive great personal satisfaction from the fact that the film, completed of necessity in such a brief period of time, has been well received by General Marshall, Admiral Leahy, Admiral King and many others. This is due in large part to your efforts. I am aware of your enthusiastic participation and strenuous work, involving frequent all-night sessions and a complete disregard for normal hours.... Your attention to duty, initiative and technical competency contributed to the favorable reception of the film. I am pleased to extend my commendation.

I suspected that Nelson had drafted the letter for McNarney's signature, as he sent me one of his own couched in similar terms. Only it began with "Despite the fact that Colonel Darryl Zanuck said that the film could not be done in one month, I am pleased to note ... *etcetera*."

* * *

It seems strange to be in jail when I think back over our war work. Particularly when I think back at the absence of political animosities in the Division in spite of the widest range of political opinions and attitudes, from the ingrained conservatism of Saarinen (whose family was close friends with that Finnish crypto-fascist, General Mannerheim), to my own developed radicalism. We had great discussions but no ill feelings. A conscious devotion to the war effort was our common ground. Also there was in the division a genuine democratic attitude of free and easy relationships without rank or formality. In part this was due to Barton, whose deep-rooted, almost instinctive, democratic approach is in the finest American tradition. In part, also, I contributed to the atmosphere out of my conscious Marxist philosophy.

It is an irony, instructive if unpleasant, that my political beliefs for which I am in jail were of great value in the war effort. My ability to analyze problems was directly traceable to Marxist training. The same is true of my approach to work in the shop, and to some extent to the content of our jobs. In some cases I was able to make helpful, if small, contributions to the content. For example, there was the controversy over Siberian bases for the strategic bombing of Japan.

In 1943 a group of congressman were viciously attacking the Soviet Union for not giving us bases in Siberia, although as a matter of fact the American military did *not* want such bases while the war with Germany was going on, fearing it would precipitate a second front against the Soviet Union. All our military thinking was in terms of having such bases after V-E Day. The Soviet government was of course informed as to our military views, yet day after day they saw themselves attacked without justification. It was not a sight to strengthen friendship, particularly because of the effect on the American people. While preparing the War Department Conference, I came across General Staff studies on the logistics of the Siberian bases and their conclusions that they would be prohibitive. The subject matter of the conference was made by us into a film, *War Department Report*, in which at my suggestion the matter of Siberian bases was discussed.

When the film came out, several New York papers headlined the Army's position on the Siberian bases, and the reactionary congressmen shut up on this particular issue. Their power throughout the war should not be underestimated; many government officials often exercised a self-imposed censorship even when in no danger. For example, on the headlines over Siberian bases, Army public relations in New York immediately notified the Pentagon when the papers came out on the street. I happened to be in Petersen's office when the news came in.

"I'll bet," I told him, "that General Surles [then head of public relations] will ask you to cut Siberia out of the film."

"Oh, I don't think so," he said.

"Bet you. It can be done of course, but it'll hold up the film a month."

"We'll do no such thing," he said. He thought a moment. "I'll just go down to Surles's office and see what he's thinking."

He came back half an hour later.

"It's all right," he said, "it stays." Then he grinned mischievously. "I won't say he didn't ask to take it out."

The Presentation Division was firmly established by the end of the war as a worthwhile organization; though several of its more talented members returned to their professions, the Division to some extent was able to compensate for their loss by its accumulation of experience. We were on particularly good terms with the Bureau of the Budget, the Nemesis of government bureaus. After V-J Day, therefore, although we retrenched somewhat, we didn't suffer too great cuts in personnel. By the end of 1945 the OSS was liquidated. It was divided by Presidential Order, one half becoming the nucleus of the State Department's Office of Intelligence and Information, under Colonel McCormack, who had done a brilliant job in Army intelligence during the war. As a result of all these high-level decisions, I found myself in the State Department without having tried to get there. As a matter of fact, I was still in the Army when the transfer was first ordered. I spent nine months in the Department, a most interesting experience.

My transfer coincided with the assumption of a new Secretary of State, Mr. James Byrnes. As Assistant Secretary for Administration, Byrnes brought in his former law partner Mr. Ronald Russell. Russell in turn borrowed General Nelson from the Army to help reorganize the Department. He also brought in several men who had been serving in the Army, including a certain J. Anthony Panuch. Panuch played an important part at my trial.

Panuch was a lawyer by profession, a short, paunchy fellow. Uncouth in speech and vulgar in manners, Panuch was something of an anomaly in the Department. He had in his thinking a quality of wooliness, together with an undertone of violence, that struck me at the time as fertile ground for fascist ideology. I happened to meet Panuch on his first day in the Department, and I happened to be in conference with a couple of colonels when we met. He assumed I was some kind of important guy around the place and he offered me a cigar. Though our minds were quite dissimilar, we hit it off pretty well primarily because my language is not free from a certain "earthiness," which is not common in the State Department. Our relationship continued on a first-name basis even after he found out my relative unimportance.

I should perhaps explain that my formal standing in the Department was somewhere halfway between the Secretary and a messenger boy. The echelons of command went something like this. On top was the Secretary on a level by himself. Below him was the Undersecretary and six Assistant Secretaries as well as the Office of the Counselor, then vacant. Each Assistant Secretary had charge of a general area—Russell of Administration, McCormack of Intelligence, Braden of Latin America, Clayton of Economic questions, Dunn of Political questions. The post of Congressional Relations was vacant. Of these men, Russell was the powerhouse by virtue of his relations to Byrnes; therefore Panuch, as his deputy, and Nelson, as his special assistant, were also in this level. Under the Assistants were the Divisions, which were in effect the third level. These were grouped for convenience into Offices, but quite often a Division Chief was as powerful as an Office Chief. The Divisions were the operating units, autonomous as to budget and hiring. There were perhaps a hundred divisions in the Department, and as Deputy Chief of one of them I was not without bureaucratic standing. However, my relations with Nelson and Panuch were much closer than was warranted by my rank.

To return to events in the first months of my State Department stint. Mr. Russell had inherited a first-class headache, for the Department at that time was a mess (it still seems to be), the result primarily of a sudden growth. During the war, as the U.S. moved to a position of primary world importance, many functions of foreign policy had been handed out to war agencies such as the Board of Economic Warfare, the Co-ordinator of Inter-American Affairs, the Lend–Lease Administration, the Office of War Information, the Office of Strategic Services, and other smaller ones. With the end of the war these agencies were abolished and their functions went back to State, together with part of their personnel. As a result State went up from a strength of some three thousand people in 1939 to over twenty thousand in 1946, an expansion that was sudden, chaotic, and exacerbated by a fierce bureaucratic struggle. Every move to streamline the structure of the Department became part of a struggle for power. Basically the struggle was that of the old-line, pre-war State Department, against all comers.

The heart of the pre-war State Department were the so-called "geographic desks." For example, there was a "desk" for the British Empire, one for France, one for Italy, and so on. These "desks" were manned by a tight clique of a few dozen men, mostly career Foreign Service men, who also manned key diplomatic posts abroad. For example, George V. Allen, Jr., of the Near East desk went as Ambassador to Iran, Dunn served as Ambassador to Italy, and so on. These men ran foreign policy as their private preserve. They had been closely associated for years; usually they were intimate friends. If these men didn't like an official decision by the President, or by the Secretary, they would quietly sabotage it. For example, the "desk" man here might send out official instructions to a diplomatic post abroad. In the same pouch would go a personal letter that might say in part, "I've sent you a notice to do so and so, but it might be better to handle it thus and so..." The man abroad would be guided accordingly. This is no exaggeration. In an investigation within the Department letters were found of this kind. This species of internal dictatorship, by its *esprit de corps*, its cohesiveness, its expert knowledge and its control of the best jobs, either captured the Secretary or frustrated him. What couldn't be accomplished by these means was accomplished by the convenient "leak" to hostile columnists and congressmen. The "leak" was widely recognized as a major implement of internal psychological warfare.

The men who came to State from other agencies were often people of considerable ability who were not disposed to submit tamely to the control of pre-war cliques. The result was unremitting warfare, expressed in terms of organizational policy. For example, take the intelligence setup. Its new head, Colonel Alfred McCormack, wished to have a central control for State Department intelligence, where all information could be gathered, evaluated, and distributed to the various "desks." Aside from being sound intelligence policy, this would have given the Secretary a point of view independent of the desks, and this was precisely what the career men couldn't afford.

The main strength of the geographic officers lay in their ability to back a proposed policy with "facts." They were the experts. They were the only ones who had all the facts and all the specific information. Their "expertness" was their first and last line of defense. To have an independent source of information was bad enough, and to have the head of that source able to see the Secretary at any time was even worse. So they fought McCormack bitterly. Their counterproposal was that each geographic area should have its own intelligence officer who could act as a liaison with a central staff in McCormack's office. Inevitably such a set up would make the intelligence officers subservient to the "desks." The old clique was smart in this internal warfare. Though they disliked Spruille Braden, they maneuvered him into fighting McCormack. In this tangle, General Nelson took a wrong step.

As a good staff man Nelson had been appalled by the confusion. He set up a committee to study the organizational problems and at my suggestion put in a certain Just Lunning as secretary. At this time, beside my official duties, I was acting as a kind of assistant to Nelson. The committee uncovered many of the practices I've mentioned and Nelson recognized that the old-line men were at fault. He felt, however, that they had to be handled carefully and by indirection. He backed Braden in the dispute and McCormack resigned. Shortly after, Braden was maneuvered out and Nelson also left. The clique was in firm control.

After Nelson left, Panuch took over his work and I continued in more or less the same relationship. Panuch carried through some of Nelson's proposals, including one to strengthen an existing Management Division to make it a control instrument in administration. Again at my suggestion, Panuch put in Just Lunning as chief of the division. It should be observed in view of all the talk about "Reds" in the State Department that in this long important struggle neither the men nor the issues involved were political. For example, I had no idea what Lunning's politics were when I recommended him for the job. I still don't know. But I had seen him at work and he was a good administrator. McCormack was a conservative; Russell even more so. Panuch was a semi-fascist; Nelson a liberal. As for me, I worked both for Nelson and for Panuch with easy conscience. My job was to help make the Department more efficient and I was doing so. I kept my nose completely out of foreign policy, just as I had done during the war.

I had not, however, abdicated the use of either my mind or my conscience. To make a government agency function smoothly when you approve of its basic purpose is one thing; to do so when you disapprove is another. After the end of the war I became aware of a slow shift in our foreign policy. China was the beginning. I knew how large was our intervention on the side of Chiang Kai-shek; how we had airlifted Chiang's divisions into Manchuria to stop the Communists; how our Navy in Tsingtao was helping Chiang, while Marshall unwittingly double-talked peace. Then our Germany policy began to crystallize. Robert Murphy, of Darlan fame, was General Clay's political adviser, and Clay began to give in to big-business pressure from America, channeled through James Forrestal. The dissolution of German cartels and the break-up of German big business was an irreducible essential for German democratization. The point of control was the de-cartelization policy of the Finance Branch of the Economic Division of the American Military Government. The head of the Economics Division, Colonel Bernstein, was forced out and William Draper, a banker, was installed. He was from Dillon, Read & Co., Forrestal's old firm. Russ Nixon, a progressive

above
"Free Carl
Marzani."
Ricky and Tony
ride in the May
Day Parade, 1951

below
Carl at the
United Electrical
Workers, 1952

above   Wedding of Carl
and Charlotte with "rabbi"
Angus Cameron, 1966

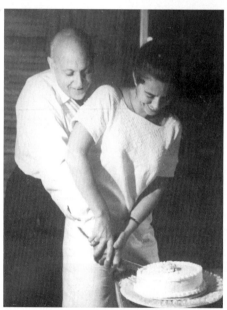

centre   Carl and Charlotte's
engagement party, 1966

below   Carl's in-laws,
Abe and Phyllis Pomerantz, 1966

Carl working on the reconstruction on 21st Street, 1966

above Carl with Daniel
and Posy, 1970

below Charlotte with Posy
and Daniel on Fire Island,
1975

Charlotte, Ricky, and Tony, with Daniel, Jennifer, and Posy,
Puerto Rico, 1973

above Carl with Ricky on Fire Island, 1976

below Daniel in a bucket,
Guanica, Puerto Rico, 1973

above The "finished" Fire Island house, 1990

below The house Carl built in Guanica, Puerto Rico, 1975

above Carl coming home from clamming on Fire Island, 1985

below Carl in his office on 21st Street, 1991

THE SURVIVOR

A Novel

by

CARL MARZANI

we can be friends
THE ORIGINS OF THE COLD WAR
by Carl Marzani

September Selection

INSIDE

THE

Khrushchev

ERA

GIUSEPPE BOFFA

A critical but friendly newspaperman
who worked in Russia for the last

The
Open Marxism
of
Antonio Gramsci

Translated and Annotated
by
CARL MARZANI

NEW YORK
Cameron Associates
1957

CUBA
VS
THE
C.I.A.

by Robert E. Light, Carl Marzani

$1

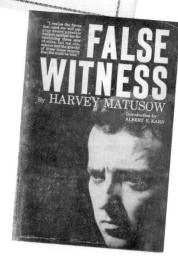

"I realize the forces
that need me will em-
ploy every possible
weapon against me for
recounting these acts
of mine, but my con-
science and the gravity
of these times require
that the truth be told."

FALSE
WITNESS
BY HARVEY MATUSOW

Introduction by
ALBERT E. KAHN

trade unionist, was forced out as head of the Finance Branch. German big business, one of the major pillars of Nazism, was on the way back.

At the same time the Baruch proposals on atomic control disturbed, with the emphasis on American domination. We were reneging on our Potsdam agreement, anti-Soviet propaganda was increasing, and finally, as a clincher, came Churchill's Fulton speech with Truman on the platform. The shape of the post-war world was becoming clear and I didn't like it. I felt I could no longer work in the government. I was helping to make the State Department efficient—but to what purpose? It was time for me to get out.

I didn't come easily to this decision. Government work in peacetime is not unpleasant. There is security, no pressure, vacation with pay, sick leave. My pay was good, close to $9,000 a year and the paychecks were steady and welcome after the financial licking of the war. At the same time I knew that I would become very unhappy in my job if reactionary trends continued, as I thought they would. So I looked around for a job, preferably in the trade unions, and I found just what I was looking for.

A group of my friends had started a business in Washington and they were asked to make a film by the UE, the United Electrical, Radio and Machine Workers of America, one of the largest unions in the country. It was suggested I write the script and produce it, which I was happy to do. In view of the redbaiting of the UE that has gone on, I might mention that at about this time I was also offered a job by Victor Reuther, of the UAW, to be his assistant.

To do the film, I took a leave of absence. During the war I had taken no vacation and had quite a lot of leave accumulated. Furthermore, I had put in a fantastic amount of overtime. One- and two-night stretches were frequent. Without exaggeration, in four years of war work I put in easily the equivalent of one year's unpaid overtime. Other people in the Division had also put in overtime. With the approval of General Donovan we had worked out a system of compensatory leave. After a long job, people were given time off. This included military personnel who worked as hard and as long as civilians. This compensatory overtime had also accumulated, since I had taken no time off. I used up about two months of this time to make the film. (Incidentally, using a technicality that compensatory leave is not transferable between agencies, the government at the time of the indictment put in a claim for a refund of my pay. There is no trick they haven't used to repay my naive attitude of working loyally for my country without thought of recompense.)

The film I produced in the summer of 1946 was *Deadline for Action*.

It turned out to be the direct cause of my indictment. If I say so myself, it was a good film. As I write this, five years later, the *Nation* in a recent review of labor films, has called it the "classic" of labor documentaries. The film was built around the great strike struggles in early 1946. It showed the UE's fight against such powerful corporations as GE and Westinghouse. It showed these companies using injunctions and police violence to break strikes. One particularly powerful sequence showed the Philadelphia police, nearly a thousand strong, mercilessly and deliberately clubbing UE strikers. Their viciousness was terrifying and the camera caught it—an unimpeachable record. It was pure accident that such a record was made; a union man happened to be an amateur cameraman. The sequel to his photography is a striking commentary on how police will break the laws with impunity.

The Philadelphia police tried very hard to find the film. They tried to browbeat the cameraman; they broke into and searched his apartment. The cameraman was so terrorized that when I went to see him in Philadelphia to get the film he was afraid to open the door until I could satisfy him I was from the union. I remember thinking this was like a scene from a film on Nazi Germany. It was the first time I felt like that; the feeling was to become commonplace in the next five years. Once I was in his apartment he couldn't find the film. "They got it," he kept saying, "they got it." He was referring to the police. Finally he found it. He had hidden it so well that he had fooled himself.

Deadline for Action was more than a documentary on strikes and police violence. It dug below the surface of union struggles to the bedrock reality of the monopoly structure of the American economy. The film was based entirely on government documents, some of them, ironically enough, from Truman's wartime investigating committee. It showed conclusively the oligopoly control of American business—how eight groups controlling 101 key corporations owned 30 percent of all the assets in America. Five of these groups are family groupings—Morgan, Dupont, Kuhn–Loeb, Mellon, and Rockefeller; and three are area groups—Boston, Chicago, and Cleveland. The film named names. The Morgan group, for example, controls GE, AT&T, U.S. Steel, N.Y. Central, and so on. Dupont has General Motors, Mellon has Westinghouse, and so on—the roster of American economic royalists. The film contrasted our current domestic and foreign policy with FDR's promises made during the war. It exposed British intervention in Indonesia and Greece and exposed American intervention in China. It attacked our newly formed "atomic diplomacy" under the leadership of Churchill. It was a fighting film, painstakingly accurate, unanswerable and utterly damning—the first exposure of U.S. responsibility for the Cold War.

The closing sequence of the film was built around the Lincoln Memorial in Washington. The union hero of the film, a toolmaker, goes to the Memorial to renew his faith in the American democratic ideal and his determination to fight against reaction. Into this sequence went my own aching sorrow that the peace was being undermined, my own love for Lincoln, my own faith in the democratic progressive forces in our country. Even now, sitting in a cell, which seems to mock my belief in America's democratic tradition, I still hold unshaken to my optimism. I remember the end of *Deadline* with pleasure—and with pride.

I left the State Department officially on November 15, 1946, sending in a written resignation through channels. The resignation had been accepted, my pay stopped, my desk cleared out. Furthermore, I had gone around to various officials making my goodbyes, including our Office Director, Colonel Humelsine, and Panuch. Both were extremely cordial. I told Humelsine I was going to make labor films and he told me about his father, an old trade unionist. He seemed to approve of what I was going to do. Panuch told me that while he was sorry to see me go, he thought I was doing a wise thing since as a radical I could go no further in government service. He was effusive in his declaration of friendship. He escorted me to the door, with such shaking of hands and repeated assertions of goodwill. If he could ever do anything for me all I had to do was to let him know. And so on.

I can write verbatim Panuch's last words. I remember them because they struck me as typical Panuchiana, boastful, unclear and vaguely ludicrous. In view of later events, they were not so funny. What Panuch said was: "After all Carl, you and I belong in the Big Leagues." The next time I saw Panuch was six months later in a courtroom, where he lied under oath, swearing away my liberty.

Five

I was indicted in January 1947, the first domestic repercussion of the developing Cold War. The indictment itself came as a complete surprise, although I had about two days' warning that something was afoot. The warning was vague. One evening I received a long-distance call at my home in Arlington, Virginia. On the telephone was an old friend from the Lower East Side of New York, where we had lived before coming to Washington. My friend was a progressive trade-union leader, mature and level-headed.

We exchanged hellos and he started right in without further preamble.

"Carl," he said, "I thought you had left the State Department."

"I have, months ago. Why?"

"Something's fishy. An investigator came to see me from State Department. He had your photograph, wanted to know about your politics, were you a Communist and so on. I've found out he's been around to see a lot of people."

"I can't understand it," I said.

"Well," he rejoined soberly, "I don't like it. Something is up. I've been called before the Grand Jury tomorrow." Secure in my knowledge of no wrongdoing, I didn't take it seriously.

"Don't worry," I told him, "the government may be preparing a smear of some kind. Call me when you get through." He promised to do so and we hung up. The next evening I waited, more curious than anxious. When he didn't call, I called him.

"What's up," I asked. "Didn't you go?"

"I went all right." His voice sounded troubled.

"Why didn't you call me?"

"I was told not to get in touch with you. I hoped you would call me so that I would be in the clear."

"Well?"

"Well, I can't talk. I've been warned not to say anything about the hearing."

"Why not?"

"They say it's illegal and I'd go to jail." (This is coercion of witnesses and is itself illegal. The witness may repeat what he has said. This was the first instance of illegality on the part of the government.)

"Okay," I told him, "don't tell me. "Answer my questions. Is it serious?"

"Very."

"About Communism?"

"Yes?"

"Should I see a lawyer?"

"Absolutely. I think that's enough. The telephone is probably tapped."

"I realize that," I told him.

"I feel like a heel," he said miserably, "not saying anything and knuckling down to those rats."

"Don't be silly, it's okay and you've been fine. Don't worry about it. So long and thanks." We hung up.

That night Edith and I beat our brains trying to guess what might be wrong. It was two months that I had been out of the government. My work had been irreproachable and indeed something more: I had some pretty glowing letters of praise from the highest government officials. I had an honorable discharge from the Army, the friendship of my former superiors. There had never been any question as to my professional integrity, nor could there be. So what could the government be up to? The only indication was that a few weeks before I had a cold, curt note from Panuch saying I was fired. Since I had been on leave for months, and my resignation was formal, the letter was silly and I had dismissed it. Could Panuch be planning something against me? But what? And why? The whole vague formless threat seemed incredible. Yet the warning could not dismissed lightly. My friend in New York would not be so concerned without tangible and substantial reasons. Edith and I decided I should see a lawyer, though we both felt a little silly. What could I say to a lawyer?

The next day I had lunch with Frank Donner, a CIO attorney, who made me feel even sillier. He said a Grand Jury investigation didn't necessarily mean trouble, that there were all kinds of fishing expeditions going on, and probably nothing would happen. I felt like a fool, and a melodramatic fool at that, but I was stubborn and I said lamely that it didn't do any harm to be prepared. So he ran over a few lawyers with a thumbnail sketch of each. Of one of them he said, "He's a little on the academic side, but he has a first-class mind and real integrity." The name was Allan Rosenberg; it was the first time I had heard of the man. I called Rosenberg and made an appointment for the next day. I told Edith about the luncheon, and our friends' opinion. We were somewhat reassured, though there still remained a substratum of uneasiness. It wasn't too serious, just a feeling of possible unpleasantness, like being called as witnesses in a case, or something of the sort. Never did it occur to us that I would be indicted.

The next day I went to Rosenberg's office. I took to Allan right away. He was about my age, a friendly, mild-mannered, intelligent man. I told him the episode and he questioned me for some time. He was satisfied that I had no reason to fear the government and his offhand reaction was similar to that of the union lawyer—that nothing serious was going on.

We were exchanging amenities when the phone rang. He answered it and turned to me. "For you," he said. It was Edith. "Darling," she said, her voice tense. "It's happened. It just came over the radio. You're indicted. Subversive activities or something. The announcer said 110 years in jail. It's just crazy. The newspapers are calling up. What shall I do? It's like a nightmare." I made sympathetic noises and informed Allan.

"Tell her to say nothing," he instructed. "No comment until we find out what the score is." Thus began a struggle that was to last many weary years, a struggle between a lone individual and the most powerful government on earth. Allan told me to leave the office and stay away from my usual places so that the FBI couldn't pick me up. I was to call at half-hour intervals while Allan found out the score. If the Department of Justice wanted me, we would meet at the entrance of their building. "That way," said Allan, "they can't pick you up somewhere else and say you were trying to avoid arrest." "Oh, the government wouldn't do that!" I said, and Allan looked at me curiously. "Wouldn't they, though?" he countered.

I tramped the streets of Washington for three hours. Allan was having difficulty contacting the proper officials so I walked, block after block. My mind was in turmoil, my emotions roiling. I had a feeling of being hunted, of being on the run, threatened by sudden, unknown dangers. I tramped the streets, a part of my mind still objective enough to jeer at my walking around, like a scene from a Hitchcock film. For the second time since the night in Philadelphia when the union cameraman had been afraid to open the door, I felt like a character in an anti-Nazi film, with a sense of being hunted and outlawed. Yet this was the United States, the year was 1947, FDR had been dead less than two years.

I realized that an indictment is no joke. One hundred and ten years in jail was a scary statistic, not because I thought I would ever serve such a sentence, but because by the very enormity of that possible penalty the government showed its deadly hostility. I can't remember now, as I write, everything I thought then. I do recall thinking, "this wouldn't have happened had Roosevelt lived," for even then I realized that this attack on me was part of the government's swing towards reaction which I had so sharply attacked in *Deadline for Action*. I remember I had a bitter sense of futility about the value of the war, of my own participation in it, a bitter sense of my naïveté in hoping that perhaps this war-torn world of ours might at long last find its way to peace and prosperity. I felt a mean, overwhelming anger against the new men of the Pendergast tradition, the Trumans and the Tom Clarks, these moral pygmies whose narrow, parochial ignorance made them so easily pressured by the hard-bitten Forrestals and the devious Byrneses.

Today, four years after the indictment and two years in jail, that bitterness is tempered by contempt. The sense of futility vanished soon after the indictment, and, I'm glad to say, has never returned. In my darkest moods, when worries over my wife's health and my children's welfare have driven me into anger and depression, I've never regretted the war, never regretted our participation in it, never regretted my own freely given, full-hearted work. The world is a mess and people are suffering in it; but an Axis victory would have been infinitely worse. Yet while I don't regret having fought, I am the more determined that our brass-hats and power-mad monopolists shall not succeed in bringing their anti-Soviet crusade to the bitter fruition of World War III.

One further incident of that afternoon I do recall. I had on me letters, cards, addresses and so on—nothing in the slightest way of concern to the government, but I didn't want them on me if arrested. I had no wish to act as fingerman for the FBI. I went into a stationery store, bought an envelope and stamps, made a neat package and mailed it to a friend. Again I found myself acting as if in Nazi Germany; acting as if the FBI were the German Gestapo. This may strike the reader as an exaggeration. Perhaps it is. Perhaps to feel, as I did that afternoon, the chilling shadow of cormorant fascism is to be guilty of unbalanced judgment. But it is important to remember that I, an American citizen and an American veteran, only nineteen months after a bloody war against fascism, felt in the capital of America the fear of a political police. This may be hysteria—it is also a fact. To me the FBI represented not the shielding arm of democratic justice but the irresponsible fist of vicious reaction. I still feel like that. It may be that I am mistaken; that the pudgy J. Edgar Hoover, the chinless Tom Clark, and the complaisant McGrath have no points in common with any fascist, living or dead. The resemblance, as novelists say, may be purely coincidental.

Late in the afternoon, on calling, Allan told me that arrangements had been made. He had pledged himself to have me in court whenever the prosecution desired. He also had obtained a copy of the indictment; why didn't I come over to his office. I might be interested. I was.

The indictment had more than personal significance. It was a declaration of war by the federal government against the left wing in American politics. It gave notice that the government would be as unrestrained in its attack, as dirty, as unethical as any cheap machine politician in a corrupted country. The ethics of the Pendergast machine ruled in the

Department of Justice. This was clear from the very basis of the indictment. It used my patriotism against me. Had I not wished to fight and
to contribute to the war effort there could have been no indictment. The
indictment, in a sense, was the culmination of a long-running fight I had
from the beginning of 1942 to retain my simple basic rights as a citizen.

The struggle started when I applied for work in Washington. One of
the officials in Donovan's agency was Dr. Baxter, President of Williams
College. Kind mutual friends had informed him I was a Communist and
he was reluctant to hire me. He characterized me as "brilliant but eccen-
tric," the eccentricity being no doubt my long anti-fascist record, what
in Civil Service jargon is known as a "premature anti-fascist." However,
after being cleared by Army and Navy Security, I was hired.

Two months later, in the spring of 1943, I was interrogated by both
the FBI and the Civil Service Commission. They had been informed by
the N.Y. City Police Department that I was a member of the Communist
Party and what did I have to say about it. I admitted signing Communist
Party petitions, being a radical, fighting in Spain against Franco and
similar horrendous acts but denied membership of the Communist Party.
A few weeks later the Civil Service Commission found me "unfit" for
government service. This at a time when the war was going badly for us
and high army generals were praising my services. Still I was "unfit."

I appealed the decision. The Civil Service Review Board heard the
case. I made no secret of my radicalism; I didn't apologize for it; I didn't
recant. One of the questions they asked me was whether my wife was a
member of the Communist Party. I replied pointedly, that I, not she, was
on trial and that I couldn't, and wouldn't, speak for her. There is little
doubt that the Review Board considered me a fellow traveler, if only
because I refused to make the usual "liberal" attack on the Communist
Party. However, the impact of Soviet heroism at Stalingrad was having
its effect even on hardened government officials. The decision was reversed; I was granted the privilege of fighting fascism. A few days later
I was drafted into the Army, sent to training camp, and then returned to
the OSS on detached duty.

Despite the Civil Service clearance I was considered a fellow traveler
by the OSS authorities. I was refused a commission, time after time. I
had as my subordinates majors, captains and lieutenants. I was a private.
This created a real problem, for I was in daily transactions with Army
and Navy brass, and a private just doesn't talk back to a general. So my
rank was kept quiet and I was authorized to wear civilian clothes, one of
a handful of people in Washington who could do so. To the best of my

knowledge, I was the highest functioning private in the entire armed forces. The position of the OSS authorities is on record. In 1945 when General Nelson called me to Italy, he wanted me commissioned to facilitate the work. General Donovan refused. He sent a cable, which I saw, that said something like: MARZANI REPUTEDLY COMMUNIST. WE DO NOT BELIEVE IT BUT WILL NOT COMMISSION HIM. General Nelson wished to commission me anyway, but on two separate occasions I firmly refused. I did this primarily because I didn't want him to be subject to a possible future smear. The agency could have commissioned me without repercussions; for Nelson to have done so in the face of that cable would have made him open to criticism. As subsequent events showed, General Nelson did not have the sense of loyalty that I had.

The final tangle over my politics occurred in the State Department after my transfer there. In February 1946 I was called in by one of the officials and asked to resign in view of my radicalism. I refused to do so and went to see both Russell and Panuch. I saw them one Saturday morning and brought to each a copy of the hearings before the Review Board. I saw Russell only a few minutes; he asked me point-blank "Are you a member of the Communist Party?" I said, no, I was not. Russell was very friendly.

The interview with Panuch lasted two hours, of which only a few minutes were devoted to the issue of my Communism. To the best of my recollection at no time did Panuch ask me whether I was a member of the Communist Party prior to entering government service. His questions were extremely vague and loosely constructed. At the trial he testified that he had asked a number of very rigorously drafted questions. His first question to me was something like this: "Carl, what's all this about you being a Red?" "The usual bunk, Joe," I told him. I went on to say that I was known as a radical and had made no effort to conceal it, but I was not a member of the Communist Party. I also told him explicitly that I thought Communists should have the same rights as everyone else. I went on to tell him that I was thinking of leaving government work anyway; I just didn't like resigning under pressure.

The conversation turned into a generalized bull session, with Panuch airing his views on Russia, the Catholic Church, Spengler and other historians. It was the talk of a man who obviously liked to read and picked up opinions here and there without any realization that many of them contradicted each other. He also spoke at length about his superior, Mr. Russell, in terms of disrespect and animosity that surprised me by their venom. For my part I discussed our foreign policy. I told him specifically I disagreed with our policy in Greece and China, that we were riding for a fall, and that our foreign policy was slowly but surely going to make us hated by the rest of the world—not only the Soviet Union but Asia and Europe. He agreed on some points, disagreed on others, but in a most friendly fashion.

This was the interview that became crucial in the prosecution, both during the trial and before the U.S. Supreme Court. This was the interview that the government presented as a formal investigation with carefully worded questions. The interview was completely unofficial. There were no witnesses, no records of any kind; no notes were kept either by Panuch or myself. No questions were framed in a legalistic manner—the talk was rambling and spontaneous. After the interview, I discussed its contents with a couple of friends simply because Panuch's ideas were amusing, as were as some of his remarks on Russell. By repeating it, the interview became fixed in my mind and I feel quite sure that my recollection of it is reasonably accurate.

A few weeks later Panuch called me in and told me that he and Russell had agreed I should remain. By this time I was negotiating to do the film *Deadline for Action* so I warned him I should probably leave. He insisted I do nothing hastily; my work was appreciated and so long as Russell and he were in charge I would have no trouble. I made it clear that I probably would leave. Soon after I took leave of absence. In November I resigned. My resignation was accepted; as I've said before, Panuch was extremely cordial with his talk of us both in the big leagues.

Six weeks later I got a letter from this same "big-leaguer." It was a registered letter: cold, curt, official, informing me that I was fired as a subversive. Naively, I paid little attention to the letter. I thought Panuch was building up a record for himself to show congressional committees. The indictment disabused me.

All these episodes crowded my mind as I sat in Rosenberg's office studying the indictment. It consisted of eleven counts alleging false statements to the government. This indictment, drawn up *in 1947* stated that *in 1942* the Civil Service had asked me whether I had been a Communist *in 1940*; whether I had given money to the Communist Party, given services, spoken for them or used the name Tony Whales. Each of these counts was punishable by ten years in jail and a ten thousand dollar fine. Identical questions asked by the FBI were made the basis of four more counts. The last two counts stated that in 1946 a government official (Panuch) had asked me whether I was a member of the Communist Party in 1940 under the name Tony Whales. The total penalty for the eleven counts was 110 years in jail and $110,000 fine. Clearly, the government wasn't kidding.

The indictment was a masterpiece of legal phraseology designed to whip up hysteria in the press and prevent an unbiased jury. The American government prides itself on impartial laws. As the press, radio, magazines, educators and politicians tell us, ours is a land of democratic liberties. Justice cannot be bought. Men are not jailed nor homes broken up at the whim of a bureaucrat. Class bias is not the basis of prosecutions. Thought is free. Government persecutes individuals only in benighted countries, particularly those with a red flag. But in the United States the laws and the government are severely limited by certain strict forms. There must be an indictment, a trial by jury, an appeal. These forms also appear in benighted countries, but there, we are told, they are a farce. The reality there is that the government does what it pleases. In the U.S., on the other hand, these forms have real meaning, based on the Bill of Rights. These legal forms are scrupulously observed, now as in the past. They were observed for Eugene Debs, for Tom Mooney, for Sacco and Vanzetti. Jailings, executions, all legal. Legal for the Scottsboro Boy and for the Trenton Six. All quite legal, and quite efficient.

If in the process the truth is stretched a little, that's done legally too. Expert lawyers find the right words, the proper innuendo, the proper formulation to build a monstrous structure of falsehood—all quite legally. As was done in my indictment. The actual charge was false statements; the phraseology suggested treason. Inflammatory in intent, the wording was slanted for propaganda. For example, there was a charge that I had denied giving services to the Communist Party. Whereas, said the indictment, I had and such services were listed.

No. 1. I had sold tickets to a Soviet movie. Whether I had, or had not, I certainly couldn't remember seven years later. In any case that's a pretty horrendous activity and clearly designed to make the Capitol tremble on its foundations. But the "services" got more and more sinister until the next to last was, "He had stirred up racial hatred among Negroes, etc." And the last one, "He had trained and infiltrated members of the Communist Party into the Army and Navy for the purpose of taking over the Army and the Navy and overthrowing the government by force and violence." Me, they were talking about.

Reread this last charge. While the FBI had sat quietly by, I, a known anti-fascist, had been trying to take over the Army and the Navy. Think of it: that I, a trained historian and presumably intelligent man, could have believed such tripe is incredible. It is an obscene absurdity. Yet there it was, in black and white. This obscene absurdity uses the language of a Hearst or a McCarthy. But it was written by the federal government. It came out of the Department of Justice. It was used in a federal courtroom.

Re-read the next-to-last charge. Ponder it. It says I'm responsible for racial tensions. Since I object to Jim Crow I am responsible for racial hatreds. Not, mind you, the upholders of Jim Crow, *not* men like congressman Lapham, who at a committee hearing yells "Black s.o.b." to a Negro witness; no, he is not responsible for racial tensions. *I'm* to blame if Negroes object. Rankin is the hero; I'm the villain. The thesis that racial tensions are caused by the *words* of agitators and not the *deeds* of white supremacists is not an original invention of the Department of Justice in the year 1947. It is the shopworn thesis of Dixiecrat Southerners. There is no Negro problem in the South. Everything is well in hand. It is only the agitation of "damn yankees," "furriners," and "Reds" who mislead the happy Negro and cause trouble. This Dixiecrat argument is the lineal descendant of the slaveholders' argument. Slaves were happy and contented, fondly watched for and cared for by their masters in the magnolia South. It was only the abolitionists who made trouble, stirred up hatred, incited rebellion. The logic of this kind of argument may be summarized by saying that doctors are responsible for diseases by uncovering and naming them. Its most modern version is one prevalent among liberals, namely that Communism is responsible for fascism. The obvious fact, of course, is that historically both abolitionism and Communism arose to fight existing evils and the spread of reaction.

No, the thesis outlined by the indictment is not original. What is original is to see the federal government stoop to adopt the sophistry of Rankin and the language of Hearst. If the reader will think it over a moment, he too, I think, will find it passing strange.

But there was even more flamboyant cynicism and legal jugglery in the indictment. The indictment was drawn up in 1947; the alleged false statements were committed in 1942. Even were the charges true, the government could not prosecute since the statute of limitations had "run out," as the lawyers say. This statute says that the government must prosecute within three years of the offence. The statute of limitations is one of the pillars of legal freedom. The reason for it is usually given as the desirability of conducting trials while evidence and witnesses are still fresh and available. But there is a deeper reason, which is part of the essential inner structure of democracy. Without such a statute, the government could use criminal prosecution for political purposes. If a congressman, let us say, committed a theft, the government could decide to hold the prosecution over his head as blackmail, or spring the prosecution when it suited them politically. Likewise, the government might hold the prosecution in reserve for such times when hysteria in the population would make conviction easier. In effect, therefore, the statute of limitations demands that the prosecution take place as soon as the government knows about the offense. In my case, for example, the government knew of my alleged offense in 1942. They didn't prosecute until 1947. Why? The answer is obvious. They would have been laughed out of court. When the government did prosecute me in 1947, they deliberately violated the statute of limitations, exercising considerable ingenuity as well as considerable hypocrisy. Here is how they did it.

During the war, huge contracts for materials were made and some terminated. In these transactions there was always the possibility of fraud; the government investigators couldn't keep up with the great volume of transactions. In protection, therefore, Congress passed a law extending the statute of limitations *in regard to war frauds* until three years after the official end of hostilities, which turned out to be January 1946. In other words, fraudulent war contractors were subject to prosecution up to January 1949 for any fraud committed during the war. However, I wasn't a war contractor and I hadn't defrauded the government. The bright young lawyers of the Department of Justice, nevertheless, used the words "false and *fraudulent* statements" in the indictment and asserted that my statements came under the extension of limitations. Thus a law clearly intended to punish crooked war contractors was *first* used by a reactionary government to "get" a veteran who not only had not profited by the war, but had made substantial contributions to the winning of it. It was a shameful, barefaced attempt at playing with words, which was nonchalantly upheld by the trial judge as perfectly legal. The Court of Appeals later held the application illegal in a unanimous decision.

There was far-reaching grim purpose behind this legal chicanery. If it had been upheld by the Court of Appeals the government would have had a powerful weapon to use against anyone in the population they didn't like. During the war practically the whole adult population had, of necessity, made statements to the government. This was true of the millions of men and women in the armed forces. It was true of the millions who had worked in armament plants, where there were security checks. It was true of farmers who had filled out questionnaires. It was true of the millions who had dealt with OPA and rationing. According to the law as interpreted by the Department of Justice, any statement to the government on a matter within its jurisdiction could, if false in the slightest, be made the basis of prosecution. For example, suppose in 1942 a citizen had gone to a gas rationing board and had been asked how far he lived from his place of work. Suppose he had said ten miles whereas in actual fact it was only nine miles. He would be liable to prosecution until 1949 and a possible penalty of ten years in jail. Ridiculous, says the reader. No more ridiculous than the actual indictment against me. There was no doubt whatever in my mind that if this legal jugglery was approved by the courts, the government would use it as a major anti-Red weapon. So much for the first nine counts. The last two counts also broke legal ground—or, I should say, illegal ground.

The last two counts alleged statements made by me to a government official, (i.e. Panuch). There was no proof whatever that these statements were in fact made. There were no witnesses to these statements; there was no record, no notes, no objective proof of any kind. There was only Panuch's say-so and my denial. By this procedure the government was setting up a mechanism by which they could indict anyone in the government. An official would simply say that he had asked an employee a question and the employee had answered falsely. That would be that. No proof, no procedures, no safeguards—nothing. This may sound silly and impossible but it is exactly what happened, as was brought out sharply before the Supreme Court.

The flimsiness of the case is the measure of the government's dishonesty. After the trial Panuch wrote an article for *Plain Talk*, a reactionary magazine edited by the professional anti-Soviet, Isaac Don Levine, and partly financed by Alfred Kohlberg of the infamous "China Lobby" which was behind Joe McCarthy. The article said that the Justice Department was very dubious about the case. Well they might be. The Grand Jury would never have returned an indictment on the basis of the last two counts. Their flimsiness was covered up by the first nine counts with their backing of official transcripts of interviews. And the first nine counts were illegal. However, once they got the indictment the prosecution didn't have to worry about a conviction. They had a powerful extralegal weapon—redbaiting in the press.

The press went to town. Imagine the juicy morsels. A State Department official was a Communist. He was foreign-born. He had infiltrated Communists into the Army. He was planning to take over the Army! Boom, boom, went the drums of hatred and hysteria. Simultaneously the Truman Doctrine burst on the world. Guns to Greece, guns to China, guns to Indonesia! Boom, boom went the drums of the Cold War. The Russians are getting ready to dominate the world, take Alaska, subvert Panama. Communists are their tools. Marzani is a Communist. Put him away! Protect American legality? Nonsense. Fairness? Piffle. Democracy? Don't be silly. Just put him in jail; it'll teach him a lesson. Indeed it did.

Not content with the lies of the government, the press manufactured some of their own. For example, reporters kept calling up my home. Exasperated my mother said, "No, Carl's not home. I don't know where he is." Headline: RED SKIPS TOWN. Sub-headline: Marzani's Mother Says "You'll Never Find Him." The FBI flashes into action. I'm peacefully having dinner. Our wonderful free press! Our truthful, accurate, objective, democratic press, free of the terrible control of trade unions, co-operatives, local governments or national governments which is the case in benighted Red countries. Our joyful, innocent press, where a kindly millionaire boss wouldn't dream of slanting the news; where editors know they have a code of responsibility to the public; where friendly reporters come to see you, wide-eyed devotees of truth. Oh, yes. I remember them well, the reporters. So friendly, so kindly to your face, deftly slipping in loaded questions and then writing the most venomous, lying articles. If you get mad, you just haven't a sense of humor; you have no sporting blood—it's only a game, a way of earning a living.

The population takes it all in. Somewhere in the population a jury will be forthcoming, primed with hatred or primed with fear. There is no question as to the power of the press. It is expressed in the flood of threatening phone calls: "You dirty so and so—go back where you come from..." "You better get out, you ——." "We'll take care of you..." Night after night. Living in a small suburban home, with a small child, a pregnant wife, an ailing mother. Worrying that some inflamed patriot will do something. America 1947, land of the free, land of the brave. The worst elements of the population whipped up by the press with ammunition from the government. Pleasant isn't it? Democratic isn't it? Just the thing to inspire love for one's government, to inspire devotion, loyalty, civic responsibility. America 1947.

My worries about our physical safety were not exaggerated, though luckily nothing happened. But the fears were not far-fetched. In New York, shortly after, Robert Thompson, a Communist leader, was attacked on his way home and repeatedly stabbed. The police department hardly lifted a finger; the assailant was never found.

The development of extra-legal violence, condoned and often protected by the authorities, is one of the most ominous developments in

America in the post-war years. Immunity was practically guaranteed to reaction's underground. One of the most blatant examples of collusion was again in New York City. Robert Thompson had a little girl of nine. One night while her parents were out, a man broke into the home, terrorized the baby-sitter, took the child into the bathroom and began an obscene display. The sitter's calling for help frightened him away, but she had recognized him as someone in the neighborhood. He was arrested. He was identified as a private detective watching Thompson on behalf of private interests who were never ascertained. In open court the man was found guilty and sentenced. A few days later, the District Attorney, *on his own initiative,* reopened the case *on the grounds that a wrong synonym* had been used for certain sexual organs. Within a few minutes the case was dismissed by the judge. Immediately this vicious criminal was spirited away from the courtroom, whisked into a waiting car and vanished. No more flagrant example of sinister collusion can be imagined. This was the BIG FIX with unknown, but powerful influences, pulling the strings of the puppet D.A.

The culmination of this kind of incitement to physical violence was in the Peekskill riot, where patrioteering hoodlums with tacit police approval staged a full-fledged Nazi-type brawl. Months after the riot a grand jury issued a whitewash. It found that the Communists were responsible and darkly hinted of Communist "military formations" because two thousand trade unionists had protected the meeting from the projected assault.

In other words, if people protect themselves from hoodlums, it is their fault for starting a riot. This is the classic fascist pattern. I cannot too strongly emphasize this point. The use of violence, of strong-arm squads to break up left-wing meetings, and the benevolent protection of the thugs, are the clearest indications of developing fascism. It's a cynical, heads-you-win, tails-you-lose proposition. If the thugs are successful they are never prosecuted. Rather they are praised as patriots who "lost their heads." If the left wing defends itself, the police and the courts jump on them like a ton of bricks with charges of assault, conspiracy, "military formations" and jail sentences. The vicious pattern is designed to smash the left resistance to the growth of fascism. This connivance between police and the courts and vigilante groups was used to the full in Italy and Germany, where Mussolini's Black Shirts and Hitler's storm troopers developed their organizations under the protection of the authorities. Their untrammeled violence towards working-class organizations was the prelude of the Fascist seizure of power. In our country today, Peekskill is a lightning flash which illuminates the murky terrain of a sharpening class struggle.

While the most corrupt forces in our society go their way with impunity, the federal government brings the huge machinery of government to bear against those who seek to expose them. This is the meaning of my indictment. For what was the reason for my indictment? Why was I chosen as the first victim of the Cold War? What was the specific motivation? The answer must be sought in Panuch's actions, since it was he who instigated the prosecution. What made Panuch move?

The reader will recall that when I resigned, Panuch was extremely friendly. In the *Plain Talk* article, Panuch says that he didn't really accept the resignation, that I was under investigation, and that I had resigned in fear. This is pure poppycock. During the trial we proved that the resignation had been officially accepted. I am as certain as certain can be that Panuch's cordial farewell in November was genuine. It was six weeks later, in December, that I received Panuch's registered letter saying I was fired. It was of course a complete surprise, but what was I to do about it—write back by registered mail and say, "Dear Joe, how could you?" After the indictment I realized that I should have written giving in detail our various interviews, thus placing on record my version of events. I also should have gone to see a lawyer. But while this business of lawyers and records is commonplace among big business, which is always sailing close to the winds of illegality, it is not standard operating procedure for the average citizen. One doesn't expect the federal government to break its own laws. Therefore I did nothing. My feeling at the time was that Panuch was building up a record in case of redbaiting pressure from Congress. I mentally shrugged my shoulders and forgot about the letter.

Actually, as Panuch revealed in his article, the letter was part of a buildup to legal prosecution. In the six weeks between the time of his fulsome farewell and the sending of the letter, something had happened to turn Panuch's friendliness into hostility. Something had happened sufficiently infuriating to warrant a prosecution. What was it? What had happened during those six weeks? The answer was simple and self-evident. A film was released, *Deadline for Action*. As I've mentioned, *Deadline* was a pointed attack on our foreign policy and the financial interests behind it. It exposed corporate monopoly control of the American economy, giving names, dates, places, and specific details—all taken from official government documents. The film was both convincing and unassailable. It infuriated big business because it hurt. An unfailing test of one's effectiveness in a struggle is the reaction of one's adversary. In this case the reaction was prompt. The companies and their press screamed; they were particularly angry because of the technical quality of the film. *Business Screen* attacked it and so did the *New York World Telegram* in a bitter article by Frederick Woltman, bannered by an eight-column headline UE FILM WINS OSCAR IN MOSCOW. This of course was a lie: Mr. Woltman meant that it *should* get an Oscar, not that it had gotten one; but accuracy in left-wing matters is not a Scripps–Howard virtue. Woltman went on to describe the film as the slickest, subtlest Communist propaganda ever put out. That the Philadelphia police did beat up strikers without provocation was not mentioned. That the camera had caught them in the act was propaganda. The economic facts were neither mentioned nor challenged. They, too, were propaganda. Truth, if distasteful, can always be dismissed as "Red propaganda."

The officials of the General Electric Company had fits. They had good reason. Among the revelations of the film was GE's connections with Nazi cartels; also the fact that GE had been indicted for defrauding the U.S. government. Such facts are not usually mentioned in our "free" press, or if published they are phrased obscurely and tucked away in an inconspicuous corner. But the film was neither obscure nor inconspicuous. It was clear, explicit, and powerful. GE's reaction was one of foaming rage, as I happened to know firsthand through a series of coincidences.

GE, like other major companies, has been making propaganda films for years, glorifying the blessings of capitalism. The owner–producer–filmmaker happened to be in the East, at GE headquarters, when the film was shown to assorted vice-presidents and other high officials. He sat and watched the film and their reactions. When he returned to Hollywood he spoke about the session to a friend of his, who was also a friend of mine. As I got it, his narrative went something like this: "So there I'm sittin' with all these big shots and the picture goes on. Well, you shoulda seen it. It just came right out and said GE was a bunch of crooks. Yeah, just like that. No tact or nothing. Said right out, crooks. And slick, boy, I'm telling you. It's got Lincoln at the end, and good photography and mood music—the works. Schmaltzy, you know, with the sun rising and shining on Lincoln—it was something. Those GE people were so mad—fit to be tied. They said they were going to sue. But then somebody said that wasn't smart: too much publicity. But they'll do something."

They must have. GE subsequently admitted that they had planted the article on *Deadline* with Woltman. Also at a public-relations conference after my indictment, a GE vice-president referred to it as an illustration of how to handle an unfavorable attack. His comments suggested that they claimed credit for the indictment. Just what was done I have no idea. But something was done. One chain of events connects GE with Panuch via *Deadline*. I traced every link and can prove it by the individuals concerned.

GE planted the article with Woltman. The Woltman article sparked a series of attacks in the press. As a result, the New York distributor of *Deadline* went to see a friend of his, a lawyer, for advice. By sheer coincidence this lawyer was in the State Department, and when he heard that I was the producer, he showed how alert he was to State Department interests by telling Lunning. Lunning, my presumed friend, didn't say anything to me. He passed the story on to Panuch. Panuch got a hatchet man of his, named Klaus, to look at the film. Such was my innocence that I showed Klaus the film and was pleased that he should be interested.

Klaus's report must have bothered Panuch. Angry at the attacks on foreign policy, anxious lest he be attacked in Congress for having kept me on, eager to cover up his previous blessing to me, Panuch decided to get me. I found out months later that Klaus went to New York to snoop around my pre-war residence and as a result of his activities the FBI was brought in, my telephone was illegally tapped and, when they thought they had a case, they went to the Grand Jury and got an indictment. Incidentally, I know that my phone was tapped by certain remarks the prosecutor made to my defense attorney. It didn't matter because I had nothing to hide, but the invasion of privacy was not pleasant.

The impact of the indictment on my life and family was of course tremendous. Money was immediately a problem. Our small savings were flushed away and we sold our car. Because of a hobby of mine, woodworking, we had several hundred dollars' worth of power tools—they went. We were planning to build a home: an architect was making the plans and we had bought some acreage on the Potomac River. Plans and land were sold.

It seemed useless to think ahead; yet think we had to. A second baby was on the way, Edith being two months pregnant at the time of the indictment. For a couple of conspirators we certainly had given hostages to fortune. We were both sorry and glad about the new baby. Sorry in that it created further problems; glad that we could do nothing about it. We had wanted a second child and yet if the indictment had come two months earlier, we wouldn't have had it. As it was, the decision was no longer in our hands. Writing now, when the child is three years old, Edith and I are very happy it turned out that way. He has added to the burden of the last few years; he has also made it more bearable.

It is no use to give details of our state of mind at the time. It would take many pages to give an adequate glimpse of our feelings, the real sense of terror and fear, the nightmare quality of something happening while the mind said it can't happen, it can't be, the government doesn't behave like this, this is America! Alas, it *was* America and the government did behave like that. The feeling of helplessness before the ferocity of the attack is paralyzing. Underneath it all was the throbbing pulsating anger, the grim awareness of the betrayal of the Truman administration of everything decent and progressive—slaying the peace of the world in a saturnalia of redbaiting and an orgy of inflation and profits. The Lattimores, in *Ordeal by Slander*, go to some length to describe their feelings of horror under attack. Yet, in comparison with me, Lattimore had powerful friends. He was attacked by McCarthy but defended by the administration. Our family was being hounded by the federal government. Multiply his problems by ten and the reader will get some sense of our state of mind.

Frankly, as I sit here in jail, the persecution as vindictive as ever, the problems of our family as serious as ever, I just don't feel like writing about it. It only serves to intensify my anger and contempt for the un-American rotten crew that has put me here and keeps me here.

Leaving aside my feelings, I think it is more important and significant to write of the effect of the indictment on my friends and acquaintances. Whatever hope I have for the future rests precisely on their magnificent response. I should estimate that 90 percent of the people who worked with me during the war supported my case. There were a few defections, mostly from high officials, but in general the effect of the government's prosecution was to anger and radicalize people. This should be a warning to the government.

As I said there were a few defections, the most notable being that of Otto Nelson, former Major General, U.S. Army, former Assistant Deputy Chief of Staff, former Deputy Commander, MTOUSA, etc. Nelson ran like a scared rabbit. I was never so surprised and disgusted in my life. He had the impudence to tell a friend of mine that I had "betrayed" him. Like the time, I suppose, when I refused his offers to commission me. Nelson knew my opinions and beliefs. He had seen me work at close range. He knew the way in which I responded to any and all of his demands, no matter how onerous, without at any time receiving any personal reward. He said, and I believed him, that he thought highly of me. I've mentioned Donovan's cable to him in Italy, saying I was reported to be a Communist. Nelson said to me then that he considered me as good an American as he was. After the way he has behaved, I consider myself a good deal better one. There's a twist to this story. At the time of the cable, Nelson said that he didn't think Donovan was behaving well. That was a fine liberal position. But after the indictment, the contrast in behavior between him and Donovan is instructive.

General Donovan is an unreconstructed conservative, not to say a reactionary. He is quite aware of the class struggle, is explicit about it, and participates in it with full consciousness, zest and lack of mercy. He is one of the most powerful Catholic laymen in America, one of the foremost Wall Street corporation lawyers, the elite corps of capitalism, and one of the most skillful intriguers in the international field. Though ostensibly "out of the government," he keeps his intelligence contacts, very much as Churchill has always done. Donovan is always to be found, ready and willing, at reaction's barricades. For example, he popped up in Hong Kong as Chennault's lawyer in a barefaced attempt to prevent Chinese transport planes from being transferred to the new Chinese government.

The personal relations between Donovan and myself in the OSS were both slight and chilly. I had come into conflict with several of his worst appointees in the agency, some of them his personal friends, and as a result he considered me a "troublemaker." The only thing that saved me from his anger was the fact that I was obviously effective and producing services which were highly regarded by the Army. General Nelson, for example, as McNarney's deputy, had much to say over the allocation of military personnel to the OSS. If I pleased Nelson, Donovan was too good a politician to fire me. Despite this personal and political antipathy General Donovan not only refused to feed the newspaper attack on me but maintained an attitude of benevolent neutrality that culminated in a letter to the parole board asking for my release from prison. He also signed a petition for presidential pardon. Neither did any good, but he tried. Donovan's *esprit de corps* and his sense of fairness overrode his basic bias. Nelson, the liberal, scuttled.

Nelson, of course, was only rationalizing his fear. It wasn't so much that he was against me, but that he feared being smeared by association. He had just become a high executive in one of the large insurance companies and he wasn't taking chances. In a classic Americanism, "Why should he stick his neck out?" This point of view is the most effective aid to reaction and fascism. It paralyzes action. The knuckling under to political terror is an acid test of contemporary liberalism.

I saw this fear of smear by association in the most unexpected places. I had two room mates at college, both close friends. They were asked to come to Washington to testify as to my character; it never entered my mind that they would have any hesitation. When I saw them it was obvious they were on my side, they wanted me to win, but they were afraid to come down lest their companies wouldn't like it. Finally they *asked permission* from their companies; one came, the other didn't. The roommate that didn't show up was married to a plain-spoken, practical-minded woman. She expected her husband to testify; when he told me he couldn't, she gave him such a look of contempt that I'm sure their relationship hasn't been quite the same since.

In one group of people I was profoundly disappointed: my college friends. I graduated from Williams in the class of 1935. The Defense Committee mailed an appeal for funds to the classes of 1934, 1935 and 1936, a total of over four hundred names. I was well acquainted with perhaps half of them. Amongst those were scores of personal friends and some men who were very much in my debt. There was only one answer to the mailing and he was not one of my friends. He sent in two dollars with a note disavowing any sympathy for my ideas but wishing me luck. One man out of four hundred: a testimonial to the scope of intellectual terror in our country, and, conversely, a revelation of the lack of courage in the middle class. It is precisely amongst those who mouth most piously about democracy that the failure of nerve in its defense is most striking. Our "better" people are, in general, cowards.

In contrast, in the working-class district of New York's Lower East Side hundreds of dollars were raised for the defense among people of very low income. Furthermore, though scores of people who had known me were called before the grand jury and intimidated by the government prosecutor (one pregnant girl had a serious hemorrhage), there wasn't one who would help the government.

My trial was one of the first skirmishes of the bitter anti-Red war which the government has initiated, and still leads, though men like Senator McCarthy are eager to take over. The philosophical basis of the government's attacks, slowly being accepted by the courts, is that a Communist is outside American society. He is not only an outlaw but, in the Hindu sense, an untouchable. The ostensible reason for this is that the Communist has no ethics, no moral values, whatsoever. It is therefore of some interest to consider the ethics and moral values of the government. As to whether I am, or am not, a Communist, or whether I ever was, or was not, a Communist, I can give no answer, one way or the other. This is not because I am ashamed or I have something to hide from the people of the United States; it is simply that I'm afraid. Any statement I make can be used by the Department of Justice to harm fine, decent, Americans, some of them my friends. I will not be a party to the witch-hunt in any form. I will repeat what I've said many times, and that is that on the two counts on which I am serving a jail sentence of three years I am not only morally but also legally completely innocent.

For the sake of sharpening the moral issues, however, and to show the trial in its full significance, let the reader assume that I was a Communist and then see what he thinks of the government's actions. Let it be kept firmly in mind that at no time was I accused of harming the government or the people of the United States in the slightest manner. On the contrary, the prosecution admitted that my war record was excellent. Further, the full flavor of the government's actions can only be understood by stressing certain basic incontestable facts. One of those is that the government, from 1942 onwards, had in its possession all the evidence that was used against me in 1947. If the government had either believed the evidence, or considered me a menace, it should have prosecuted me in 1942. It didn't. The government made full use of my services; then, when the war was over, it paid me off with a jail sentence.

Another basic fact is that throughout my government service I made no secret of my radicalism. I was outspoken in sympathy for the Soviet Union. I often defended Communism. On one occasion I argued against capitalism in the very office of a prominent War Department official. I was considered a fellow traveler; I was denied a commission in the Army on precisely such grounds, as shown in the Donovan cable in 1945, already mentioned.

The question of the commission was not only one of prestige and recognition for my work; it had a financial aspect. I've mentioned that my work entailed dealing constantly with assorted brass. I was authorized to wear civilian clothes while my army rank of private was kept quiet. Civilian clothes solved the problem of rank, but not that of pay; they added to it. To keep a family in wartime Washington on a private's pay was not a minor matter. The average GI, if married, usually reorganized his domestic economy. But I had to go on pretty much as before. We had to maintain a house, and, because of the nature of my work, I had to maintain a car. I had to maintain a certain standard of clothing; laundry was a considerable expense. Such simple things as business luncheons were a serious drain. In the midst of work, we would adjourn for lunch. If we were in the Pentagon, I'd try to maneuver the group into the cafeteria, which was good and cheap. But quite frequently people would like to relax and get good food and they'd want to go to a good restaurant. The reader may be amused at this detailing of petty things, but at the time it wasn't funny. The petty things ran into money. As a result I used up all my savings for the privilege of serving a war-time government. After nine months of this, I remonstrated, and the OSS front office belatedly recognized the justice of my complaint. I was promoted from a private to a master sergeant. As someone said humorously at the time, in being promoted seven grades at one clip, I was halfway to a general's star.

I don't write about all this in a spirit of regret or petty bickering. I had much to be thankful for. I was at home with my wife and child. While other men my age were being bored in Iceland, sweltering in Iran, freezing in the Aleutians or killed on Guadalcanal, I was working in a safe, stimulating, and interesting job. Nevertheless, the basic fact remains that the government exploited my loyalty to the full. They were welcome to my savings—but not all this and a jail sentence too.

While my financial problems, in retrospect, are amusing, some of the government's actions were considerably grimmer. The lack of moral scruples was clearly shown by the offensive against my former colleagues. It makes wretched reading. The most brutal example was the attack on my chief, Hu Barton. I've already described Barton. He was, and is, a decent, liberal-minded New Dealer, not even vaguely socialist, let alone Communist. Government service was his career; he had planned for no other. The government moved against him with the gangster ethics of the Pendergast machine. It's a disgraceful record. Barton was fired from his job on trumped-up charges of using the Division's station wagon for private purposes. The charges were so phony and ridiculous that several months later, after Barton had hired a lawyer, they were withdrawn. By then the trial was over. It is my firm belief, shared by everyone concerned, that the government's purpose was to discredit Barton to prevent him from testifying on my behalf. When the trial was over, the charges were withdrawn and Barton completely cleared, though of course the position was not given back to him. Not that Barton would have accepted it.

I watched Barton through this ordeal and suffered with him. For a while he was dazed; he didn't quite know what had hit him. The manifest injustice, the utter cynicism of the blatant frame-up shocked his moral sense. He couldn't believe that his government could possibly behave in such a manner. He was, as it were, uprooted. Barton fought through his despair and became one of our most active supporters.

The attack on Barton was followed by a development that should be a lesson. Reaction starts with radicals but goes on wildly and blindly to smash all kinds of people, including its own stooges. When Barton was suspended, his current deputy resigned in protest and the State Department had no acting chief for the Division. Finally they found one man willing to take the job, a certain Leonard Rennie, a section chief who had previously preened himself as a socialist. This miserable opportunist took over. The sequel is both comic and sobering. A month or so later, Rennie was fired without reason or warning; the division was dispersed. As I heard the tale, Rennie went around Washington moaning, "Marzani should have been fired, and maybe Barton. But not me! Not me!" This incident is a little parable for the so-called "non-Communist" left. The Murrays, Nathans, Reuthers, Biddles and the rest of the redbaiters should think about this incident. Reaction doesn't spare them when the time is ripe. Owen Lattimore was frantic in denying Communist leaning; it didn't do him any good when McCarthy let loose.

Professor Kirkland, a historian writing in *The Key Reporter*, warns the liberals: "to discard the radicals may well seem, to those wise in the ways of this world, the most effective protection of the liberals. Such adroitness may postpone the showdown, but, when it comes, the conditions favorable to defense have been gravely impaired." Reaction always begins with an attack on the Communists and fellow travelers. But it moves inexorably against all leftists, liberals, and even apolitical independents. There is only one possible answer: to fight against the first breaches of civil liberties, no matter against whom directed. Whether one likes it or not, the defense of the legality of the Communist Party *is* the first line of defense against fascism.

Six

The story of the trials and appeals can be told with comparative brevity. In jail everyone talks about their cases and I learned to be brief. To the average inmate his trial looms as the most important event in his life. I was no exception, but with a difference. The difference was that my trial was important to me not only for its impact on my life and my family, but also for the insight it gave me into current American justice and the ethics of the administration. I learned what most people do not realize, that the federal government will stoop to any vile action to gain its end. It uses perjured witnesses; packs juries; lies, cheats and breaks the law with the same blatant abandon as a Huey Long, a Hague or a Pendergast. My trial and appeals, up to and including the U.S. Supreme Court, constitute an almost perfect specimen of class justice.

Allan Rosenberg was reluctant to take the case to trial. He said to me, "Carl, I'd love to try the case, but I don't have enough experience in criminal law and I should hate to start on you." He therefore became attorney of record and did most of the work on the briefs—brilliant work as events were to show. The trial attorney for the defense was Charles E. Ford of Washington, D.C. Ford is a first-class criminal lawyer. In my case he behaved with perfect honesty and integrity, but in dealing with a political case he had certain weaknesses, apparent in retrospect.

In general, Ford's technique was to focus the attention of the jury on a sharp dramatic point, or to sway the jury by strong emotional appeals. Our case, on the other hand, was detailed, complicated and tiring—not to say boring. As for emotional appeal, the appeal was there all right, but against us since the jury was victim of the constant redbaiting in press and radio wrapped up in patrioteering slogans. Second, though Ford was convinced that my indictment was a travesty of justice, he was himself unconsciously influenced by the pervasive redbaiting, so that he was reluctant to probe certain issues for fear they would boomerang. This left the initiative in the prosecutor's hands. Finally, Ford didn't expect the judge's hostility. His relations with judges are friendly; they are part of his professional life. When the judge unmasked his bitter antagonism, Ford was in no position to fight him and risk the kind of contempt citations that were used later in the Bridges trial or the Smith Act trials.

In short, Ford was no Clarence Darrow, and this is no reflection on his abilities. Men like Darrow do not develop often in our society—lawyers possessing not only the necessary competence in the law and trial procedures, but also the necessary political understanding and acumen to deal with problems where the jury is deeply and unconsciously biased. In all the political cases of the past four years, no lawyer has stood out as a match for the times. The best showing in my opinion was Mr. A.L. Pomerantz in the Gubitchev trial. Pomerantz got the FBI agents on the stand and, despite the judge's hostility, with great patience, pertinacity, and dexterity was able to drag out into public light the entire sordid story of wiretapping, hidden microphones, and, most amazing, wilfull destruction of evidence by the FBI.

Ford didn't have the faintest idea that the entire machinery of justice—jury, prosecutor, and judge—would be arrayed against him in a tacit, but obvious, conspiracy. As a matter of fact, when the judge was appointed and it turned out to be the Honorable Richmond B. Keech, Ford was actually pleased. "That's good," he told me. "He's one of the smartest judges in Washington. He knows the law, a scholar you might say, and he'll throw the first nine counts right out. You'll see. They're so clearly unconstitutional." Ford had a rude awakening. Keech was smart all right; in fine legal phraseology he upheld the constitutionality of the first nine counts. How wrong Keech in fact was is seen by the fact that the Appeal Court of three judges unanimously reversed him on this point. It is difficult for me to believe that an intelligent, scholarly judge could be so completely wrong in interpreting the law. In my opinion, his ruling was the first instance of the "Honorable" Mr. Keech backing the prosecution to the limit of the law—and well beyond.

I must say that, however naive I was about the law, I was not naive about Keech and from the beginning doubted Ford's analysis. Certain facts about the judge bothered me. He had been one of Truman's administrative assistants; since Truman, to put it mildly, was no flaming liberal, I had my suspicions as to Keech's impartiality in political cases. Also, Keech was a Southerner: born, bred and educated in Washington. While this does not necessarily imply a reactionary outlook, the statistical probability is all in favor of it. Finally His Honor at fifty-odd years of age was a bachelor, and I mistrust bachelors. Sometimes they are remarkably alive men, but more often than not they are narrow self-centered prigs with deep psychological maladjustments. Such were my feelings before meeting Keech.

What I saw when I did meet him strengthened my fears. He's a good-looking man, and knows it. He has a superficially impassive manner, betrayed however by his eyes, which are not under control. During the trial, the eyes blazed at me with naked personal hatred while the otherwise neutral face gave forth judicial sounds. There was about Keech an intangible, yet none the less definite, impression of a spoiled brat, a mama's darling. Finally the trial showed the judge to be a monument of self-righteousness based on insufferable conceit. There was basis for his conceit, for His Honor was an intelligent man, though hardly so brilliant as to justify his attitude. But he was intelligent. He played interference for the prosecution, alert to the prosecutor's slips and saved him from his mistakes in a most unjudicial manner. As will be seen, he was a perfect hatchetman.

A sidelight on Keech's self-righteousness I found in Washington jail. Keech is universally and bitterly hated by inmates. This is unusual, for most inmates do not hate judges. They hate the police sometimes, more often stool pigeons, false friends and opposing witnesses. But the usual attitude to the judge is that he's doing his job. If you had a sentence coming, you had it coming. Undue severity, however, is recognized for what it is: a sadistic expression of an unbalanced personality. Judge Keech was despised for his abnormally stiff sentences. This may be a source of pride to His Honor; as for me, I never did like prigs.

The choice of Keech to preside at the trial may have been accidental. If so, it was only the first of a series of remarkable coincidences of which the most important to the trial, and the most despicable, was the race of the jury. The opening day of the case, we found that the jury panel for our trial consisted of 90 percent Negroes. This is an unheard of proportion of Negroes for a jury panel. As a result, by the time the jury was chosen, out of twelve members, nine were Negroes. This is fantastic anywhere in the United States, but particularly in Washington where Jim Crow is dominant. Without any research, I venture to assert that never in the entire history of Washington, D.C., had there ever been such a preponderance of Negroes on a jury. Its value to the government came out when it became known that the three main government witnesses were, all three, Negroes. Finally, to complete the picture, most of the evidence revolved around my activities in the National Negro Congress.

Here indeed was irony fit for the Gods on Olympus: a defendant indicted for denying Communist membership and charged with stirring racial hatred because he had actively fought Jim Crow; the judge a Southerner whose animosity was transparent; the prosecution witnesses three Negroes, and the jury three-fourths Negro. On first glance it seems somewhat weird. But observe further. In the South, including Washington, one of the most common forms of ingrained racism is the refusal by the whites to take the word of a Negro for anything, particularly if in conflict with a white. Therefore to get its witnesses believed, the government deliberately got itself a panel resulting in a predominantly Negro jury. This maneuver was the reverse side of the racist shield of Jim Crow; in its own discrimination it was rooted in Jim Crow, but more subtly, of a higher order, a kind of second-degree equation in racial bias.

To top this grim jest, the Southern judge proceeded to restrict evidence on the *ground of the composition of the jury*. For example, I had first met one of the prosecution witnesses, Harper, at a meeting called to discussed police brutality on the East Side. A police car crew had stopped two Negro youths on the street, and, not liking their answers, had beaten them severely. The prosecution contended it was a Communist meeting; the defense said it wasn't and tried to show what was discussed. The subject matter of the meeting was both relevant and essential. Mr. Keech, however, prevented us from mentioning it on the grounds, said he, that it would prejudice "this" jury—his exact word.

What the judge was saying was: police brutality against Negroes will prejudice this predominantly Negro jury against the police, and hence against the prosecution. His Honor also gave a broad hint that I was doing it on purpose, as propaganda. The fact was that I was speaking the truth. That it would make the jury angry was very likely, and indeed so it should. But (a) I hadn't chosen the jury, and (b) it was the *action of the police* that would cause the anger, not *my talking about it*. If police brutality wasn't so well known and widespread, my words would have had no effect. Police departments in such cities as Washington, Detroit, Chicago, New York, as well as those in the South, have notorious records of brutality against Negroes. This brutality is not sporadic but goes on all the time, because the bias which causes it is present all the time. Only the more flagrant cases of unprovoked shootings, unwarranted arrests, inexcusable beatings and downright frame-ups are reported in the liberal and left-wing press. The constant attrition of day-to-day intimidation is known only to the Negro people. But they know it well.

The subtle use of Jim Crow by the government was to me one of the more obscene perversions of democracy during the trial. The point was generally missed, including by people who are usually perceptive critics of dirty finagling, such as Mr. Harold Ickes.

Another subtle aspect of the trial was important. The government knew I was a radical; I'd never made a secret of it. The government knew that I'd been active in the National Negro Congress and believed in racial equality. It would therefore be abhorrent to the defense to object to having Negroes on the jury. I am convinced that the government *counted* on our making no objections; it was counting on my principles to hang me. The shoddy cynicism is most revolting, and very much in character with the prosecutor, Mr. John M. Kelley.

Kelley was a tall, thin, grim-faced man moving in an aura of self-righteousness. He was a caricature of what a fanatic Communist is supposed to look like. He behaved throughout the trial with the zeal of a crusader, and I am sure felt deeply that I was the lowest form of life. I think he was a Catholic and brought great religious convinction to his defense of civilization-as-he-knows-it. He also brought a characteristic Jesuitical approach to the facts. There was no trick so low or petty that he did not use it to discredit me. For example, he asked me on the witness stand whether I hadn't told relief investigators in 1939 that I had no bank account. I said that was correct. "But you did have, didn't you?" "I did not," I replied. "Yes you did. Here's proof that you had a bank account in England at the Barclay's Bank." Now there was a lulu of adroit lying! When I had left England I hadn't formally closed my account and had forgotten all about it. But there was no money in it; actually I owed two dollars for service charges. So actually I had no account, i.e. no money; legally I had an account, i.e. my name was on an open ledger. Kelley knew the facts perfectly well, yet by his semantic juggling he made me out a liar. This may seem petty, but it was also very harmful to me.

In general, everything Communists are accused of doing in the press, Prosecutor Kelley did. He lied, twisted, perverted facts and justice. There was in him no honor, no decency, no integrity. This pharasiacal, walking mummy had the nerve to consider himself a Christian. The use of Negroes as a weapon could well have originated in his diseased mind as a very clever maneuver.

His behavior illustrates a point of ethics in the struggle between progress and reaction. For definite reasons, all ultimately related to the survival of the species, most people are more decent, moral and law-abiding than otherwise. Left-wingers are no exception; if anything they are more ethical than the average. Reaction uses this very decency of people against them both to spread its lies on a gigantic scale and to hamstring the people's self-defense. Hitler was very explicit on the subject; he spelled it out in *Mein Kampf*. For progressives generally this is the hardest lesson to learn: that reaction stops at nothing. It will use all the rotten, filthy, vicious unscrupulous tricks, lies and stratagems whether it's the British Tories using a forged "Zinoviev letter" to steal an election, or the Massachusetts government murdering Sacco and Vanzetti on a frame-up, or Goering burning a Reichstag. Reaction will stop at nothing. The process of learning to beat reaction is a hard bitter lesson. In my education, the trial has played its part.

Applying this point of view to the trial as a specific case, we of the defense should have challenged the entire method of selection. I wanted to do so at the time, but I didn't have enough legal knowledge to make my point prevail. We should have challenged the panel as unrepresentative of the community and forced the court to examine how it was chosen and by whom. I do not believe it would have had any effects on the results of the trial; any jury under existing hysteria would have convicted. But challenging the panel would have helped to strip the government of its pretense of legality.

The current reactionary drive is two-pronged; the more blatant McCarthyism coupled with the administration's spurious legality. The administration drive is different in kind from the terrorism of the Palmer raids after the First World War. Many liberals tend to underrate its ferocity. I was told, with paternal overtones of being too young to remember, that the terror was much worse in the 1930s and that civil liberties are not as endangered now as then. I think this is nonsense. The instigators and executors of witch hunting have become more sophisticated. Hence more effective. It is instructive to note that one of the most evil influences of our period is J. Edgar Hoover. Hoover was in charge of the Palmer raids. His flouting of the Constitution was so crude that he had to apologize before a congressional investigating committee and admit that he had been guilty of illegal acts. His extenuation was excess of zeal. I think he learned a lesson and now piously maintains the utmost respect for the law. In actual practice, of course, his intellectual thugs still disregard the law whenever they think they can get away with it. The proof was during the Coplon–Gubitchev trial, where FBI agents perjured themselves in open court and were finally forced to admit that they had destroyed evidence.

The lesson that Hoover and others learned is that crude repressive measures tend to mobilize public opinion. In the 1920s a group of fine legal minds, including Frankfurter, Dean Pound and others, issued a stinging public rebuke that did much to stop the deportations delirium. Today, no comparable action has taken place, though a few individuals such as Professor Commager of Columbia have been doing yeoman work to bring the truth to the American people.

Crude repressive measures are also more difficult today because American progressives are considerably stronger. There has been some degree of general political growth as the result of the struggles of the Depression and the New Deal. There has been a great advance in labor organizations. In spite of the disgraceful sellout of many labor leaders, the existence of these unions forces reaction to demagogy. This, by the way, is one of the hallmarks of fascism.

To expose the government's spurious legality is one of the major tasks of progressives. These witch-hunting trials conducted under a veneer of criminal law must be exposed for what they are—political persecutions. If the issues are clarified and truth made known, large sections of the American people will respond. Reaction may yet be stopped before the ultimate enormity of a third world war.

During the trial, the government ran the gamut of trickery, ably assisted by the Honorable Keech. One of their more elegant examples of fairness was to allow the government to place in evidence any documents from federal files they wished, and prevent the defense from securing any such files on the grounds of "national security." For example, they refused to let us obtain my personnel file, which included the Donovan cable stating he wouldn't commission me. Not only did the government use whatever documents they wished, but in at least one instance falsified the document, deliberately. This was in their attempt to prove that I had been fired from the State Department, whereas I had in fact resigned many weeks before Panuch's letter of "firing."

To this end, the prosecution introduced the State Department record on my resignation, which turned out to prove falsification. After the printed "Action requested" was typed the word *Resignation*. Under that, was typed *November 15, 1946*. Both had been scratched out and an illegible word substituted for resignation and a new date, December 20, both handwritten. The illegible word had been heavily scratched out and the word "Removal" handwritten, with a new date above it: 12/27/46. However, the writer had been careless. In the corner of the document was stamped a round seal marked "Division of Budget Control." Underneath was the word "APPROVED" and underneath that a date. The date was washed out but under a magnifying glass clearly legible: "NOV 20, 1946." When this was pointed out, the prosecution immediately dropped the issue and the judge covered up by ruling it immaterial.

The court refused to allow my wartime record into the trial. To make a dent in this iron curtain we tried to think of something I had done, sufficiently dramatic to impress the jury and sufficiently simple so I could say it before the judge stopped me. We finally decided on the target selection for Doolittle's raid. So the next day, while I was on the witness stand, the defense lawyer said abruptly, "Mr. Marzani, what *did* you do during the war?"

"Well," I said fast, "I picked the targets for Doolittle's raid on Tokyo, and then..."

"Stop!" snapped the judge, but for once he was too late. The jury had gotten the point. Kelley was furious. He was determined to show me up as a braggart and a liar. For two hours he pounded at me, trying to twist me up, or catch me in contradictions. In vain, I had spoken the simple truth. Finally the court adjourned and Kelley turned to typical underhanded trickery. He decided to bring into the courtroom the executive officer of Doolittle, a handsome beribboned colonel, who was to testify he had never heard of me. He would testify that he had selected the targets. This was perfectly true, but my statement was also true.

The point is that as an operations officer the colonel never saw the map with my name on it. He received a series of individual target maps, one to a target. These maps had been made up at headquarters from my original selection, but he wouldn't know my name. From the targets which I had selected, the operations officer would make his selection depending on various operational considerations. In other words, he did make his own selection, but he could only choose among my selection. Therefore every target he chose had been selected by me. Kelley's ethics can be seen from the fact that although *he knew I was telling the truth*, he was counting on this distinction and on the officer's impressive uniform to impress the jury and make me out a liar.

Fortunately for me, the original map, as the reader will recall, had been signed. Because of a captain's zeal, what should have been an anonymous map was a speaking document. We demanded to subpoena the map, describing it in detail and we also prepared to subpoena people who had seen me do it. This proved too much for Kelley. He quit on the point and the colonel was never called. He agreed to a statement which was read to the jury; namely that I had in fact picked the targets but I did not claim to know which of them had been bombed. The point is of importance primarily as an illustration of the government's ethics.

On still another document the government lied brazenly and maliciously. We wished to show that the government was aware of all the alleged "evidence" against me as early as 1942. In spite of it, I was cleared by Civil Service. Obviously the government had not believed the evidence. There was a report from the FBI to the OSS giving the "evidence," which was exactly what the government was using in 1947, five years later. I had seen this report and I could get a copy from a friend in personnel.

We subpoenaed this report. The government denied its existence, flatly. We insisted that it did exist. I'll never forget Kelley's cruel smile as he said to the defense attorney, "produce it." Since all security reports are secret, if I had obtained a copy and produced it, the government would have indicted me for possession of secret documents. The government was laying a trap, which we declined to enter. But the facts are indisputable. The government lied without the slightest qualm in a case where I was accused of lying. They lied again and again. They lied in big things and they lied in little things. They were unspeakable. The prosecution not only lied itself but used perjured witnesses deliberately and consciously. Some of this I can prove, some I cannot, some I dare not. For example, Panuch was a government witness. He said he asked me six questions: was I a member of the CP, did I give money to the CP, etc. I had answered "no" to each question. The questions were never asked.

I cannot call Panuch a liar. There are libel laws. He has money, I haven't. He's a lawyer, I'm not. He might take me to court and convince another jury as they convinced the one at the trial. Therefore I cannot say that Panuch, deliberately, maliciously and in full consciousness perjured himself on the witness stand. No, I cannot say that. But I can say this: Panuch's recollection of the interview and my recollection of it is flatly contradictory. Nor is this the only area of contradiction.

Panuch maintained on the witness stand that when I resigned I was under investigation and that my resignation was not accepted. We could prove his contention one way or another by looking at the security files. This they refused to do. Those documents that were introduced supported me and not Panuch. We tried to show that Panuch had actually been influenced by *Deadline for Action*, but we were not allowed to bring the film in. The court and the prosecution were fearful that once the film was shown, the jury would approve of it and I would never be convicted.

From Panuch we go on the prosecution star witnesses, three men, all Negroes. Their names were Drew, Harper, and Hewitt. With those men the government reached new lows of falsehood and half-truth. Remember, this is a trial where my crime is false statements. I keep harping on this because it is the crux of the case. The government that was accusing me of making eleven false statements was producing false statements, either its own or others', not by the dozen, but by the gross. The prosecutor perverted the truth wholesale.

The basic issue of ethics lay not only in the falsehoods themselves but also in the motives behind them. For even if there had been falsehoods, what was my crime? That in order to participate in the war effort, to be patriotic if you please, I had made false statements to the government—in exactly the same spirit and for exactly the same purpose as a boy might misrepresent his age when enlisting.

What of the prosecutor and of the government? Their lies and falsehoods were designed to put a veteran in jail, a veteran who had done his
best during the war; designed to harm a family, including two small
children, whose innocence was self-evident; designed to be the opening
gun of a campaign of witch hunting and hysteria that will destroy democracy if unchecked. In short, my alleged false statements were made to
fight fascism; the government's proven false statements were made in a
step to fascism. Keeping firmly in mind this fundamental fact, the reader
should now take a look at the three key witnesses, see what kind of men
they were, and remember that not McCarthy but the *federal government
was their proud sponsor*. Let us start with Hewitt.

Hewitt was a renegade Communist known as Tim Holmes. Although
I had no recollection whatever of meeting him, he miraculously remembered that seven years previously he had met me for a few minutes upon
the introduction of a man named Drew. My personality, I thought, must
be atomic to have made such an impression in such a short period of
time so long ago. There was a less flattering explanation. Hewitt might
be lying. He was. The corroboration for his story came from Drew, who
turned out to be a police spy. The renegade and the police spy vouched
for each other. It was touching.

My trial was the first appearance of Hewitt as a professional witness
for the government. He came to be known as the "pet perjurer" of the
Justice Department when he was caught in flagrant perjury in the State
of Washington and was indicted by the Attorney General there. It is not
a pretty story. Hewitt testified against Professor Rader of the University
of Washington, swearing that the teacher had attended a Communist
school conducted by Hewitt in Kingston, N.Y. in the month of July,
1938. Rader proved conclusively that he was three thousand miles away
at the time, and the State of Washington indicted Hewitt for perjury.
Immediately, Hewitt was flown out of Seattle and the FBI pressed the
Attorney General to drop the charges since the indictment impaired
Hewitt's usefulness. Imagine! This by the way is not the only occasion
where federal agents intervened with local officials to get favors for their
witnesses. In Bridges' case, Rathbone, the star government witness, had
a police record in Los Angeles which was destroyed. In Hewitt's case,
the FBI did not succeed: the indictment stands.

There was a fitting end to Hewitt. In 1949 a man was taken into
Bellevue Hospital in New York suffering from a nervous breakdown. He
was stricken with aphasia, which is a loss of speech and nervous controls
due to mental breakup. The man was Hewitt, renegade, perjurer—the

star federal witness for three years! What shall we say of a government that stoops to such filth?

Then there was Harper. Harper had been a member of the Communist Party, but on the witness stand he said he was no longer a member in 1940. Drew said Harper was a member. More important, according to Drew's reports produced in court, Harper had once asked Drew's advice. He confided to Drew (the police spy) that he, Harper, had once been arrested in the South on left-wing activities, that he had given a false name (the name was Michel Angel), and had gotten away with it. Now, went on Harper, he was going to take a government job. Should he say anything of his arrest on his application? Did Drew think the FBI might know? Not at all said Drew, the police spy. Perfectly safe, go ahead and take the job. (Incidentally, this is entrapment, the standard activity of an *agent provocateur*.) Harper went ahead and took the job while Drew sent his name in to the FBI. From then on, Harper was open to blackmail. He was guilty of the crime I was accused of, false statement to the government. Harper had to jump through the hoop under threats of prosecution. He jumped. I had known Harper on the East Side of New York; we had been friendly. He was married, with a child and on relief or WPA most of the time. In 1940 he had not been a bad fellow—weak, but not vicious. At the trial in 1947 he showed great reluctance on the witness stand; he tried to give his answers as innocuously as possible. It was evident that he was acting under duress and was conscious of his cowardly role. This does not lessen the contemptible nature of his actions; but if he was contemptible, what shall we say of the government that used him and blackmailed him into perjury?

The third witness was the star, Archer Drew. Drew was a cop. A well-built, virile, good-looking Negro, he was intelligent and self-confident. He exuded trustworthiness. He was a bitter symbol of the obscene irony which underlay the trial. Drew, the Negro, was the tool whereby a basically Jim Crow administration, using a Jim Crow judge, was sending to jail a man who fought Jim Crow. To understand Drew, we must think of the structure of Negro life in America. Kept in a position of inferiority and ignorance, any degree of achievement by a Negro enhances his position in the Negro community. A Negro postman, for example, has a substantial social position in the community. He has a security beyond the dreams of his fellow men; he has a decent wage; he is somebody. Drew was even more of a somebody: he was a detective, a rare achievement. He had been a rookie for only a year and suddenly made detective. This was a tremendous step forward, financially and socially. To Drew,

American democracy was meaningful. He couldn't realize that his very advancement was an exploitation of his color; that he had been chosen because a Negro acting as a spy would have more room to maneuver in the Communist Party. To Drew, the present society was a fine thing and naturally he was against Communists, who, he was taught, were leading his people astray. To himself, Drew was something of a hero. In reality, he was a tool in the hands of unscrupulous men, in a police department whose brutality to Negroes is a matter of record. Drew saw himself, I believe, as a defender of democracy.

Drew had none of the sense of embarrassment of the other witnesses. He was doing his duty. I knew this from a curious incident. Pending appeals, I lectured around the country to raise funds for the defense, and I was flying back to New York from Detroit. As I entered the plane, I heard a welcoming voice say to me, "Well, look who's here." I turned around and there was Drew, smiling friendly. His attitude both amused and angered me. "Why, you pig!" I blurted out. "Aw, come on, don't be like that!" He was genuinely aggrieved. It was apparent that he considered my anger unjustified. There was nothing personal between us. The trial was just so much red tape. Why should I be angry at him? He was only doing what he was told. My retort to these unspoken arguments was not courteous. "You're a rat," I told him inelegantly and walked away to find a seat. My feelings toward him were those of mingled pity and contempt. I sat in the plane aching with sadness that qualities of intelligence, education, and leadership which are so desperately needed in Negro communities should have been perverted by the police. Instead of being of service to his people, Drew was serving people who operated on the basis of racial superiority. I looked out of the plane taking off, and my mind went back ten years to another occasion when I had felt the same feeling of mingled pity and disgust.

It was the Christmas season of 1937. Edith and I spent it in the German village of Reit-im-Winkle, a tiny hamlet south of Munich on the Austrian border in fine skiing country. Our village and the others in the area were full of Austrian Nazis who were being organized in a Nazi Legion for the invasion of Austria, four months later. One evening in the local inn several of them joined our table—without invitation from us. Although around us there was laughter, jollity, music, dancing and singing, our own mood was not a happy one. The news from Spain was bad. The very season of Christmas reminded me of the previous Christmas, which I had spent in Bujaraloz, on the Ebro sector. At this very moment, I knew, Spanish Republican soldiers were shivering in the Aragon cold, on the exposed, snowbound, windswept plateau which was the front. They would have one blanket apiece and their food would be a handful of chick peas, lentils or beans with perhaps a hunk of dried codfish.

All the gaiety around us was so much froth on the European cauldron of evil forces which seemed at the time almost irresistible. Into this depressed mood came the Nazi boys, happy, spirited, bubbling over with beer and animal spirits. They proceeded to cheer me up. I watched them, joking and laughing. Physically they were fine, healthy youths in superb condition. They were intelligent, articulate, self-confident. Yet their minds were cesspools of superstitions and prejudices—anti-Semitism, racial superiority, elite theories, and anti-democratic practices. These good-looking heroes were the cream of Austrian storm troopers; they had won their spurs beating up Jews, Communists and workers in the streets of Lins, Innsbruck, and Vienna. These fine, fair-haired boys had murdered and tortured and maimed.

It was horrible. It was horrible to sit there and watch them and know what they had done and what they would do. They were in training for mightier and more resounding atrocities, these unthinking robots manipulated by the most evil men of our generation, the Hitler gang. In my feeling of horror there was also a tragic awareness of the waste and the sorrow inherent in the malformation of these boys themselves. And even as I hated them, I pitied them. Yet I also knew I would fight them to the naked death so that their world might not come to pass. They kept pressing me to drink and give them a toast. Out of my churning feelings I did a rather juvenile and indiscreet thing. I lifted my glass and said in English: "Here's to the time when we'll beat the hell out of you! Skoal!" "Skoal!!" they shouted and drained their glasses merrily. It was a silly to do, but I did feel a lot better.

I thought of them in the plane, and I thought of Drew, there ahead of me. I thought how arrogant and confident the Nazis had been, their war machine the mightiest the world had ever seen. It was only ten years ago. Now they were nothing. In ten years their own blind arrogance had destroyed them. Our own streamlined warmongers, with their Drews, might well think twice before unleashing new struggles.

As for Drew, my understanding of his development did not lessen my contempt for him. True, I had greater contempt for his superiors, but Drew himself was by no means the innocent dupe I may have unwittingly described. If he was a product of a vicious setup, he was also a part of it. Police spying is not pleasant work and Drew was not a pleasant fellow. I shouldn't want the reader to feel unwarranted sympathy for him. His motives may have been understandable, but his acts were despicable.

One of his activities gives the true measure of Drew. On the Lower East Side of New York there was a small Negro community of some three hundred families. There was no Negro organization outside of a couple of tiny churches located in run-down stores. According to his story, Drew had been instructed to investigate the National Negro Congress. There was no chapter of the Congress in the area, so Drew, on his own testimony, got Harper to help him and he, the police spy, proceeded to organize the outfit he was supposed to investigate. The police spy solicited Negro members; the police spy every night turned in the new members to the police department. The mind recoils from this sordid picture. It is the classic story of the agent provocateur. He makes a fine record by creating the conditions he is investigating. This is Drew, the defender of the Negro people.

I was among his victims. Drew and Harper asked me to speak in a Negro church on behalf of the National Negro Congress. I did, speaking on housing and the necessity of joint Negro–white action. I pointed out that racial antagonisms are harmful to both groups, sapping their strength. This is what the government in the indictment called stirring racial hatreds. At the lecture, a collection was taken which was turned over to the pastor for the use of his church. I shall never forget him for something he said to me. He was a fine old man, a biblical figure, with a brooding, dignified face. He said to me at the end: "Mr. Marzani, I thank God for people like you." It's a proud memory to have in jail. A proud memory for a stirrer-upper of racial hatreds.

Drew had good reasons for his corrupt actions. He had to build up a good record because he had failed on his first assignment. He had been originally detailed to join the Communist Party in Harlem. He reported he couldn't find it, a rather silly excuse since its address is in the telephone book. Moreover at that time it wasn't difficult to join the Communist Party—about as easy as joining the Kiwanis or the Rotary Club. Newspapers speak of "undercover" FBI agents with a flavor of derring-do, secrecy and risk of life, which is plain silliness. The activities of the Communist Party are about as secret as the World Series. The only reason the press and the FBI publicity men have been able to build up the Communist bogey is because in the past there have been so few Communists that John Q. Public has rarely met one. As I've already mentioned, prior to Spain I had only met one Communist and he would hardly talk to me.

Drew's despicable work among the Negro people was never fully brought out before the jury because Judge Keech intervened to exclude the testimony. He went so far as to overrule the prosecutor to prevent me from talking in response to the prosecutor's invitation. It happened after I had been on the stand several hours. Kelley handed me a sheet of papers; it was an election petition for a Communist candidate. Had I signed it? I said yes. "Why did you sign it?" sneered Kelley.

His invitation pleased me mightily. I had been trying for hours to tell the jury my side of the story; to present to them the true picture of my beliefs, my activities, my background, in short myself. I felt sure that if I could show them how much my experience was like their own, if I could establish the human contact, then the government's case would stand exposed for what it was—an unprincipled, reactionary attack against a man who, whatever his personal faults and weaknesses, was an infinitely better American than prosecutor Kelley or Justice Keech or Attorney General Clark. However, I thought he might stop me when I got started so I asked cautiously, "Do you want *all* my reasons?" "Sure," Kelley waved his hand, "go ahead and talk."

He was expecting me to hang myself by spouting Marxism, using unintelligible words, sneering at the government, attacking bankers and Wall Street, in short talking both over the heads of the jury members and against their beliefs. Presumably, I would totally alienate them. Kelley didn't know how wrong he was. I was going to talk about my father coming to America, about his life among the workers, and my childhood. I was going to tell the jury how we had lived, saying to them, you know how it was, you also had to keep families going in the Depression, sending children to school with shoes not so good, with clothes not so good, with food not to plentiful and so on. Somewhere along the line I would make the jury see me as they saw themselves, as one of them, someone similar to one of their own, like a son, a friend, a brother.

Once I made that identification Kelley would be lost. For then I would talk about going to school, working my way through school, being lucky enough to get a scholarship to Oxford and so on, and the jury would no longer be antagonistic to me for having had a good education, but they would be glad to listen, for I would now be identified in their mind as one of themselves. I would point out that ordinarily when a man receives as much education as I had, he would turn his back on the friends of his childhood, the poor people he grew up with, sometimes even his family. This, too, the jury would understand because it happens often enough. But I didn't, I would say, for my father had taught me that money and success are not as important as decency, integrity, and justice. Also I was lucky enough to have married a woman who felt the same way. That was why on the East Side of New York my wife worked in the Tenants League; that is why I spoke at the National Negro Congress. Finally about Fascism, I would tell the jury about my father, how he had left Italy, how Fascism operates, its racial superiority and so on. I would tell about Spain, my learning about Russia. I would tell them that I too had believed that Russia was a bad country until in Spain I saw that Russia helped the side of the people, while England helped the side of Franco. And so on, through Spain, and the war, and my desire to work in the war.

These, I would finish, are the reasons why I signed a petition to put the Communist Party on the ballot. Because the Communist Party said it was for decent wages, for good housing, for racial equality, for victory over fascism. And I thought they had the right to present their ideas to the people. Finally, I would make the point that they were the ultimate authority in that courtroom—not the judge, not the prosecutor. They the jury; if they said I should go free—I would go free.

Such was the outline of my comments. Here would be the crucial struggle for the sympathy of the jury. The prosecutor was in a sense challenging me—here, he was saying, is a group of Americans; go ahead and talk, see if you can convince them. I was not only eager for the challenge; I was so confident, so certain of winning their sympathy, that I thought the case won there and then. Kelley didn't realize he was challenging me on a strong point, the ability to deal with a hostile audience. He was due for a rude awakening.

I started to speak. "Stop," said the judge. The prosecutor waved his arms. "Let him talk." "The Court doesn't wish to hear it," said His Honor. That was that. It was completely illegal. The rules of law are very explicit on the subject. Once the prosecutor has asked a question, or opened up a field of evidence, the defense has the full right to answer it or explore the field opened by the prosecution. Furthermore the defense has a traditional right to a good deal of leeway on the witness stand. The court is supposed to let the truth emerge and freedom of speech is essential. But not our "Honorable" Mr. Keech. He violated specific rules of law. He violated legal tradition. He violated democratic tradition. Unfortunately, my defense attorney did not take an exception to be used as foundation for a point of appeal.

Keech was smarter than Kelley. He wouldn't take the chance that I might win over the jury. He was making sure that I wouldn't break through. He was the real brains of the trial; he was the true villain of the piece. He skillfully broke all the rules of the game, biased, vindictive, and sanctimonious. He hated me, personally and directly. While I was on the witness stand, his face was only a few feet from me. Again and again I saw his eyes blaze with uncontrollable, murderous hate. His eyes reminded me of something, I couldn't quite remember what, and then I placed the experience. In that fine film *Native Land* there is a sequence where the Ku Klux Klan is torturing a minister. There are several close-ups of the fascist vermin, white skullcaps with slits for the eyes. The close-ups show the eyes, fixed, insane with hatred, the glint of murder naked in the pupils. Keech's eyes were exactly the same way—the eyes of a lyncher. Keech was a fitting judge for the trial, a faithful representative of a rotting ruling group, fearfully and venomously striking out. As reaction grows in America, Keech will go far. I despised him then; I despise him now.

Summing up those days in the courtroom, they had that eerie quality of impossibility, yet actuality, that Kafka describes in *The Trial*. There was the same sense of a vast remorseless bureaucracy at work, a pervasive sense of being trapped, of being menaced, of being hopeless. Besides this generalized sense of oppression, I have one other memory of the trial: that is the repetitive monotony of the government's villainy and my inability to get used to it. Again and again I would be, as it were, shocked anew, at some bit of government trickery. I was aghast at the travesty being perpetrated.

It was as if, in 1865 the seceding Jeff Davis should be the judge in a trial of a captured Union officer, with a period-piece Rankin as the prosecutor and a fearful group of slaves as a mock jury. The charge, abolitionist sedition. Or as if, in the Nazi Germany of 1943, the anti-Semitic Julius Streicher should be the judge in a trial of a captured Communist, with Ilse Koch as the prosecutor and a fearful group of Jews faced to sit as a mock jury. The charge, anti-Aryan subversion.

As I sat in the witness stand of this incredible courtroom of this incredible America of 1947, a veteran badgered and baited hour after hour, I was not altogether immune from doubts. Not doubts of my rightness and the prosecution's deviltry, but doubts as to the worth of the struggle. The mocking thought came insidious into the brooding mind—why are you here? Why bother? Who cares? Looking at Keech and Kelley, I thought if these are Americans, then I don't want to be one. If this is the New World, let's go back to the Old. For the first time in many, many years I was conscious that I had come from across the seas. I was born a Roman; I have traditions older than this courtroom. For all its evils, the city of my birth is untainted by running sores of Jim Crow. I said to myself, what are you doing in this courtroom of shadows and racial guilt? What is it to you? What do you care?

The simple fact was: I did care. I may have once been a Roman, but I was now an American, raised in American schools, a veteran of the American Army. Here my father is buried, my wife rooted, my children born. This is my country. To the Clarks, the Keeches, the Kelleys I fling back the challenge of the grammar school: "I pledge allegiance to the flag and to the republic for which it stands; one nation, indivisible, with liberty and justice for all." Yes, I did care, and do care. Struggle I must. Within me, as within all, there is good and there is evil, in little things and large. Reason knows the difference. I will not accept Jim Crow, anti-Semitism, the exploitation of man by man, atomic mass murder. Against the dark forces of our times I assert my human-hood "in one irremedi-able, invincible, inflexible repudiation." The words are those of a Southern writer, William Faulkner.

* * *

The jury was out five hours. They returned with a verdict of guilty. Reaction had triumphed, with some legal trickery, it is true; with perjury, it is true; with some intimidation, it is true—but to the outside world little of this was visible.

Even without dishonesty the government had big advantages. These are discussed by a legal expert, Mr. John Hanna, Professor of Law at Columbia University. In a letter to the *New York Times* of March 12, 1950, he examines jury verdicts in terms which are peculiarly relevant to my case and generalize my narrow personal experience. "The most unfortunate defendant," he writes, "is one who is charged with an offense against the nation at a time when popular feelings are aroused." (Aroused—by whom?) "When the issue is a simple one of veracity, the defendant may be doomed if the jury is hostile for any reason." (Or intimidated by the witch-hunting.) "The jury is the average man, or less, multiplied by twelve. The government with its investigative resources has an enormous advantage over the defense in advance knowledge of prospective jurors." (Plus the ability to rig up jury panels to their advantage.) "The greatest danger is that once the prosecution has been announced, the Government will regard its prestige as involved in a conspicuous case and will suppress evidence for the defendant..." (Such as government documents under pretext of national security.)

So far Professor Hanna has dealt only with what may be called semi-legal manipulations of procedures. But this professor has an eye for reality and goes on to cover the nub of the question, government corruption of justice. He relates how a lawyer friend of his "asserted that he knew of a recent instance where a crucial prosecution witness was under treatment for a mental disturbance. The prosecution not only concealed this fact from the defense but took drastic steps to isolate both witness and physicians..." (Could he be talking of Hewitt?) "Power still corrupts," concludes Professor Hanna. "A former student in a responsible position once boasted to me, 'We can get anyone we don't like.' ... It is salutary to recall that in many criminal cases the only real protection of the defendant depends upon the integrity of the prosecution." It is salutary to recall, I may add, that the integrity of the prosecution is precisely what is lacking in the administration witch hunt.

To the last moment, the trial had a few dramatic twists. In the summation Charles Ford made a long emotional appeal to the jury, harping on the fact that I was being persecuted. He kept saying, "you know what persecution is," thereby making the jury uncomfortable. Charley was sincere but he was embarrassing. Unless he showed up the witnesses, unless he challenged Drew's credibility, all talk of persecution was so much "lawyer talk." He didn't attack Drew largely because the judge had prevented the necessary ammunition from going into the record. But without the foundation of fact, Charley's summation was obvious theatricality.

Prosecutor Kelley was smarter. He underplayed the part. He was very quiet, very composed. He said to the jury, in effect, "Drew has no reason to lie. Marzani has. You believe Drew or you believe Marzani." His last words had a fine Jesuitical touch. He quoted Lincoln, "You can fool some of the people all of the time, and all the people some of the time; but you can't fool all of the people all of the time." It was a fitting ironical finish. At the peak of a trial which was the epitome of injustice and reaction, the prosecutor struck a lofty, moral tone. The quotation he used may well serve some day as the epitaph of the corrupt government that hired him. But the final culminating irony of my trial lay elsewhere, in another courtroom. On the very day I was convicted, in a South Carolina courtroom, twenty-four white men indicted for lynching Negroes were acquitted by an all-white jury, despite the fact that several of the defendants had made confessions.

In fairness, some of my jurors were not taken in: a friend of mine, a reporter, went around to interview them. Most of them wouldn't speak to him, but four did. They were all Negroes and all indicated embarrassment. Said one of them, a woman, "What could we do? Anyway, he'll get off on appeal?"

Seven

I entered a federal jail for the first time in my life at the age of thirty-five. It was in June 1947. The Honorable Mr. Keech had refused bail pending appeal, a clear case of animosity. (His hatred backfired, for as a result of being in jail I obtained the aid of the finest lawyers in the country for a fighting series of appeals. But this productive side of jail was some way in the future.) I was numbed. One moment free; the next shackled and led away. Part of the impact was the unexpectedness; we never thought the judge would refuse bail. The following few days were miserable in the extreme. I was lonely and depressed. Worries beset me. My wife was seven months pregnant; we had little money. I knew that our personal friends would rally round. I knew that all over the country tens of thousands of people would help in all ways necessary. I knew that I was not alone and abandoned. But I couldn't help my emotions. I felt alone. Moreover, I was aware that the days of reaction were just starting, that redbaiting and witch-hunting would sweep the land; that the most hateful forces in American life would scum up to the surface from their submerged positions during the New Deal period. This did not help my feelings.

I was prey to dark moods as I contemplated the government's pernicious techniques shown during the trial: the mixture of intimidation, chicanery, and demagogy; the calculated disregard of basic laws through spurious legalisms abetted by complaisant judges. I was close to despair such as I had experienced only once in my life, the day in Prague we learned of Munich. I fought against my mood. I told myself that the fight for continued American democracy had only just begun; that reaction could be defeated. I believed this, but the oppressive reality of prison bars could not be dismissed; the dreary regimen of prison life could not be ignored.

The tremendous power of government is nothing to joke about. The average citizen is utterly helpless before it. The government can, and does, pour hundreds of thousands of dollars into a case; it can, and does, put hundreds of investigators onto a case; it can, and does, use whatever number of lawyers it finds necessary for the legal preparation of a case. In political cases, the sky is the limit. The areas in which appropriations are skimped is in the Civil Rights Unit and the Anti-Trust Division of the Department of Justice.

Against this huge power are only three controlling influences: the existing laws, public opinion with the ultimate sanction of the vote, and the independent organizations of citizens. In political cases the government (executive, legislature, and judiciary) subverts the law with impunity. Public opinion is rigged by the interested press, radio, magazines, and so on. Organizations which can fight the government, like trade unions, find themselves subject to external attack and internal dissension. In any case they are slow to move. Thus, in any case of a left-wing character the government can get away with anything, literally. Even a state government, like Massachusetts, can get away with murder. It did so in the execution of Sacco and Vanzetti.

In those first few days in jail, I felt very removed indeed from the outside world, very conscious of federal power, very helpless. Worried, lonely, and depressed I wrote a letter to Arthur Garfield Hays, the civil liberties lawyer. I knew Hays was politically anti-Communist but I felt that my case was outrageous, regardless of political belief. In my letter I gave expression to my sense of outrage, my sense of the wanton use of governmental power, my sense of helplessness. I don't have a copy of the letter but it must have adequately reflected my state of mind, for in a few days I got back a cheerful note from Hays. He was looking into the case.

I'm sure that if I hadn't been in jail, I wouldn't have thought of writing to Hays. I also have a hunch that if I hadn't been in jail, so clearly helpless, Hays might not have taken the case. I feel morally certain that the "Honorable" Mr. Keech by refusing bail had unwittingly forwarded my defense. Six weeks later the Court of Appeals granted bail, reversing Keech. This doesn't happen often, and points up the judge's bias. I immediately got in touch with Hays, who asked me out to see him at his summer home in Long Island.

Many things have been written about Arthur Garfield Hays, by many people, including himself. I gather he has lived a full life, with all its inherent consistency and contradictions, and I imagine you can get any kind of an opinion on him depending on who is giving it. My relationship with Hays is of no more intimate degree than that provided by the case. I have read little about him, or by him, and my opinions are based strictly on personal experience.

Hays was by then in his sixties. He is a short, still muscular man, with a massive head on powerful brooding shoulders, to me vaguely reminiscent of a buffalo. He has heavy-lidded shrewd eyes and a slow, very knowing smile of considerable charm. His face is hardly handsome, but I found it attractive and I imagine this is a very general reaction, both from men and women. He likes good living; he also likes good talk, his curiosity is resilient and there is nothing blunted about his intellect. He seemed to me restive about theories. I have no idea at all how closely my impressions correspond with reality. Like most men in public life, he has built up consciously or unconsciously a certain picture of himself, so that he is, as it were, constantly on parade. It is hard, therefore, to get at the inner man, but I should add that he did not seem to me excessively mannered.

In short, I liked him. I think he was honest with me; I know I was honest with him. Consequently, outside the area of civil liberties we clashed violently. Our conversations tended to be undisguised intellectual warfare, with obstinate frontal clashes and slashing guerrilla raids. The first day I met him we argued for six solid hours with a neutral break for lunch. I didn't want him to take the case with any illusions about my political beliefs; I was pro-Soviet, I was pro-Communist, I considered myself a Marxist.

During those six hours there was little we didn't touch upon. We argued over the Finnish War and the Chinese guerrillas, over Munich and the Nazi–Soviet Pact, over Marx and Keynes, Trotsky and Stalin, Tito and Mikhailovitch, Greece and Czechoslovakia, on and on, a long, unrestrained, sometimes bitter wrangle. By the end of that day there could be no question as to where I stood. Whether he knew such was my purpose I didn't know, but since he's a shrewd man I've always assumed he did. His daughter, who had heard most of the arguing, told me later that she had never seen her father so wrapped up in arguments. She added she thought he had enjoyed it; I had too. In any event, at the close of the day, Hays told me he would take the case to the Court of Appeals, without fee.

As I got to know him a little I found it hard to categorize him. Hays is a liberal, with all the vagueness that term implies. In economics I found him strongly conservative. I don't think Herbert Hoover's economics or even Von Mises would be outside his range. Yet, maverick, I'm sure he approves of TVA. In politics again, he's right of center. I can see him voting for a Taft as well as for a Lehmann. It is only the realm of civil liberties that Hays is entirely liberal, and here he puts most liberals to shame. His position is in the great American tradition, with a maturity and realism which exposes most liberals of the ADA stripe for what they are, camp followers of witch-hunters in our country. Not for Hays the Jesuitical lubricity of a Sidney Hook or the junior Schlesinger. On the crucial question of Communism, Hays, while strongly anticommunist, is one of the few in his position who do not accuse Communists of being agents of a foreign power, any more than Rhodes Scholars are agents of Whitehall, or Catholics agents of the Vatican.

The clarity and quality of Hays's thinking on the subject is shown by a small, but to me extremely significant, fact. Hays never asked me, at any time, whether I was or had ever been a member of the Communist Party. He properly considered that question irrelevant. Even the question of guilt was irrelevant! The government had no business prosecuting me in the first place, the indictment was invalid, the case was a clear-cut violation of civil liberties. With an insight rare indeed today, Hays realizes that the civil liberties of Communists and fellow travelers are precisely those most under attack, not because they are most dangerous to reaction but because they are most exposed. Reaction uses redbaiting as the channel to the vitals of our democratic structure. I think Hays might agree with what I consider to be a basic political truth of our times: the defense of the legality of the Communist Party is the first line of defense against fascism. I know I've said it before, but I can't repeat it too often.

While Arthur Hays and Allan Rosenberg were preparing the briefs for the appeal, I settled down to the problem of finances. Justice in America is expensive—particularly for the poor. This seeming joke is a literal truth. On an income of $100,000 a year, a legal expense of $10,000 is an inconvenience. The same expense with an income of $5,000 becomes a debt-creating burden; with an income of $1,000 it becomes an impossibility. We had very little money and my earnings were barely adequate to maintain the family. Court fights are expensive, despite the fact that everything was done as cheaply as possible. Arthur Garfield Hays took no fee; neither did his partner, Osmond K. Fraenkel, who later argued the case before the U.S. Supreme Court. Both men even paid their own substantial incidental expenses such as railway fares, hotel bills, and so on. Their behavior is beyond praise. Allan Rosenberg had to be paid something. He neglected his practice to give nearly full time to the preparation of the appeals. He did arduous and brilliant work on the briefs, and his financial returns were meager in the extreme. It was a standing joke between us as to which family pinched more on its budget.

Printing the briefs was one of the big expenses. The requirement to print briefs is one of the many anachronisms surrounding our courts, vestigial remains of ancient needs. The total printing run of a brief is only thirty or forty copies, rarely a hundred copies. Yet it's as expensive as publishing a couple of volumes. Due to the need for accuracy, and specialized requirements such as type, abbreviations, layout and so on, legal printers charge stiff prices. Mimeographing or multilithing would be completely adequate at a fraction of the cost.

The needless expense of printing helps to keep justice beyond the reach of the majority. Nothing is done about it; nothing will be done. Too many interests are involved and it is one of the ways in which a class justice parades under a Platonic leaf of impartiality. To complete the record I should mention that in theory a man may take a pauper oath and submit typewritten briefs. In practice, those poor enough to qualify are so ignorant and downtrodden that they have neither the knowledge or the presumption to follow through with appeals. The large group who, like myself, do know enough to press for justice, are not poor enough to be paupers. A few hundred dollars in the bank is sufficient to disqualify one as a pauper, while insufficient to pay for an appeal. In most cases the individual simply folds up and goes to jail.

I don't know exactly what we spent on the trial but it seemed to me as if every time I turned around there were more thousands of dollars going to printers. I made four tours of the country, more or less extensive, in eighteen months. As an offhand guess I imagine that, including lawyers, printing, court fees, publicity and expenses in travel and raising funds, the Defense Committee spent around $30,000, using volunteer labor. That's six years' wages for an industrial worker. This $30,000 is dirt cheap in a political case; the case of the eleven Communist leaders will cost its defense an estimated quarter-million dollars.

When I first came out of jail on bail, the defense was only a gleam in our eyes. We had no organization, no experience in this kind of activity. We had lawyers but they needed to be supported by funds. The American Civil Liberties Union was silent; the Civil Rights Congress was overburdened. The Congress was defending Eisler and Josephson and its resources were scanty. We therefore set up a "Committee in Defense of Carl Marzani," with Paul Sweezy as chairman and Betty Lundquist, wife of a wartime colleague, as secretary. For a while my wife and I were the only staff. Later we found some volunteer helpers.

The start was like trying to steer a becalmed boat. There was no response to the rudder. Slowly our activities agitated the air, there arose a little wind, a puff here, a puff there, a little breeze. Presently the boat was moving, the rudder responding. We wrote a pamphlet on the case and got it printed on credit. We distributed a couple of hundred thousand copies. We approached the press, where I had some contacts. But reporters don't make editorial policy and many were frightened. The *Washington Post* teetered but never came out for the defense. They did maintain a benevolent neutrality and I could usually get a letter in its columns. The *New York Post* was editorially silent, though their columnists helped publicize the case favorably. Later the *Daily Compass* was a staunch friend. The *Daily Worker* supported us throughout.

Our greatest support came from I. F. Stone, who wrote several articles for *PM* and the *Nation*. From the beginning Stone was outraged at the bare-faced villainy of the prosecution and said so with his usual vigor. I got to know Stone. "Izzy" is one of the liberals who in the post-war era have kept their eyes on the ball. There are many things he doesn't like about the Soviet Union and the Communist Party but he believes that they are historically progressive. He is largely immune to the ADA propaganda of "Red Fascism," and he certainly won't swallow the domestic fairy tale of Harry S. Truman as the Great Fair Dealer. There are many reasons for this, not the least being Stone's intelligence and political acumen. But there was one additional factor. This was the post-war history of Israel, which Stone followed in great detail. The maneuvers of the British Foreign Office over Israel are one of the most despicable features of Bevin's foreign policy, and the State Department has again and again supported the British, often running interference for them. The resounding victory of the Progressive Party in the New York Congressional election of Leo Isaacson was a main factor in Truman's recognizing Israel. Yet this was only a zag in our zig-zagging policy in the Near East, deeply influenced by American oil interests. Stone saw at first hand the tacit support of Britain for the armed intervention of its Arab satellites. The achievement of Israel's independence against great military and political odds is one of the epics of our times. Though not comparable in scale, grandeur, or achievements with the Chinese Revolution, the people of Israel nevertheless showed the same quality of fierce tenacity, pertinacity, and willingness to die that characterized the Chinese Communists.

As Stone followed closely our foreign policy, it was not difficult for him to follow its relationship to domestic policies. As I say, he has great political acumen. He knows the mechanisms, crosscurrents, surrenders, the myriad positive acts and negative calculated inactions that go into the development of fascism. He was not only conscious of the broader political implications of my case (within two months of the indictment the government instituted the "loyalty oath") but he was also acutely aware of the sinister legal techniques the government was developing. He knew they were dangerous; he didn't think me overwrought when I pointed out their evil. He spoke out clearly and forcefully. He became helpful in defense activities.

Another columnist who came out in my defense was Jennings Perry, now with the *Daily Compass*. The occasion that moved him to write on the case was an accidental meeting between us, which was rather amusing. It took place on the Washington–New York train the day of the 1947 Army–Navy football game. Usually on a train trip, I polish off a mystery story. I bury my nose in a book and pay no attention to my fellow passengers. On this day, there came to the empty seat beside me a slight, medium-sized man carrying *PM* and the *Nation*. His face seemed vaguely familiar but I had no idea who he was. He had a quiet, infectious smile of a most friendly nature. Because of it, and the magazines, I didn't withdraw into my books as I usually did, but, as people will, began chatting. He said he had come up from Memphis, Tennessee. I remarked I had once hitchhiked through Tennessee and remembered its fine concrete roads. I said I really knew little about the state except that Hull came from there, that it was the namesake of the TVA, and that it had a good newspaper, *The Nashville Tennessean*. At that his face broke into an enormous pleased grin and with a quizzical twinkle in his eyes he said he was glad to hear that: he had been the editor for fifteen years.

He hadn't given his name (I hadn't either) and I racked my brains to think of who he might be. There aren't that many liberals in the South that it was a prohibitive guessing task. Meanwhile we discussed foreign and domestic policies and found ourselves in considerable agreement. We discovered we had mutual friends in Washington. We were passing the slums of Baltimore and I mentioned that it was a shame to bring up children in such an environment. Children, I said, should have yards, and trees, and green grass. I regretted, said I, that I was leaving a little house in Arlington, Virginia, to go live in New York. I didn't know it at the time, but the remark stuck in his head. A couple of hours later, our names came out, we discussed the case for a while and went on to other subjects. Two weeks later he wrote a friendly touching column.

I was sharply disappointed in one columnist, Samuel Grafton of the *New York Post*. I didn't know him personally, but during the war he had written wonderful columns, characterized by a lucid prose and hard-hitting content. I went to see him at his office. It was a horrible experience. His glacial reception, the studied aloofness of silent treatment, was as repelling as he had intended it to be. I got out of his office as quickly as possible, in a couple of minutes, conscious that he resented my putting him on the spot. I resented his resentment. In the following months the reputation for courage and directness acquired during the war evaporated; his columns came to be filled with a cumbersome, vapid prose vainly camouflaging a phony liberalism. It's one of the clearest examples of style following content that I know. Grafton really went out with a whimper. When I saw him, he had obviously decided what side his bread was buttered on. It was a sad spectacle—and slightly disgusting.

I made several attempts to get into magazines. Stone got two articles in the *Nation*; I finally got a letter in the *American Scholar* after weeks of negotiations. This was the extent of publicity in periodicals, though I came close to success with the *New Yorker*. I wrote an article on my six weeks in jail, severely restrained as to the case itself, no politics, dealing only with actual jail experience with stress on the humorous aspects. I called the article "A Reporter Not at Large" in deference to their department of nearly that name. The article would have been valuable publicity; it would have been seen by the judges; it might have been the necessary straw. Who knows?

I assume the editors realized its importance; I have reason to believe there was some soul-searching in the editorial offices of that basically decent weekly. The article was kept four months, itself an indication of uncertainty in a magazine that prides itself on prompt acceptance or rejection. Finally it was turned down, with a friendly letter that quoted a couple of their editorial readers as praising the article; but, said the editor, it was finally rejected because the *New Yorker* tried to limit itself to the New York area. The implication was that my case was of Washington or national interest only, and too far removed from Manhattanite concern. Obviously I should have got myself tried in New York City. The polite evasion was hardly meant to be believed.

Since for all practical purposes the press, magazines, and radio were closed to the defense, we turned to speaking at public meetings. It is an effective medium as far as persuasion goes, but it is terribly limited as to numbers. With the most indefatigable speechifying over eighteen months, the number of people reached was probably below a tenth of a million people, hardly a dent in the population, and two-thirds of them were already conscious of the attack on civil liberties. The most important group of non-leftists reached were college students. I spoke to perhaps twenty thousand students all over the country. We had audiences of over a thousand at places like Harvard and Chicago Universities where the authorities adhered to their standards of free speech and allowed use of the campus auditoriums. We had audiences of around a hundred in places like the University of Michigan at Ann Arbor. There the authorities not only prohibited the use of university facilities but, through pressure on local businessmen, prohibited the use of town facilities even in a case where the owner was eager to help. By pressure on the local politicos, they prohibited the use of public areas such as parks.

The hypocrisy of reactionaries is nowhere so clearly seen as in the actions of these university authorities. We are not dealing here with aberrant or ignorant chiefs of police, or political hacks of city halls. These deans and presidents who denied us meeting places were the flower of American culture, theoretically aware of the meaning of democracy and its implications. The most disgraceful aspect of the current witch hunt is the knuckling down of academic people to reactionary trustees and state legislatures. It is very widespread with a few honorable exceptions. Hutchins at Chicago is one. The faculty at University of California put up a good fight against the loyalty oath, and then, with victory won, compromised it away. I was pleased to see President Baxter of Williams College stand up for a professor attacked by the trustees for supporting the Progressive Party.

My meetings were organized and sponsored by a variety of organizations such as trade-union locals, UAW in Detroit, UE in Cleveland, Packinghouse Workers in Chicago, Longshoremen in San Francisco, Fur and Leather in Minneapolis, Carpenters in Los Angeles, and so on. In major cities there were local chapters of the Civil Rights Congress, Young Progressives, IWO lodges and similar organizations; here and there a chapter of the American Veterans Committee, but that organization, rent by factional struggle, was rapidly declining. In some places like Hollywood, there were temporary committees formed by a few friends. Some of the largest meetings were joint efforts of individuals and organizations under attack. Yet, as I've said, despite all the work and all the people helping, fewer than 100,000 individuals were reached. When contrasted to the huge propaganda machine at the disposal of the government in the shape of press, radio and magazines, it is no wonder I felt comparatively helpless.

The chief purpose of all this effort was to raise money for the defense costs, and in this we were successful. In large part the money came from poor people in dollars and half-dollars. If, in one sense, the tours gave me a feeling of comparative helplessness, they also gave me a feeling of the potential power and strength of the American people. There is a fundamental decency in the majority of our people, which, if tapped and organized, will stop reaction cold. Never, with the most hostile audiences, did the facts at last fail to elicit sympathetic response. Obdurate anticommunists were silenced. I debated with an ADA lawyer at Brown University, who agreed from the platform that my case was a disgrace.

I found sympathy in the most unexpected places. An amusing example was a businessman who had sat down next to me on a plane to Chicago. He took for granted I was a businessman or professional with opinions like his own, and began telling me of the evils of unionization. The country was going to the dogs, business was being stifled, unions were crippling production, and so on. I managed to keep quiet for some time. Finally, as an illustration of the union's mingled stupidity and arrogance, he told me that a union organizer had told his workers (he emphasized the possessive) that they didn't need bosses; they could get along without them. Imagine!

"Really?" I said ironically, but he misunderstood me.

"Yes, he really said that. We had his speech on a wire recorder."

"How'd you get that?"

"Oh," he smiled, "we had microphones all over the plant."

"You mean," I said gently, "sort of spying on them?"

He looked disconcerted and slightly uncomfortable.

"It was my plant," he said defensively.

"It was their privacy," I retorted. "It doesn't seem very nice."

He stiffened belligerently, then just as abruptly, relaxed.

"Truth to tell," he said confidentially, "I'm sorry we did it. I've always felt ashamed of it." "Still," he recovered himself virtuously, "can you imagine such stupidity? They could get along without me!" His anger rose in retrospect. "Humph!"

I tried to be very gentle and very friendly.

"Please," I said, "please don't be angry but..." I smiled at him kindly, "but you see, I agree with them."

He gave me a sharp, startled look. Was I kidding? Was I... crazy?

"No, no, I'm serious," I answered his look. "Now before you get angry," I said urgently, "try me out. Listen." He looked as though he had nursed a viper in his bosom. "I'll make two statements, you say yes or no to each." He was intrigued, listening, interested enough to suspend judgment. "Now, the first. If every worker in the United States dropped dead tomorrow morning, wouldn't the factories close down?"

"Naturally," he answered promptly.

"Okay, we agree on that one. Now for the second. Suppose, instead, that tomorrow morning every stockholder, every owner, every corporation director—yes, even every plant manager dropped dead. I'm not wishing it, mind you, but just suppose. Do you think the factories would shut down?"

He thought that one over for quite a while. He saw the point all right. Finally he said reluctantly.

"No, I guess not."

"That's right," I told him. "We agree."

"They wouldn't be efficient," he maintained groping for arguments.

"Possibly," I conceded, and went on to tell him of a textile factory in Spain I had seen going full blast, months after its owner had run away to Franco territory during the civil war. But I didn't have to belabor the point. He understood very clearly what the union organizer was getting at. It didn't make him very happy. "Who are you?" he now said. "I mean, what do you do?" He was very curious.

So I told him. I gave him some background, told him about the case. At first he was very stiff and disapproving. He resented the fact that I should be in this upper-class world of an expensive plane, that I should be wearing the clothes of his environment, using the speech and manners to which he was accustomed. I was either an imposter or a traitor to my class. Yet another part of his tradition reasserted itself as I talked— that one American is as good as another, that everyone had a right to his opinions. Slowly, visibly, he warmed up toward me and by the time we reached Chicago he felt almost as strongly on my case as I did.

"I've got some influence in Washington," said he. "I'm going to do something about this." "You do that," said I without illusions, and gave him a pamphlet on the case. "You do that and let me know how you make out. The address of the Defense Committee is on the pamphlet."

I never heard from him; I hadn't expected to. This incident is illustrative of the fact that in all strata of American society there is a large reservoir of genuine democracy, which I believe will prove important in the current struggles against reaction and fascism. But the real strength of democracy was in the meetings in working-class areas.

I am by no means a sentimental individual. Yet the human warmth, the respect, the explicit palpable love manifested by people at those meetings touched me deeply. Out of the solidarity, strength, and devotion of these people, I drew renewed strength and commitments to my beliefs. I think it was Lenin who said that contact with people for a political fighter is like Antaeus touching the earth. In the eighteen months of weary, and sometimes seemingly hopeless struggle, those meetings revitalized my will, recharged my determination.

To my surprise, I found I was something of a speaker, able to establish intimacy with an audience, to infuse in them my own emotions, evoke their participation and stir their minds. There were many reasons for my unexpected success. Least important, but first in point of time, was my appearance and manner of speech. I discovered this early in the touring, in Chicago, when a veteran came up afterward and said in fine Hemingway style, "Holy —— mackerel, you talk like a —— GI." "I —— well ought to," I replied in style. "I was one."

The point is that audiences were surprised at the very outset. Advance publicity billed me as a "former State Department official" and "Oxford scholar" so that people expected to see the popular misconception of the striped-pants diplomat complete with broad As. They saw instead a run-of-the mill individual, something of a cross between their corner druggist and their union organizer. It was a surprise and to them, a pleasing one. It tended to create friends.

This led to a second more important reaction: the audience's self-identification with my problems and feelings. I tried to get across to them the emotion of shock and helplessness under the attack of the government; I described step by step what we had been forced to do, the effect on my wife and children, until somewhere along the line the imagination of the audience caught on and each person began to relive my experiences. A powerful emotional potential was generated.

A third emotional element toward speaking success was anger. I got across my very profound and sincere sense of outrage at the government's actions. Outrage in personal terms, outrage in political terms. The audiences responded immediately, since the sense of the fitness of things in a democracy is basic in our culture. Therefore, when the audiences added to their identification with my personal problems, their own objective indignation as citizens, we had a powerhouse.

Finally, the most important reasons were the determination to fight and my confidence in the ultimate victory of progressive America. This was primarily an appeal to the intellect. I didn't kid them, and they knew it. I didn't minimize the difficulties, the defeats, the setbacks. But I analyzed our advantages, our strengths, and our reserves. I convinced them because the facts themselves were persuasive. I told them why I did this. My theme was the necessity to maintain the will to fight, the morale, of progressive forces in our country. I was very explicit about it, and indeed, besides raising money, this was the main reason for my tours and speeches.

The essential problem in the political life of America today is, in my opinion, the maintenance of progressive morale in the face of a reactionary offensive unprecedented in American history since the Civil War. The post-war period has been for progressives a period of retreat, and the line between retreat and rout, between severe losses and complete disaster, is indeed a razor's edge. Since reaction is obviously winning battles, it is important to judge whether it is winning entire campaigns, whether it will win its strategic objective of fascism. It is important, it is essential, to estimate the extent of reaction's success in view of the relationship of forces, or, the same thing from the obverse side, the scope of progressive defeats in view of the power that reaction has brought to bear. A clear-eyed view of the political struggle must be the basis of progressives' will to fight.

The assertion of willpower may itself be the decisive factor in a struggle. This statement should be carefully hedged in. I have no sympathy whatsoever with Nietzchean philosophy concerning the will, and its vulgarization by Hitler and Mussolini. The fascists idealize the will, make it both causation and determination of events. To Marxists, this is nonsense. Reality exists objectively, i.e. outside of men's minds. "Facts are stubborn things," and all the will in the world will not change certain causal chains. You can will all you want, but if you jump off a roof you won't fly upward. To a fascist, to will is to achieve. The ultimate results were the Italian defeats in Greece; the German defeats in Russia. The basis of action, therefore, must always be the rational knowledge of facts. In those situations where willpower is itself a factor, it is important to be objective about its limitations.

Having made all this clear, however, it is also true that there are situations where the balance of forces is so close that the assertion of the will becomes decisive. In such situations, the superior will wins. This is true whether it's two boxers, two strategists, or two political groups. The essence of warfare is to impose your will on the enemy, to break the opponent's will. This is what the Nazis did to the French; what they could not do to the British and the Russians. In the period of their defeat, British and Russian morale remained virile—battered yes, but indomitable. In periods of defeat, the fibers of one's courage are strained to the utmost. A weakening of morale can flare into panic, into irreparable disaster. That is why I have stressed incessantly the necessity to maintain our will to fight.

To maintain morale in 1948 was not easy. For one thing we Americans were spoiled. We were babes in the woods about fascism. While Europe was undergoing its Gethsemane of Spain, Munich and rampaging German blitz, we in America were enjoying the fruits of our political victories under the New Deal, our successful Popular Front. The war itself strengthened our optimism, with its development of Allied unity, the unleashing of the tremendous productive might of American industry, the string of brilliant victories, the creation of the United Nations.

We were disarmed. Reaction, when it did hit, was most successful because most unexpected. The first blows came camouflaged by an administration that called itself the Fair Deal and was touted by its touts as to the "left of the New Deal". There was solid power in reaction's drive; there was sordid treachery in the progressive camp. There were the Mike Quills and the Joe Currans. The leadership of the great militant CIO cravenly caved in, undermined by the Catholic Church, cajoled by the anticommunists, subtly threatened and overtly flattered by the administration. A Secretary of State addressed a CIO Convention. Labor had arrived! The appeal to be a "labor statesman" proved irresistible to Philip Murray; he took the well-worn path of a Ramsay MacDonald. Contrary to all his bitter experience in decades of labor activity, Murray allowed the right to precipitate a fatal fraternal struggle.

The fragmentation of the left in America is the major reason for reaction's victories, just as the rise of Hitler was possible primarily because of a divided working class in Germany. Over this German division, a long historical controversy has crackled. The Communists blame the Social Democrats; the Social Democrats blame the Communists. I never felt I knew enough to assess responsibility but in the current situation in America, in many ways a deadly parallel, I *know* beyond shadow of a doubt that the split in progressive forces is squarely the responsibility of the Social Democrats and their stooges. This fact is cardinal in contemporary politics. The split in the New York American Labor Party was engineered by Dubinsky. The victory of the Socialist Reuther in the UAW marked the watershed of CIO unity. Within that labor organization I saw how the coalition of Socialists, Catholics and phony liberals went all out, reckless of the cost, in smashing CIO unity. I saw at close range the efforts of the left wing to compromise, to maintain unity. The left went to what I thought were embarrassing extremes—all in vain. In other organizations it was the same story. In the once flourishing Washington chapter of the American Veterans Committee, I saw Robert Nathan shamefully and ruthlessly precipitate a struggle for expulsion of pro-Communists, from which the outfit never recovered. Nathan, himself so often redbaited, nonetheless used the most virulent redbaiting. The right wing in committees actually threatened to inform the FBI as to who opposed them. Everywhere the right wing rode roughshod over all opposition in a hysterical orchestration of redbaiting. The formation of the Americans for Democratic Action marked the coming of age of American social democracy. Its theoreticians, like Professors Hook and the junior Schlesinger, have been busy confusing liberal thought and supporting the hair-splitting arguments of the administration in their knifing of the Bill of Rights. It will do them little good; the Peglers and the McCarthys have already opened fire on them. But it has never been a source of consolation for me to know that Schlesinger and I may share the same concentration camp. In fact, if any motive were necessary, this in itself would be sufficient for me to fight so that it might never come to pass.

No, all in all, 1948 was not a year of joy. Yet it was my considered opinion that in the face of formidable attacks, the left at that time was not doing too badly. The left-wing unions stood firm, except in the few cases where the top leadership betrayed. Within the CIO they were fighting a stubborn delaying action. In the political field the American Labor Party re-elected Vito Marcantonio. On the national scale the Progressive Party carried through the significant achievement of placing the party on the ballot in some thirty-six states in the face of the most calculated opposition of local political machines. Even in the field of civil liberties, the government's demagogy and circumspection was a tribute to its fears of repercussions.

In the international sphere there was ample ground for optimism. The citadels of Nazism, fascism and Japanese feudalism had been smashed beyond repair. The socialist world stood stronger than ever. The British Empire was crumbling; only the United States stood as a center of truly vital capitalism. Asia was on the move and events in China were heartening. Though I didn't foresee the torrent of victories that 1949 was to bring, it was evident that the Chinese Revolution was unfolding with refreshing rapidity. In the Near East, Israel's establishment seemed certain, profoundly affecting the rotting fabric of the Arab world. In Europe I felt certain that the Marshall Plan could not possibly bridge the dollar gap, so that sooner or later Britain and Western Europe would have to rebel against American plans, defy the Almighty Dollar and resume trade with their natural markets in Eastern Europe. As I remembered Munich, and my dreadful feeling of unrelieved despair at the time, I thought that 1948 was hardly the year to give up. It was up to us, the progressive forces in America, to keep a stout heart and a steady head; to fight back with energy, time, and money so that we might draw our country back from the precipice of Cold War into the path of world amity and peace. Such in brief were my sentiments at the time; writing now two years later and in jail, I find that my basic confidence remains unchanged despite the acceleration of domestic reaction.

In part my confidence is sustained by international events. Soviet development of atomic weapons has given salutary pause to American blitz strategists. Equally important, the overwhelming, fantastically rapid achievement of the Chinese Revolution has shaken the world. It is now fearfully apparent to the blindest reactionary what was clear to Marxists in 1948: capitalism is no longer the unchallenged system in the world. It has become impossible to organize a world crusade against Communism, or to isolate the USSR as was done between 1919 and 1939. In fact, the basic question behind current diplomatic struggles is not whether the Soviets will be isolated, but whether or not American reaction will be. If India and China should develop an alliance, however loose and tenuous, its effect on Europe will be such as to make the isolation of American reaction a probability. For the capitalists, world war has become the riskiest of undertakings. There is no question in my mind that by 1950 the position of progressive humanity has been vastly improved on a world scale.

Domestically, the reverse is true. Reaction has gained great victories, at least one by the accident of death. The death of Justices Murphy and Rutledge, and the consequent Trumanizing of the U.S. Supreme Court has been a most severe blow to prospects of civil liberties. I have no confidence whatsoever in Justices Douglas and Jackson; I don't believe the present Supreme Court can be counted on in the slightest to stem the attacks on civil liberties. I feel reasonably sure the Communist Party of the USA will be declared illegal and the thirsting FBI turned loose upon the land in a saturnalia of arrests, persecutions, and intimidations. Government proscription is upon us and tough days are looming.

The trade unions have gone from weakness to supine surrender to craven complicity with reaction. The infinitely contemptible agreement whereby maritime unions collaborate with the FBI to weed out "Communists" from employment is an indication of the degeneracy of certain sections of the leadership. In left-wing unions much strength has unquestionably been lost.

Throughout the land extralegal violence has been on the increase, often protected or abetted by the authorities. One cannot minimize the daily defeats suffered by progressives, nor dismiss the seriousness of the situation. I desire to do neither, but, once again, though the picture be somber it is not completely dark. Progressive organizations, the hundred-odd groups named as subversive by the Attorney General, are battered but unbroken. Left-wing unions have suffered grievous losses, but most are still sound. There are millions of determined men and women in the United States who are fighting. On the periphery of the struggle are the formidable battalions of organized labor. If they once break through the fog of redbaiting hysteria, reaction is lost. They do not seem capable of doing so, but one never knows. Their very existence is a massive threat. They are, as it were, an army in being, restraining the worst excesses of reaction, or, more accurately, forcing reaction to legalistic demagogy.

A profound uneasiness is permeating American society; although at the moment that anger is directed against Communists at home and the Soviets abroad, the possibility for channeling this discontent against the real enemies of the people is ever present and not to be discounted. Reaction is not unaware of all this. It acts viciously, but it is itself uneasy. There is little confidence in American reaction today. The impact of world events is having, and will have, increasingly profound effects on American politics. The Chinese Revolution and the Korean War, the increasing resentment among our allies over our sterile diplomacy, the mounting evidence that our foreign policy is not producing results, are undermining our ruling groups and will finally split them wide open. Bipartisanship in foreign policy is, I believe, in a process of disintegration, and when thieves fall out, honest men may get their dues.

Much depends on unity among liberals, progressives, and left-wing forces in America. Admittedly, this seems like whistling in the dark, but here too reaction may have overreached itself, as it often does. McCarthyism has shown to liberals that they are not immune and has stiffened some backbones. If the progressives continue to fight, inch by inch, without despairing, I think the turn will come.

This I do know: unity will not be achieved without courageous struggle. The morale of the progressives must be maintained, though the stresses are severe. Some of our finest progressives, beset by many problems, suddenly find the struggle too much. As I write these lines, in April 1950, the newspapers carry the news that Professor Mathiessen of Harvard is dead. He jumped from a window, leaving a note that said, "I have been depressed by conditions throughout the world for many months..." Like John Winant. Like Jan Masaryk. Broken by a sense of despair that after a bitter antifascist war, the suffering seems to have turned out in vain. To a man like Mathiessen the American domestic scene was a nightmare. Here is what he wrote returning from a visit to Europe:

> I was home in time to find that, during my absence, many of my activities have now become "subversive." The Attorney General has apparently drawn up a "list." It includes nearly all the groups who have been militantly anti-Fascist ever since the rise of Hitler, who have honored the Abraham Lincoln Brigade and have tried to help the Spanish refugees, who have defended labor's prisoners and the Negro and the foreign-born, who have supported the cause of a people's democracy, whether at home or in China or in Greece. I have believed in the work done by these groups, whether or not some of their members are Communists. I have been proud to belong to them.
>
> I have a renewed sense of the responsibility of the intellectual—a word honored by William James and scorned by Fascists—of the necessity for him to be as true as possible to what his experience has taught him, and to speak for those truths as fully and as fearlessly as he can.

Professor Mathiessen engaged himself fully and fearlessly in the struggle for a progressive America. I met him once, when he chaired a meeting for me at Harvard. I was struck by his gentleness, his kindliness, his tranquil transparent goodness. I thought then how difficult it must be for this quiet, retiring scholar to be the target for reaction's unceasing assault. He did not recant, but the emotional strain was tremendous. It proved too much. The gentle, kind souls are favorite victims of reaction.

This is nothing new in the world, or in America. I've just read Ginger's biography of Debs. There is in it the story of Julius Wayland, publisher of the *Socialist Appeal to Reason.* Wayland, with Debs, had been indicted for violating postal regulations. In addition Wayland was brazenly framed by the federal government of President Taft on a morals charge. Though completely innocent, he knew that the indictment had been made, and the trial would be conducted, so as to smear the left-wing movement. He put a bullet in his head, leaving a note: "The struggle under the capitalist system isn't worth the effort. Let it pass." Kate O'Hara gave an epitaph for Wayland then, that applies to Professor Mathiessen today: "We shed no tears of grief; grief is for the naked lives of those who have made the world no better."

No grief no, but anger and determination. Not grief but resolution that reaction shall not triumph, that rotten men shall not cackle over these deaths as the despicable Senator Mundt cackled over the death of

Larry Duggan. Duggan had died from a fall from a window after a smear by the un-American Activities Committee. Said Mundt to the press: "We will release more names as they jump out of windows."

Killing is pleasant to these putrid butchers. Harry Dexter White, wartime Under Secretary of the Treasury Department, died of heart failure after a session at which he had asked for pauses because of his heart. The rest was denied. These are only the well-known names; there is no record of the hundreds, indeed thousands, of beaten, broken-hearted men and women terrorized by the witch hunts, the Cold War, the gut-searing sense of futility and despair. Against this assault we must harden ourselves. We must extirpate those feelings of softness that play into the hands of the Mundts, the Rankins, the McCarthys. There is an anecdote that Lenin, after listening to music, said that he really should stop listening. Music makes you soft and the mad dog of reaction bites your hand off. It is not the least of reaction's sins that by its lawlessness and lack of scruples, it forces normal, decent people into an unnatural, unwanted bitterness and intransigence. Yet it is either that or be beaten, and to be beaten by fascism is to die. Progressives must, for sheer survival, put iron in their souls.

I hammered away at those points at every possible opportunity. The response was heartening, and over a period of time I gained something of a reputation. It would take too long to give details of the tours. A few meetings will give the flavor of them all. One of the first meetings was in Congressman Sabath's district in Chicago. It's a working-class area, but it was not a large meeting—about three hundred people. In the middle of my speech I was interrupted by a long-distance call. It was from Washington, about my wife. A new baby had arrived, several weeks ahead of schedule. It was a boy and both he and my wife were doing well; I should not worry but go on with the tour. When I told the audience about it there was great cheering and happiness. The collection was five hundred dollars, a phenomenal sum for the low incomes present.

Another meeting in Chicago was that of the Packinghouse workers. About six hundred people came, almost entirely Negroes. I told them about the case, particularly about the use of Negroes on the jury and the use of Negro witnesses. They got the point of the subtle Jim Crow at once, whereas many whites, presumably smart and educated, never have understood it. There is on these issues the greatest perceptiveness and sensitivity among Negroes. My frank and straightforward discussion made me instantly accepted, appreciated, and welcomed. They knew that the real villains were the prosecutor and the judge, but they knew also that the witnesses had to be exposed, and their role in the Jim Crow setup explained. In San Francisco a strike was going on of the Marine Cooks and Stewards. I spoke at their union hall and showed them *Deadline for Action*. Many of the union members are Filipinos or Puerto Ricans and their English is sketchy, but I could tell by their laughter and their healthy swearing at the proper places that they were following the arguments.

One meeting was of particular importance. In the winter of 1948 I was scheduled to speak with Gerhart Eisler at the University of Michigan. The university authorities refused a hall for the meeting. A private hall was rented in Ann Arbor. The university authorities brought pressure to bear and the hall was reluctantly refused. A meeting was then arranged in the open park and the police gave a permit.

It was snowing, hard. In spite of the snow and the bitter cold, over one thousand students turned out. We were about to start when the police appeared. The Mayor had withdrawn the permit and the police would arrest any speakers. Since Eisler and I were out on bail, an arrest could be used as an excuse to cancel the bail. We had to submit, and we went on to a private home, a students' cooperative, with a couple of dozen boys and girls who wished to have a bull session. After we got to the house we were besieged by about a hundred students, most of them from the Business School. These were supposed to be the "better" students, i.e. more middle class. They behaved like the worst kind of hoodlums, trying to break into the house, breaking cellar windows and working themselves up for violent action.

The police were called; they said they were too busy. The president of the university was called and he wouldn't speak to the students. So finally I got on the phone and succeeded in speaking to him personally. I was courteous and polite. I told him the police were apathetic, had refused to come though there was considerable disorder. I suggested that if he called the police there might be some action; otherwise it looked as if some students would be hurt. The conversation went something like this: "I won't do a thing," he said. "Someone will get hurt," I repeated. "That's your lookout," he said tartly. "You got yourself into this mess. Get yourself out!" He hung up.

Had I not heard him with my own ears, I wouldn't have believed it. This had been a university president speaking, the president of the University of Michigan. I stood there, the man's intolerant tone still present in my ear, and thought of this "educator" with mingled incredulity, contempt, and a sense of shame for him. This was a man of some academic standing, he must have had some kind of education, was presumed to know something of the nature of democracy, its ethic, its history, its conditions of life and survival. Yet he had talked to me like the most backward desk sergeant in a company town. This man who was supposed to represent law and order didn't care whether there was a riot or not; violence didn't bother him, it would serve us right! What an abdication of responsibility! What a cesspool of vigilante thinking! No words of condemnation are too strong for a man of that kind. No other incident could show so clearly the degenerating influence of hysteria in our country, the indecent surrender to the pressure of witch-hunting, the craven adaptation to a fascistic climate of opinion. "Get yourself out of the mess!" Just so might a timorous German official have answered people attacked by storm troopers in the streets of Berlin in 1932.

As I turned from the phone, the electric wires were cut and the house plunged into darkness. It was decided I should get out, find a car, and arrange for a get-away. Outside I found that more students had come, attracted by the crowd. There were perhaps three hundred of them outside, a very sizable crowd. These newcomers weren't hoodlums; they wished to hear Eisler, and Eisler came out. When I returned with a car soon after, Eisler had the people well in hand, and the size of the group defeated the hoodlums, who were isolated on the outskirts. Finally Eisler drove away, while I spoke for a few minutes, to mark time while Eisler got clear, and then I went off. There was no disorder, much to the disappointment of the police and the authorities.

I use the word "disappointment" advisedly. These fine people were not averse to disorder. If the hoodlums beat us up, that would be a regrettable "excess of zeal." If we beat them up, we would be arrested for disturbing the peace. It is the classic pattern of extralegal violence protected and abetted by the authorities. The extent to which this is happening in our country is frightening. As I write, two workers in Linden, N.J., were beaten up by some right-wing fellow workers. Arrested, the attackers were charged with disorderly conduct and released on $1,000 bail. The attacked were charged with "criminal syndicalism" and held on £20,000 bail. Why? Because the ones attacked were left-wingers—that's the meaning of criminal syndicalism.

Instances could be multiplied. The most notorious, large-scale example is the Peekskill riot which I have already mentioned. In the South, authorities consistently abet strong-arm gangs. No one is immune where racial supremacy is concerned. In his tour of the South in 1948, Henry Wallace had to travel by back roads in greatest secrecy when he was going to a dinner in a Negro home. This was the former Vice-President of the United States.

Another group of meetings that always held great interest for me were those held in Italian communities—as, for example, around Boston. Italians are generally considered backward in American politics, and so they are. Primarily this is due to the fact that as immigrants they settle in closely knit communities dominated by a few ward healers. The influence of the Catholic Church is also important and, finally, the older generation is afraid of sticking its neck out in a strange land. But, as a point of fact, the average Italian worker is extremely class-conscious. More often than not, he is also anti-clerical. He will resent an attack on Catholicism as an attack on his religion, and, basically, on his being a foreigner; but he will go a long way in distrusting the hierarchy, bishops, archbishops, cardinals and pope, as pillars of reactionary governments. Their class-consciousness is often inarticulate, but very deeply felt. There is a knowingness about it which seems almost instinctive, though really the result of long, bitter experience thoroughly assimilated. My mother is a good case in point.

Mother is not highly educated; on the surface she is apolitical. As a child I loved her dearly, but after we came to America I grew away from her. My interests centered in the school, with which she had no contact because of the language difficulties. Also the rather authoritarian parental controls which were natural in Italy became irksome in the freer atmosphere of America. Finally there was the inevitable element of alienness. She remained to a large extent Italian in customs and speech as I grew more Americanized. She remained Catholic; I grew up like my father, a freethinker. As a result I grew away from her, in contrast to my father, who understood me a good deal better.

After my father's death, my mother came to live with us. Our family was happy, when the indictment hit us like a thunderbolt. To my mother, the idea of the huge federal government smacking me down was terrifying. She broke down and went about household chores weeping incessantly. I tried to console her but it seemed in vain. She said something that struck me deeply: "We saved your father," she wept, "but we can't save you." She meant, of course, saved him from Fascism. Her insight, acute and instantaneous, into the essential nature of the attack was a lesson to me in working-class reaction. I thought often of her remark when government prosecutors orate about their love for civil liberties, or when the Sidney Hooks mumble about the difference between heresy and conspiracy to justify governmental reaction.

Because of what she said, I half-consciously tested her to see how far her understanding went. Pretending irritation at her crying I said, "All right, all right. If you're going to break down I'll fix it. I'll go to the government and make a bargain. I'll tell them all about my Communist friends and to hell with them. Let them have trouble; I'll be all right." My mother turned to me, wide-eyed, unbelieving. "Oh, no," she cried impulsively, "you can't! You can't do that!"

I know this sounds like bad melodrama, but it is absolutely true. There was in her eyes a kind of horror, a fear *of me* and *for me*, as if suddenly I had turned out to be something she couldn't understand. It was the age-old contempt for the stool pigeon, the betrayer, the coward. As for me, I was close again to her, as I hadn't been for many years. "Okay, then," I said grinning, "I won't." She realized I had been pretending and smiled timidly, coming out of her shock. I gave her a hug. "Now will you stop crying?"

She nodded, wiping her eyes. From that time, right through the trial, right through the appeals, right through the pressures, the anxieties and the long months in jail, there wasn't a murmur out of her. Whatever her private feelings, she was always cheerful and uncomplaining. In a funny way our family ordeal was no longer a "tragedy" but "trouble," just plain, familiar, working-class trouble, like a dirty job, illness or the worst thing, unemployment. Although not well, during the months I was in jail, she took odd jobs whenever she could, to help the family budget.

A fine woman, my mother, symbol of millions upon millions of working-class mothers all over the world, inexorable enemies of war, and hence a potent problem for Fascism. They are part of a world dike against reaction, integral bricks of flesh, blood, and longsuffering hearts. I spoke of her to my Italian audiences. They knew just how she felt. Their opinion of the Truman administration would be unprintable. We got along famously.

The last set of meetings I want to mention were those in which I had a partner—Gerhart Eisler. I never knew Eisler until after we had both been tried and sentenced. Then we planned a tour together to raise money for our respective defenses. The tour was primarily designed to cover universities, and we made an odd pair—he the hard, uncompromising German Communist with heavy accent and little rapport with the students; me, the soft fellow traveler speaking the language of the campus and very much at home there with the students. We were something like a vaudeville team, and, as a team, we were a great hit. I got to know Eisler, and thought that his treatment by the House un-American

Activities Committee one of the most shameful pages in their record. Eisler thought my prosecution more unjust than his. The reason is that while I thought in national terms, he thought in class terms. His thinking went something like this: "Naturally the American government hates me. I'm a foreigner and a Communist. I hate capitalism, and they know it. I want to see the end of capitalism, they want it to go on forever. I'm its enemy; they its defenders. Naturally they hate me and try to jail me. There's a bitter realism about it, and what's the use of my being angry. Since when has capitalism shown any justice or mercy in the class struggle. So they prosecute me. But Marzani! Now here's a different story. Here's a man who has served his country. He worked in the government. He was in the army. He loves his country. He's so woolly minded he even expects justice under capitalism, the dope. And what do they do to him? Use his services in the war and jail him at the end." All this Eisler said to his audiences and hammered home the point: "If they can do it to him, they can do it to you. He's one of you, a student like yourselves. You don't have to sympathize with me, the German Communist, but how about Marzani, the American veteran?"

We both held firmly to our points of view and argued about it privately. We carried these points of view onto the platform and our individual indignation was so transparently honest that it carried great weight and conviction. In short, we ended up as a mutual admiration society. He'd talk about my case and get mad, I'd talk about his and get furious. The audiences seemed to love it.

Eisler was uncompromising in his Communism and his speech. But he had a very definite charm and it worked its spell on the audiences. He was a short man, rather plump, with a cherubic face. His accent can only be described as cute. He spoke a precise and fluent English, but you had to pay attention, for now and again his accent would derail your train of thought. You'd have to do a mental double-take to catch on. I remember one example, the sound of "way-toh!" Try to guess what it means. It hit me dazedly and I could see the audience was lost too. The word he was saying was "veto" but it took some figuring.

Eisler, though, had great dignity and at the opening of his lecture he was very impressive as he drew himself up straight and said, "For thirty-five years I have been a Communist and I'm proud to be a Communist." He would hurl the fact at a hostile audience. His manner plainly said, "I know you don't like it, but you can damn well lump it!" "I've been convicted," he would say, "of contempt of Congress. That is a lie. I have no contempt for your American Congress. No Communist has contempt for the democratic institutions of another country. No Communist has, or can have, contempt for the revolutionary traditions of America, for your Lincolns, your Jeffersons. No, I have no contempt for your national institutions but I do have contempt for your reactionaries. I have contempt for a Parnell Thomas, for a Tom Clark—just as I had contempt for a Himmler or a Goebbels. I never gave in to German reactionaries; I certainly will not yield to American reactionaries."

One had to hand it to Eisler—he was a man. You might not like his ideas, but you had to respect him. The most impressive thing about Eisler was precisely his Communism. Left-wing clichés assumed meaning and dignity in his mouth. At question time, there was always someone who asked, "Mr. Eisler, what is Communism?" Eisler stood straight, the light gleaming on his spectacles. "Communism," said Eisler, "is the ending of the exploitation of man by man." The exploitation of man by man. The phrase has been mouthed a thousand thousand times, but with Eisler it lived. In Sandburg's phrase, the words "threw long shadows." Egyptian slaves toiling at the pyramids, chained captives dying in Roman galleys, mutinied Sepoys tied to cannons' mouths, uprooted Negroes in the magnolia South—up and down the striated course of time, the bitter, barbaric inhumanity of man to man; the endless suffering of misshapen bodies and violated minds.

The exploitation of man by man! Echoes upon echoes of whimpers in a merciless world. Wars, famines, unemployment, religious and racial hatreds—there aren't enough books in the world to write what is going on now, this very minute, let alone to write of all that has gone on in human history. There is no mind sufficiently knowing to comprehend the vast infinity of human tears. No mind could bear it. To me this has always been the symbolism of the crucifixion.

The exploitation of man by man! It's a battle cry. The German Communist had seen enough of suffering; he knew enough of suffering that it had sparked within him an unquenchable fire, just as it had sparked such a fire in a Spartacus two thousand years ago, in a John Brown a hundred years ago, in a million unknown men and women ten years ago, one year ago, yesterday. The German Communist stood there, and said he was going to stop it. He and millions of people like him all over the world were going to put a stop to the exploitation of man by man. I know there are learned men who will prove to you that such a phrase is meaningless. Or if that isn't convincing, other learned men will prove to you that exploitation is a law of life and that it cannot change, that it is silly to feel moral condemnation towards a *law of life*. Or if this doesn't convince you, other learned men will prove to you that the phrase only covers the drive to power of ambitious men, who only want power for power's sake and are willing to destroy civilisation (as we know it) to get such power.

I know the explanations of the learned men. I have read them, all those and a hundred others. They have one thing in common: to blunt your hope for a better world. Well, perhaps they are right. Perhaps the phrase "the exploitation of man by man" is a cliche, a slogan. It could be. But for Eisler the phrase had substance. It had stature. It has for me. With Eisler, the phrase was no cliché. This was no slogan; this was a proclamation of war, flags flying and drums rolling. It was arrogant; it was also magnificent. The little plump man stood inflexible against the mightiest capitalist machine the world has ever seen. At such times, Eisler towered morally over reactionary America. At such times there always flashed in my mind a picture of Parnell Thomas presiding at his committee table. Newsreel men used to put a couple of telephone books under his behind to overcome his short height and make him look impressive. Eisler needed no telephone books. Thomas really believed Eisler was a Comintern agent, the Kremlin representative, boss of the American Communist Party. Personally I don't believe in such nonsense. I offer, however, a few first-hand observations.

I saw a good deal of Eisler. With the indictment of the eleven Communist leaders I saw something of them as well. If Eisler was their boss, they were all magnificent actors. For Eisler's behavior was more that of a poor relation than of a master. Eisler was on the periphery. He was liked, helped, admired, his opinion sometimes asked, but not necessarily taken. Eisler's attitude, unconscious as far as I could judge, was a half-apologetic one that he was a drain on Party and defense funds. I could see that it bothered him. On trips he would travel long distances, such as New York to Chicago, in a train coach, whereas I traveled by air as a matter of course. I'm sure he did it to save money. I argued with him that it was a false economy, for he was often tired, run down, subject to colds. If he got sick it would cost a lot more. It was no use; he was gently stubborn.

Part of the same pattern was his eagerness to be used, to travel and speak, not only because he wished to fight, but also, I often felt, as a repayment for the Communist Party's financial aid. He wanted to be as light a burden as possible. Both he and his wife dressed extremely modestly, ate cheaply, and in general led a rather penurious life. For a Kremlin potentate, he sure took a beating.

Eisler's desire to go home was tremendous. I saw glimpses of deep nostalgic homesickness. He had a lot of self-control; but once, late at night, driving back from Ann Arbor to Detroit, we started singing German revolutionary songs. I watched him unnoticed. He sang introspectively, if I may use the expression, as if to his inner man, and I could literally hear him caress the German language, the German syllables, the German cadences, the tiny mannerisms within the language. There was always an air of sadness about Eisler, very reminiscent to me of my father's attitude in America, a sadness covered by Dante's heartfelt phrase: "how bitter to eat the stranger's bread." I'm sure this parallelism was part of my liking for Eisler.

The reader should not get the impression that Eisler was treated shabbily by the progressive movement; far from it. He was welcomed as a Communist and liked as a nice person. The same is true of his wife. But I think they were not happy. Many Europeans are not happy in the United States. The tempo of our life is different—more electric, not to say hectic, not only physically but culturally. Novelty is at a premium; extroverts tend to rule. Leisure and reflection are not commonplace. America exhilarates visitors, but after a while many become vaguely disturbed. Eisler, I felt, was out of his cultural environment and it bothered him. Basically, he remained a stranger amongst us, despite the five years or so he had spent here. America was constantly surprising him. I am thinking of a particular illustration of this; it is perhaps my most favored story.

I've mentioned the trouble we had at the University of Michigan and how finally Eisler got away in a car. I walked to an apartment we had previously fixed as a rendezvous. We waited for ten minutes; no Eisler. We waited for twenty minutes, for half an hour. We were seriously worried when he showed up, looking slightly dazed, but with a great twinkle in his eyes. He kept murmuring, "America, what a place!" We finally found out where he had been. It seems that as his car went off, another big car started to follow. Eisler's driver tried to shake off the pursuers, but in vain. The car behind was big, black, powerful—we got the impression of a movie thriller. Trying to get away, Eisler's driver maneuvered himself onto a highway, and before he knew it he was out of town, on the highway, the black car gaining. Finally they were forced off the road to a stop. Eisler said he felt sure they'd take a beating. Two big fellows came over, looking even bigger because of their sheepskin coats.

"Such shoulders," said Eisler. "Big! I think, 'What a beating!'" The two men came up and one stuck his head in the window.

"You Eisler?" he demanded. Eisler gathered all his strength. "Ja!" he said defiantly. A huge hand came through the window.

"Say, can we have your autograph?"

We exploded with laughter. Eisler couldn't get over the episode. "Autograph," he would snort. "America, what a place!"

So much for the Kremlin potentate. I'm convinced that Eisler was what he said he was: a German Communist refugee caught by the war in a strange land. I'm glad he's in Germany, working. I think of him often.

Besides the tours to raise money, I was engaged in one other major activity during the time of the appeals. This was the Wallace campaign in 1948. I was anxious to do campaign films for them, but national headquarters kept me at arm's length for many weeks. This was amusing in view of the fact that they were supposed to be Communist-dominated, yet here they were doing a little redbaiting on their own. I finally got approval only after I had raised a couple of thousand dollars to do the film. The total contribution of the Wallace National Committee was $800 for a three-reel film, whose commercial cost would have been at least $15,000. All labor was donated and I personally was out of pocket by a very considerable amount. After the film was agreed on, the Speakers' Bureau used me as an emergency speaker in small out-of-the-way meetings. I didn't mind; I was glad to do what I could, but this further instance of redbaiting was not pleasant.

The film we produced was *Dollar Patriots*, which was aimed particularly at showing business domination of the major parties through their campaign contributions. I laid out certain lines of research and the Progressive Party staff came up with some pretty amazing statistics compiled entirely from government sources. There emerged a clear, unmistakable pattern of business using its contributions strategically across the forty-eight states, with a contribution placed here and one there, like a vast chess game, assuring them the most politicians for their money, and resulting in a hard solid core of reactionary congressmen and senators.

I met Wallace at this time. To cover certain scenes for *Dollar Patriots* we had to photograph at his farm so I took a crew up to his place in Salem, N.Y. It is a lovely farm, spacious and well kept, with a considerable area devoted to his experiments in plant and animal breeding. Wallace likes to farm, runs his tractor and farm implements himself, and seems good at it. At the time the vituperation against Wallace was at its height. He was shocked and hurt, I think, not so much at the personal slander as at the depths of bitterness and intolerance of supposedly liberal Americans. Actually I was sure at the time that, whatever his ambitions in the past, Wallace was then campaigning only out of a profound sense of duty. Not only was the vilification campaign a severe burden, but the great fight Wallace was making was physically demanding and left him little home life or privacy. When we arrived, at around noon, Mrs. Wallace, who wasn't expecting us, let out a spontaneous "Goodness, when will he rest?" Then she smiled half-apologetically, half-humorously. "He's been seeing people all morning and I was counting on a quiet luncheon." I told her we would make ourselves invisible, wait till he was through, and that there was plenty of time. We could survey the land and plan our shots, keeping his appearance to a minimum. She thanked us warmly as Wallace came over to greet us. They made a handsome couple. She's a gracious woman with great charm and serenity. Wallace too has charm, an infectious smile, and a modest unassuming manner. I was greatly taken with both of them.

We filmed our sequences and chatted for an hour afterward. Wallace was curious about our business—did we make money, and so on. A few worlds were exchanged on the case and then the conversation meandered. Winant had just committed suicide. Wallace felt very upset; Winant had been a good friend. He told us the farm we were on had belonged to Winant. I remembered saying something to the effect that Winant's death paralleled that of Jan Masaryk in Czechoslovakia. Both had suffered greatly throughout the war—Winant had lost his son—and both had hoped for a decent post-war world. The renewed struggle must have given them an overpowering feeling of despair. Wallace shot me a keen glance and nodded. "I feel the same way," he said.

There's no question that Wallace disliked the tightening controls of Communist Parties in Eastern European countries; there is also no doubt that he saw this as the inexorable result of the Cold War, for which he holds both the USSR and the U.S. equally responsible. I do not agree with him on this. I think it is a misreading of the actual situation. The United States, in my opinion, is much more responsible for the Cold War, because we have so much more initiative and power. This may strike the reader as a joke, a poor joke, in view of the way the Soviet Union seems to have the initiative in current diplomacy, but I am serious. American power is autonomous; it is founded primarily on our tremendous productive capacity, within our borders. Soviet power is much less autonomous, depending to a large extent on the strength of Communism and its appeal in other countries. But this appeal is most powerful where the *status quo* is intolerable, like colonialism in Asia, or the corruption of the Nationalist government in China. It is because American policy is aimed at supporting the status quo that the Soviet Union has the initiative. Their power is in many ways derived from our blunders and our reactionary policies.

This discussion is not academic. If the inception of the Cold War is primarily American in origin, then its solution may well depend on our desires and initiative. Each event, such as the Korean War, must be judged in the broader context of the Cold War. If, on the other hand, each nation is equally responsible, each event is judged on its own. Wallace, therefore, on the Korean War does not blame the Cold War; he blames Soviet policies. On this issue he left the Progressive Party.

This problem needs greater development. I only mention it to show that Wallace's resignation is not inconsistent with his previous positions. I think he is wrong, but I respect his integrity and, for me, his superiority to a man like Truman is self-evident. During the 1948 campaign Wallace did great courageous work. I believe time will show, when government files are opened, that Wallace's campaign upset many plans. But of this more later.

For me the Wallace campaign was a catharsis. When it was over I felt I had spent my time well, the fourteen months out on bail. I know that by my unceasing fight I was angering the government and stirring up trouble for myself. But I knew I was being useful. I did all I could, guided in my own small way by the magnificent defiance of Bartolomeo Vanzetti in his last speech to the despicable court in his case. I came across the speech again in prison. It is printed as a poem in a Modern Library anthology edited by S. Rodman. Said the "uneducated" Italian immigrant:

> If it had not been for those things
> I might have lived out my life
> talking at street corners to scorning men.
> I might have died, unmarked, unknown, a failure.
> Now we are not a failure.
>
> This is our career and our triumph. Never in our full life could we hope to do such work. For tolerance, for justice, for man's understanding of man, as now we do by accident.
>
> Our words, our lives, our pains—nothing! The taking of our lives—lives of a good shoemaker and a poor fishpeddler —all! That last moment belongs to us—that agony is our triumph.

In my own—immeasurably lesser—sacrifice I was content. After the Wallace campaign, I was ready for jail if the appeals failed.

Eight

During the appeals the government finally came out in the open, admitting what had been no secret from the start, that they were prosecuting me for my ideas. Marzani is a Communist they said; jail him and never mind the law. This was the essence of their argument, but it was made orally. In their briefs the government still went through the legal hocus-pocus about statutes, violation of statutes and so on, quite as if I had stolen an automobile or forged a check. This, however, was window dressing, for they knew well that they were on shaky legal grounds; when they came to convince the judges, the prosecutors moved onto a more solid platform—redbaiting. Their speeches were studded with such phrases as "in times like these…," "given the circumstances…," "subversive activities," "the government must defend itself," and so on. At first subtly, and then in desperation quite openly, the prosecutors reminded the judges that I was a Communist—by implication a traitor, a pariah, a danger to society, to civilization as they knew it.

The first appeal was heard by three judges of the Federal Circuit Court in Washington, D.C., each side having an hour for oral argument. Edith and I attended with great curiosity. The government's arguments were woefully weak and it was obvious the judges thought so too. One could tell this by the kind of questions the judges asked. The questions were aimed almost exclusively at the government, and were antagonistic in nature, legally speaking that is, for they probed the government's weak points. The more they probed, the weaker the points seemed. As the prosecutor's answers became more and more absurd as a result of logical contradictions, there appeared increasing references to my subversive character.

Kelley (who was prosecuting here too) was at his Jesuitical best, or, should I say, his Jesuitical worst; a sanctimonious defender of a democratic administration. No doubt he saw himself as a spare, alert, modern Saint George slaying the Red Terror. To my prejudiced eyes he was a whited sepulcher, pious, vindictive and intellectually utterly dishonest. He was obviously uneasy about the judges' questions and about the prestige of Arthur Garfield Hays. Therefore in his peroration, Kelley suddenly acknowledged that my case did touch upon civil liberties by saying that although some people argued this, it wasn't so—this was not a case of civil liberties. He was himself, he said a great defender of civil liberties. Vibrant with righteousness he told the court what a great liberal he was, how he had in the past defended the rights of citizens, how he stood uncompromising for full freedom for every American citizen. In short, Kelley wouldn't harm a hair of dear old Democracy. But this case was different. This was Subversion. This Marzani was a destroyer of democracy. Given the times (i.e. the anti-Soviet policy current), I must not be allowed to destroy the government. This was a case of a criminal caught red-handed (he didn't say doing what), a man without principles, loyalty, morals and so on.

After this outpouring, Hays had one minute for a rebuttal. He stood before the Court, an aged man with a long successful career behind him. Slightly hunched forward, his massive head as if too heavy for him, he was an impressive figure. He spoke in a kind of reflective mood, yet there was no mistaking the deep feeling in him. "May it please the court," I quote him from memory, "the defense rests. The government has seen fit, however, to maintain that this prosecution does not infringe on civil liberties. I have had some experience in that field, and I say with deep conviction that in all my forty years at the bar, I have never seen as clear a violation of civil liberties as this case represents." In the deep silence, the voice rose ever so slightly, ever so challenging. "May I be so bold as to remind the court of the words of Justice Holmes: 'There is nothing in the law which prevents judges from seeing what is apparent to all other men.' We thank the court." It was very moving. He had given high expression to my feelings.

Some weeks later the court handed down a unanimous decision, covering two main findings. In the first part, the court unanimously declared the first nine counts invalid. Their unanimity showed up clearly the unconstitutional hocus-pocus with the statute of limitations. It also showed up the "impartiality" of Judge Keech, for obviously he could hardly have been so stupid or so blind as not to see what the appeal judges saw. If Keech had behaved correctly and invalidated the first nine counts there would have been no trial. This first finding was a major political victory. It meant that the government could not use the war contracts extension of the statute of limitations to prosecute whomsoever they pleased for false statements allegedly made during the war. This particular road to dirty work was blocked.

However, as far as my particular case was concerned, I was still going to jail. In the second finding the Appellate Court upheld the legality of the last two counts of the indictment, which the reader will remember were based on the Panuch interview. The defense had argued that such an interview, informal in character, without witnesses, notes, transcripts or safeguarding procedures of any kind, was not proper ground for an indictment. The court disagreed with the defense and when it was announced that we would appeal to the Supreme Court, my bail was continued.

Hays and Rosenberg were dejected by the decision, and surprised at my comparative cheerfulness. I felt that the political victory was vital and important, though naturally I was disappointed that I was going to jail. But blocking the government's legal hocus-pocus towards other people was a fine thing. The operation was successful but the patient had died.

We planned for future action. The next step was to obtain certiorari from the U.S. Supreme Court. As is well known, this Court is under no obligation to review a case. It does so only if it wishes to. Therefore to appeal to the Supreme Court one must first obtain their permission to do so, to be certified, so to speak, that the case is important. Obtaining this permission is known technically as petitioning for certiorari. Briefs are presented by both sides if one of them opposes the review (as the government did in our case), and in effect this step becomes a preliminary hearing. There is, however, no oral argument. If certiorari was granted it would be a setback to the government.

I wasn't too hopeful. It seemed to me that the Circuit Court decision was nicely balanced. On one hand, the Court had thrown out the more glaring unconstitutional counts. On the other hand, I was sent to jail. The government hadn't got everything its way, but it had obtained all it could get. Furthermore, with all the fuss they had stirred up in the newspapers, their prestige was involved in my going to jail and on this score they had won. Honor was satisfied as well as their basic purpose of intimidating government workers through my prosecution. It seemed to me that the Supreme Court would just forget the whole thing. After all, only 15 percent of the cases that petition for certiorari get it. These are odds of seven to one. More important, for the Supreme Court to take the case, discuss it, give opinions on it would be bound to slow down the administration witch hunt. It would set the Court smack against a bipartisan political tide of great force and I couldn't see the Court bucking it. This aside from the prejudices of the judges. I just didn't see it. It's true the lawyers felt I was unduly suspicious of the Court's motives, but if there is one thing I learned during the trial it is that in their hands the law is extremely flexible, not to say accommodating. No matter how bad you think reactionaries are, when the evidence is in, they are usually worse than you imagined they could be.

We had a new attorney for the Supreme Court appeals: Osmond K. Fraenkel, one of the foremost constitutional lawyers in America. An associate of Hays, Mr. Fraenkel has a great record in defense of civil liberties (he served without fee). His presence for the defense was an important asset. I didn't get to know Fraenkel as well as Hays. There was a dinner and a few short meetings. I liked him immensely. Fraenkel is in his late fifties, I imagine, white-haired, unhurried, affable and dignified. He has a serene, warm personality, a gentle humor and no trace of affectation. Like Hays, his mind is as impervious to redbaiting as a duck is to water. The caliber of his mind and his prestige before the Court were defense assets of the most sterling quality. In the hearing before the Court, his eloquence was moving.

Fraenkel and Rosenberg felt there was a definite chance of receiving certiorari. Allan went to work on the briefs with indomitable energy and an aggressive attitude that scorned defeatism. Throughout the case, Allan behaved magnificently. As it turned out, he and Fraenkel were right; I was wrong. I had reckoned without the integrity of three or four men on the Court who were as devoted to American ideals as Tom Paine ever was. Because of them, the Supreme Court appeal has been one of the fundamental experiences of my intellectual life. Certiorari was granted; the case would be heard in the fall of 1948. While I went on with fund-raising, Allan buckled down to more briefs. The printer was our mutual master.

The Supreme Court hearing took place at the height of the Wallace campaign. Edith and I went to Washington for the occasion. We had never attended a session of the Court, although we had always meant to when we were in Washington. The nearest I came during the war was the basement of the Court, which has the best cafeteria in the city. The Court is a monumental Greek temple. Inside is a vast entrance hall where the few people walking by only accentuate its emptiness. Beyond is the courtroom, very light, very cool and sedate in its marbled dignity. Behind a raised bench sit the justices, each in an individual leather chair that both swivels and rocks. Mighty comfortable. The justices are very informal during the hearing, breaking in on each other.

On the day of our hearing, Justice Jackson was not present. He was away making a speech somewhere. Chief Justice Vinson sat in the center, with his right wing composed of Frankfurter, Black, Murphy and Rutledge, in that order. Vinson's left wing was Reed, Jackson's chair, Douglas and Burton. Politically, the right wing was the left and vice-versa.

As the clerk called the case, *The Government of the United States* versus *Carl Aldo Marzani*, I felt a thrill of excitement. I was suddenly aware that I was now a grain in the written history of our country. I also thought that I was being sent off to jail with all the frills and furbelows. I remembered grimly how Sacco and Vanzetti were electrocuted with all possible pomp. The Governor of Massachusetts had appointed a final Pardon Review Commission of most eminent citizens: President Lowell of Harvard University, President Stratton of MIT, and Robert Grant, a former judge—infinitely distinguished men. A great honor for two unknown Italian immigrants to be condemned by such august minds. As the old gag has it, nothing is too good for the working class.

When the clerk called the case, Justice Douglas gathered his papers and left. He did not participate in the case. Why, I don't know. The Solicitor General, Philip B. Perelman, opened the case for the government. He was a pompous character with a somewhat porcine face and I thought slightly pop-eyed. When he got excited, he waved his arms and ranted. The combination of pompous language and arms waving made him look pretty silly. As he spoke, the government's strategy was transparent. It was redbaiting, pure and simple, backed by the patrioteering hysteria of the Cold War.

Said Mr. Perelman to the Court, this is not an ordinary case, this is not an ordinary criminal. The defendant, Carl Aldo Marzani, is a well-educated man, a graduate of fine universities and colleges. He described my accomplishments at great length and in the most flattering terms. Adjectives such as "brilliant," "exceptional," "outstanding" flew thick and fast. Then came the switch. How did this man get his education, his training? Why, through the kindness of the United States! Perelman elaborated the point. A poor immigrant had received a free education that developed his talents. He had received scholarships to college, scholarships to Oxford; he had received the best that America could give him. Finally he had reached a high government post, a dazzling height for one of his beginning. And what had this man done? He had bitten the hand that fed him. He had destroyed his benefactors, tried to subvert the country that had sheltered him, the society that had helped him. This man Carl Aldo Marzani was a moral leper, the more reprehensible because he was intelligent, because he knew exactly what he was doing. All this occupied Mr. Perelman for thirty minutes of his allotted hour.

In the next fifteen minutes he wrapped himself up in the flag. He stressed the perilous times in which we were living, the war in Greece, the threat of Communism all over the world, and how America was pledged to fight against it. This was official government policy, the Truman doctrine, and the country must be protected internally as well as externally from Communists. The security of the country must be protected from such dastards as I, termites, borers from within, and so on. At this time the Solicitor General used a sentence which he was to use so often that it has become embedded in my memory, "The government must defend itself," said Mr. Perelman, in effect calling on the judges to do their patriotic duty and help the government in its self-defense.

In the final ten minutes, the Solicitor General condescended to discuss the merits of the case. He touched upon the legal points involved in a sort of offhand manner that said plainly: here are some of the legal issues of the briefs but the real issue is government security against Communists, which the Court of course would not undermine.

I have presented Perelman's arguments faithfully; if anything I have understated his redbaiting and spread-eagled oratory. Remember he had spent nearly forty minutes on it. I sat there and listened, half-amused, half-disgusted, wholly incensed. I was amused because by his personal attack to obtain a kind of hammy dramatic effect (biting-the-hand-that-fed-him theme) he had painted such an intriguing picture of me that he was stirring the judges' interest. For if the individual was no ordinary individual, and his crime no ordinary crime, the Court might seek the motives for my alleged conduct and reach conclusions different from that of the government. Moreover, the more closely the Court examined the case, the more apparent would be the government's unethical conduct and all the dirty finagling of the trial might come out.

I was disgusted because this ham actor of a high government official was intellectually bankrupt. The Solicitor General of the United States was in effect saying to the Court: away with constitutional guarantees; the government's security demands it and we are the judges of our security. This was the first time this vicious argument was presented. A year later, in the Bailey case, the Appeals Court of Washington, D.C., gave it a judicial prop in these words: "The exigencies of government … must prevail," even though these may involve "harsh rules which run counter to every precept of fairness to the private individual." This is the language of tyranny. It was first used by the federal government.

However, what really incensed me was the spectacle of this political hack passing moral judgment on my actions, on my beliefs. For Perelman was a politician from Baltimore, as corrupt a municipality as any in America. What he must have done to be advanced within the political machine of Baltimore beggars the imagination. No one works through the years in the filth and muck of our city machines without doing things which must be kept hidden. Not a Truman within the Pendergast machine; not a Perelman within the Baltimore machine. Yet this cheap politician had the nerve to speak of integrity, of responsibility to the people of America.

Perelman was very eloquent about the blessings I had received in America, about my free pre-college education, about my scholarship and sympathetic help from Williams College, the fellowship to Oxford, and so on. He was very eloquent and said many things, yet not half of what I could have said, or as significant. For while I agreed with him about my education, even more important was the democratic character of that education. Even more important was the sanctuary from fascism which America provided my father and my family. The most blessed thing America gave me was the chance to grow up with a free and decent mind. This statement is no studied rhetoric or sentimentalized hyperbole. It is the bare truth.

The depth of my feelings, of my obligation to this country, can only be appreciated by someone who has seen Fascist youth at close range. I was made sharply aware of it when I returned to Italy in 1945 in the U.S. Army, and looked up my childhood schoolmates in Rome. One man in particular gave me an insight into my good fortunes. This fellow had been my closest friend as a child. We had been in kindergarten together, then in elementary school, and then in secondary school. We were about equal in ability, and shared scholastic honors together year after year. If he was first, I was second and vice versa. We had similar interests, similar temperaments. We had the same kind of home background, his perhaps a trifle wealthier. We were Boy Scouts together, altar boys together. We were inseparable and, in a real sense, alter egos.

When I saw him in 1945 he had become a polished diplomat. He had charming manners, a witty mind, a pleasant, hospitable attitude. Although he was still interested in art and literature (he was remarkably well informed on contemporary American authors), his main interests had shifted to history and economics, just as mine had. He was married to a beautiful woman and they had a delightful little girl the same age as my Ricky. All in all, he a fine product of European civilization. He shocked me. Beneath the polished, delightful exterior, beneath that surface culture, was the rot and viciousness of Fascist mentality. The rudest, most inarticulate Yankee farmer was infinitely his superior as a man. For this "cultured" character was a mass of poison inside. His contempt for people and for democracy was immense, complete, unequivocal and quite taken for granted. He was arrogantly full of Fascist elite theories. He was merciless in his indifference to the suffering of the war.

This fellow had been one of the top leaders in the Fascist Youth Movement, national inspector of universities and *chef du cabinet* to the Minister of Agriculture in Mussolini's war government. He was now against Mussolini, called him a fool, but that was because he had lost. Otherwise, there was no question in his mind that the economic and political structure of Fascism was *the* way of life. "Oh," he said to me confidently. "You'll come to it in America. You'll see. It's the only defense against Communism."

This was my childhood buddy. I realized with a scandalized impact of horror that I might have well ended up like that. We had been so very much alike; growing up in the same environment, with the same education, the same subtle corruption of Fascist ideology, we could have ended up the same. There is great ego flattery in the idea of elite stratification—when you are one of the elite. Moreover, my buddy had changed in religion. From a somewhat agnostic kid he had become a pietistic Catholic of narrow clerical outlook. Add to these factors the nationalistic romanticism and phony drama of Fascism, the bombastic yet powerful references to ancient Rome, and you get a hodgepodge of sentimentalism and cruelty, of sanctimoniousness and snobbishness, of surface culture and basic irrationality, which was revolting. Yet I might have ended up the same—but for the grace of my father and the sanctuary of America.

Mr. Perelman can orate about patriotism. I know what it is to have it. My gratitude and loyalty to this country, its people, its magnificent democratic traditions are, have been, and always will be far beyond Mr. Perelman's cheap oratory. Precisely because of my awareness of my debt to America do I fight in the progressive camp. It is real patriotism to fight against a war-mongering administration and profiteering monopolies; to educate our people in the reasons for depressions and war; to struggle for clarity and unity of all democratic forces in America. This is true loyalty to America.

There is dishonor and subversion and disloyalty in America today. It comes from the Perelmans, the Keeches, the Kelleys, the Tom Clarks, the Trumans—the initiators of hysteria and witch-hunting, the people who are undermining the Bill of Rights and the democratic institutions of our country. We can see the extent of their subversion as the hysteria they started is recoiling on them. The administration becomes the target of McCarthyism; Mr. Perelman is attacked by name as a Jew and a

Radical by that great American patriot, Congressman Rankin. I could say, I told you so, but I read the news with no sense of gratification. Should fascism come, it will crucify the Perelmans—but that's no comfort to me, my family or the millions of decent people who will suffer because of their destruction of the Bill of Rights.

Such were my thoughts as I watched Perelman in action. But he didn't hold my interest long. Standing there, full of sound and fury, his waving arms made him look just what he was—a straw puppet of the administration. The focus of interest was the Justices. The drama was in the open battle between the ideas of the administration and the ideas of the Justices. They held the center of the stage.

The most active at first was Frankfurter. He impaled Perelman on a series of sharp legal points. The Solicitor General wriggled and blustered, but there he was, stuck on a series of intellectual pikes. He didn't have the ability to get off, and he didn't have the means. He was simply in the wrong. He was a pitiful exhibit of intellectual bankruptcy. The points themselves were not too important, for they related to the statute of limitations which the Circuit Court had already unanimously upheld. Frankfurter hammered the validity of the decision home in a series of questions which had Perelman reeling.

The basic thing, however, was that Frankfurter was explicitly against the government; he had studied the briefs and didn't like the government's arguments. Frankfurter is supposedly the most acute, legal mind on the Court. I am told by lawyers that he believes in a strict interpretation of the Court's function. He believes, that is, that the Court should lean backwards not to interfere with the executive or legislative departments. He also believes in a strict adherence to the letter of the law. If he, the legalistic mind, seemed against the government, this was a great thing for us. His questions probed the prosecution's weak points and demolished them in the process. It was very heartening.

Incidentally I didn't like Frankfurter at all. He's a show-off in a finicky, academic way. Long years as a Sacred Cow at Harvard have left him with a quiet arrogance and a didactic manner which isn't nice. He does have a fine gift for the illuminating phrase, the incisive epigram, the *mot juste*. His command of the English language is prodigious. The trouble is, he knows it, and gives the impression of listening to himself talk—more, of liking it and approving of it. It is a common professorial failing, harmless if annoying. But basically, he was a cold fish.

The men, however, who made my heart beat were Rutledge, Black, and Murphy. Murphy sat up there like an El Greco portrait of a suffering early Christian. His face was drawn and he seemed in pain. He asked few questions, but the questions were vigorous and sympathetic to us. He gave off a sense of great probity. More active were Justices Black and Rutledge. They went to town.

I should emphasize again the informality of the Court. It approaches that of a group around the stove of a country store. The justices break in on the lawyers, and on each other, with questions, comments, asides, sometimes jokes. Under stress, the dialogue crackles, criss-crosses, rapid and sharp. Justices Black and Rutledge gave Perelman a very tough time. They went to the heart of the matter, the question of civil liberties. Was the government exceeding its power? Was the indictment invalid? In fact, had a crime been committed?

Edith and I sat there holding hands under her coat. We were thrilled. I was so excited I could hardly sit still; I wanted to jump up there to help the Justices, be in the ring as it were, serving in their corner. For Black and Rutledge minced no words. They made no secret of their displeasure and disgust. Their words were sharp, their tongues lashing. They were in there fighting. In existentialist jargon, they were *engagé*, completely committed intellectually and emotionally to the struggle. They were also *engagé* in the sense that they were rabidly angry. They were outraged at the government's actions and became increasingly angry at the government's arguments. Their anger warmed my heart as I sat there and listened. For the first time someone in high position seemed to have the same feeling about the case as I did. I had not exaggerated the importance of the issues; I had not gone overboard. These men affirmed my feelings.

I sat, watched them, and loved them. They were an interesting study in comparisons and contrasts. They were ethically so similar; so different in temperament and appearance. Justice Black's features are fine and chiselled; Rutledge's blunt and rough-hewn. One has a head like a cameo intaglio; the second is an unfinished study in granite. Black looks like what he is: an intellectual, a scholar, a keen jurist. There is a fastidiousness about him, a touch of asceticism, a kind of repressed fire. He reminds you irresistibly of the fashionable stereotype of historical fiction—the antebellum Southern aristocrat, cultured, hot-blooded but restrained, well-mannered but aloof, finely bred, finely tempered. Rutledge, on the other hand, looked like a farmer, or, more precisely, like a schoolteacher brought up on a farm—a rocky, infertile farm where a living meant stubborn, tenacious work; the bread earned in the sweat of the brow. I say a schoolteacher because, although he looked taciturn, he was in fact fluent and highly articulate. But there was an earthiness about him that was reflected in his speech, a certain practicality and homeliness of phrase. I thought he came from the Middle West out of Vermont stock. I found out later he was born in Kentucky, though educated in Wisconsin.

The two of them in their manner and in their thinking were great tributes to American democracy, exemplary of a way of life which we must maintain. Black was in some ways the greater. For this former senator from Alabama, product of the Deep South, has become a leader of progressive life in America. He is one of that small but growing band of Southern men like Jennings Perry, Clifford Durr, Statton Kennedy; women like Lillian Smith, Rose and Black's sister, Virginia Durr, who are the conscience of the South. The conscience, the prod, the yeast in that huge region of our country, so important to American political life and so reactionary. Yet someday this backward South will, out of its profound class struggles, turn out to be the most progressive area of our nation.

Justices Black and Rutledge set upon Perelman and stripped him, morally and intellectually. The Solicitor General tried snarling and even bullying, but to no avail. The Justices would not be intimidated. The probed and jabbed with questions until Perelman was reduced to only one answer, the theme song of his opening speech, "The government must defend itself." This was his argument; it turned out to be his refuge. It became a substitute for thinking, whether to affirm or rebut. He used it like an incantation: "The government must defend itself." Without rhyme or reason the phrase came out. Whenever he didn't know what to say, and it was often, Perelman would bring the talisman forth, "The government must defend itself." He used it in every tone, cajoling, pleading, with the air of a man of the world speaking among equals, with the air of a portentous professor uttering a great truism, and yes, with the faintly sinister overtones of a powerful administration—threatening.

The Solicitor General was a fit representative for the administration. No more thinking, he implied, away with unorthodox opinions, away with the Bill of Rights! The government must defend itself! This Decatur-like slogan of anything goes, this degenerate indentification of the nation with a rotten administration so that to be anti-Truman is to be unpatriotic, this basically un-American slogan has seeped deep into every aspect of American life, poisoning the roots of our liberty. As I've said, it comes up in court opinions, like the Bailey case, that "the exigencies of government" must rule however unpalatable the actions. This is no new doctrine, as I. F. Stone has pointed out. The tyrant Roman emperor Tiberius said it a long time ago: "The guardian of the constitution must subvert the Constitution to guard it." It is sound tyranny; it is not the spirit of '76.

The implications of this attitude were so monstrous that Justice Black could hardly bring himself to believe his ears, to believe that such could be the official government doctrine. At one point he leaned over and asked Perelman in a tone of awed incredulity, "Do you mean to stand there and assert on behalf of the government that the government can do whatever it pleases, anything at all, and call it self-defense?" There was a small pause and then Perelman plunged. "That's right," he said defiantly. "The government must defend itself." Justice Black gave a powerful snort of disgust. As if jet-propelled by his snort, his body snapped back in his chair with such violence that the seat swiveled half around. The Justice was clearly appalled.

How fantastic the doctrine is, and how dangerous, was brought out by another series of questions which had Perelman on the ropes. To understand the questions I must outline a point of law. It is a fundamental of our jurisprudence that an act must be defined as a crime before it is committed. Otherwise law becomes retroactive. The defense contended that my so-called crime had not been defined. The indictment charged false statement to the government. Did the government mean all false statements to the government were criminal? This was obviously absurd. Obviously only such false statements as were clearly specified in statutes and regulations—as, for example, answers to questions on an income tax form where there were specific provisions, statutes, warnings and so on. Now on my alleged false statements there was no prior definition. There were no procedural safeguards, no witnesses, no transcripts, no oath taken, no formal notification of any kind that this conversation was official, or that I was liable to criminal action. Nothing.

It was my contention that Panuch had not asked the questions he had asked. But even supposing that he had, Osmond Fraenkel pointed out for the defense that the novel interpretation of the government made every employee liable to prosecution who made a false statement. He gave an example. A messenger boy in a government agency comes in late and his superior asks why is he late. Says the boy, "I went to my grandmother's funeral." Actually he went to a ball game. The government could prosecute him and sentence him to ten years in jail. This was manifestly absurd. Perelman was quick to pour ridicule on the story of "grandma's funeral." The whole example was ridiculous, silly, irrelevant. Someone, I think Frankfurter, quietly asked him why. Because, said Perelman, it must be a false statement that obstructed the government in the exercise of its functions. Well, said the judge, the boy was late; his tardiness obstructed government's activities; his superior had the right to know the truth, i.e. the matter was under his clear jurisdiction—in what way was the example different, in logic, from asking a man whether he was a Communist?

Perelman began to realize too late that he was in a blind alley. The example, silly as it seems, was, logically, rigorously equivalent to my case in legal forms. As the Solicitor General paused to think, Chief Justice Vinson murmured tolerantly something about relative importance. Perelman clutched the lifeline and expounded at length the difference between a messenger boy, a nice American lad who liked baseball, and a subversive Communist who was clearly un-American. In one case the false statement was on a matter of importance, the security of the government; in the other the importance was minimal. When he was all through, Justice Rutledge asked with deceptive mildness, "Who determines what is important?" "Why, you do," said Perelman promptly. I marveled at his obtuseness. I was no lawyer, but even I could see what was coming. Not, however, the Solicitor General of the United States. He opened his big mouth and further put his foot in it. He added complacently, "That is why we are here." Rutledge's thick forefinger shot over the bench straight at Perelman. An imperative forefinger. There was a grim fury in his next question. "You admit then that there was no definition of the crime until this Court has given it?"

Again too late, Perelman saw the trap. For that is exactly what he had been saying. It was a fatal admission since it was the kernel of an important defense argument. The issue of the prior definition of a crime is so basic that it cannot be overlooked. Yet here was the government of the United States, committed to upholding law and order, blithely smashing a main pillar of our civil liberties. It was a sorry performance and Rutledge's unwavering forefinger emphasized the importance of the discussion. Perelman seemed stunned for a moment. Then he gulped and gave his answer, in a sulky, mean tone. He said—you guessed it: "The government must defend itself!" Rutledge drew back in his chair with a snort of contempt that matched Black's recent snort. As in Black's case, his temper was so violent that the chair spun half around.

Two snorts! They don't sound very polite in the chaste, august atmosphere of the Supreme Court. They weren't polite. They weren't meant to be. They expressed contempt and disgust, a contempt and disgust aimed straight at an administration that was violating the very justice it was sworn to uphold. Two snorts! Two of the most eloquent orations I've ever heard.

There is no need to go into further details. The hearing lasted well over three hours, which is unusual. As a rule, hearings are held down to the allotted two hours. The length of time was an indication of the extent of the intervention of the Justices and their estimate of the importance of the case. I've said nothing about Justices Vinson, Burton, and Reed because there is nothing to add. They sat there, Chief Justice Vinson slouched back, his jowly equine face often relaxed into a tolerant smile. His was a seeming attitude of kindly impartiality; actually he was shrewdly alert to every opportunity of helping Perelman in his flounderings. There was no question where Vinson stood. A crony of Mr. Truman, he was up there to see the administration got its way.

The hearing was so unexpectedly dramatic, the liberal judges so upright, the entire development so favorable that our post-mortems were rosy indeed. Three votes were certainly for us: Rutledge, Murphy, and Black. Three votes were certainly against: Vinson, Burton, and Reed. Douglas we assumed would abstain, leaving the decision in the hands of Frankfurter and Jackson. If they were both for us, we would win five-to-three. If they were both against us, we would lose five-to-three. Frankfurter seemed to us most important, for it was quite possible that Jackson might also abstain since he hadn't been present. Frankfurter would then be the deciding vote for a four-to-three decision, either way. We thought he was for us since his questioning of Perelman had been critical. On the other hand the questioning was entirely on the statute of limitations and we never had any worries on that score. It was impossible to tell.

The one decision we didn't think about is precisely what we got: a split decision. The Supreme Court voted four-to-four, Douglas abstaining. This meant jail, for in a split decision the judgment of the court below remains operative. We had made a good fight and we had come close, heartbreakingly close, but it was over.

Even in this defeat, there was a silver lining. The door was slammed shut on the government's attempts to stretch the statute of limitations. This was politically a great victory. Furthermore, the government was on notice that it couldn't continue its attacks on civil liberties without meeting a hostile court. Without the slightest question in my mind the Court of 1948 would never have upheld the constitutionality of the Smith Act. Finally, the closeness of the decision was a moral black eye for the government. It exposed as nothing else could do their hypocrisy. People can easily disregard my opinion as to the illegality of the indictments, but no one can disregard a four-to-four decision of the Supreme Court. I was going to jail, yes, but four Supreme Court Justices said I was going to jail illegally. The fig leaf on the government's attack had become transparent.

Newspapers and magazines were quiet about the decision—the briefest announcement. When the indictment had been made, they had a Roman holiday. When the conviction was obtained, they splattered it all over. Now, hardly a peep. This may seem reasonable to the reader. But just suppose that an important corporation official was accused of false statements concerning his business. Suppose he was going to jail on a four-to-four decision of the Supreme Court. Can't you imagine the furor in editorials and in columns on the obvious injustice of jailing a man on such tenuous grounds?

However, the fact remained: I was going in. There was a last possibility: petition the Court for a rehearing. This was a forlorn hope, for a rehearing is rarely granted. In the entire history of the Court, I believe only seven rehearings had been granted. However, defense submitted a brief asking two points: Jackson had voted but he wasn't present at the argument. We respectfully suggested that on such a close vote, it might be better, more just, if he did hear the oral argument. Second, Justice Douglas had abstained. Again given the importance of the case and the fact of a tie in an area of civil liberties, we respectfully suggested that it was to the general interest of the nation that he sit. The defense stated that without knowing why he had decided to abstain, the defense affirmed its belief in his objectivity and asked that he sit.

As I say, we all considered it a forlorn hope. I set about putting my affairs in order, expecting to be in jail within two weeks. Then the bombshell came: the Court would review the case! Our spirits soared. Our confidence in victory was nearly a certainty. We reasoned thus: obviously Justice Douglas would sit since the point about Jackson was a relatively minor one. Douglas had a reputation for liberalism and it wasn't likely he would array himself against the other four liberals. Furthermore, it wasn't necessary for him to sit if he was going to vote for the government. The government had for practical purposes won its case without Douglas incurring any stigma. He hadn't participated in the decision. Ergo, he would sit only if he intended to vote against the government. Ergo, we would win. Q.E.D.

When the day of the rehearing came, Edith and I were in the audience once more. All the judges were present. The clerk called the case. And then we sat dumbfounded. Justice Douglas gathered his papers and left the bench. He had disqualified himself; our thinking had been all wrong. The reason for the rehearing was that Jackson intended to hear the case. What did it mean? Was he going to reverse his decision? I looked at him, young face, jet-black hair, and wondered. Would he? Somehow I didn't think so. He had been making speeches that indicated his once crusading liberalism was sadly tarnished.

The hearing was similar to the first one. No new arguments were presented, but the defense had sharpened its points, brought them into focus. Fraenkel seemed to me more eloquent, Rosenberg more confident. The government didn't redbait as much, but their legal position hadn't improved a bit. Vinson still quietly helped Perelman whenever possible. Jackson said almost nothing. I think he asked one minor question and made a couple of remarks on some subsidiary point. But in general he hardly paid any attention. He lolled back, seemingly bored. I felt his attitude was indicative. He was saying: "You wanted me to hear you, okay, here I am. What of it?"

Black and Rutledge again lashed out. I thought there was a new bitterness in their attack. It was as if they had been stewing over the events and become more sharply aware of how serious the witch-hunting and the hysteria were becoming—how widespread and unrestrained. It may have been my imagination but I had a sense that this semi-fascism was striking close to home; that Rutledge and Black were saying to themselves—a little more and *we* won't be safe. Perhaps I am exaggerating, but as I watched them fighting, fierce and uncompromising, I couldn't help get a sense of deep personal involvement. They were fighting as if for their freedom.

One incident is worthy of notice. As the reader may recall, one of the defense's main contentions was that there had been no record of the Panuch interview, no notes, no transcript. It was purely Panuch's word against mine and I disagreed with him on what had been said. At one point of the defense's arguments, while Allan Rosenberg was speaking, Vinson interjected a remark that after all I had agreed that I had made the false statements. Rosenberg did a double take.

"No, your Honor," he said slowly, "Marzani disagrees. Panuch says he made certain statements; Marzani says he didn't."

"Oh, well," said Vinson, "it doesn't matter."

Justice Black, sitting next to Vinson, sat up abruptly and made an inquiring noise so the Chief Justice amplified.

"It's all written down in the transcript," said Vinson.

"I don't understand," said Rosenberg, puzzled. "What transcript?"

"The transcript of the interview."

"You mean," said Rosenberg unbelieving, "the interview between Panuch and Marzani?"

Chief Justice Vinson nodded complacently.

"But if it please your Honor," said Rosenberg, "there was no transcript. There were no witnesses. There were no notes. Nothing!"

Interjected Justice Black. "*That* is precisely the point."

"Oh, well," said Vinson in a dismissing tone and slouched back. He gave a wave of his hand that said plainly, "Forget it, it doesn't matter." Justice Black was looking at Vinson, his astonishment apparent. His low-voiced comment was clearly audible where I was sitting in the front row. "Well, indeed!" said Justice Black, in a tone that said plainly: "How can you dismiss so cavalierly the crux of an argument?"

I was as shocked as Justice Black seemed to be. It was not only the idea of dismissing an important key point; there was a deeper question in my mind—how could Vinson miss the point in the first place? How come that at this stage *he didn't know there was no transcript?* The case had been argued twice before the Court at great length. Aside the oral arguments, which covered a lot of ground and Vinson might have missed the point. The question of the Panuch interview was perhaps the central argument of the defense. The lack of constitutional procedures and of safeguards had been treated exhaustively in the brief. Not once, in one written brief, but in *three* separate briefs, once at the certiorari, then at the original hearing, and finally at the rehearing. The lack of transcript, witnesses and notes had been reiterated again and again. How could anyone read the briefs and miss the point?

The further question rose in my mind: had Chief Justice Vinson read the brief? It seems an incredible question to ask, but on the basis of Vinson's own statement he could not have read it. There isn't even the possible excuse that he read it carelessly because the point was so important and took so much space that no lawyer, however careless or ill-trained, could have missed it. And Vinson was a trained lawyer and judge. He had sat on the Washington Court of Appeals for some time. The question is still unanswered. I feel morally certain Chief Justice Vinson did not read the brief; that he gave his decision on the basis of considerations other than the law. Politics ruled, not justice.

At the end of the hearing, defense attorney Osmond K. Fraenkel said, "it is unthinkable that the government should be allowed to claim such broad, oppressive powers." It was unthinkable, but it happened. Some weeks later the decision came out. The vote was four-to-four! It was a bitter disillusionment. On top of our confidence it came hard. There was one fact that we didn't know until later and that is that a rehearing is granted if four justices vote for it. Jackson had not voted for it and his presence was a cheap stage play to give an illusion of objectivity—to make a record. He hadn't sat the first time because he was out making a speech and this might be open to criticism. Well he'd fix that. He would sit again, but the decision was foregone.

If the heroes of the trial were Justices Black and Rutledge, the villains are undoubtedly Justices Jackson and Douglas. Both preen themselves as liberals, both have political ambitions with their eyes on the presidency. It isn't considered polite to ascribe selfish motives to a judge, but it isn't polite to be in jail either. In my opinion both these Justices are playing politics from the bench. Justice Jackson has been consistently to the right of Justice Douglas, giving proofs and assurance to the people that count that he is a safe conservative. The wild oats days of his liberalism are gone forever.

I have also fancied something else about Mr. Jackson, from the tone of his public speeches. I think that his work at Nuremberg as Chief Prosecutor has given him a deep horror of fascism, and interpreting fascism as a "revolution" (of the right to be sure) he has withdrawn into conservatism almost as a reflex action. In his further development against Communism I think he has accepted two widely held liberal fallacies: one, that fascism and Communism are essentially the same; two, that Hitler came to power because the Weimar Republic was "weak." If I am correct then Mr. Jackson has resolved that he will make democracy "strong" to control Communism. This is the pro-fascist trap. Bruening, Daladier, Dolfuss all made democracy "strong." How? By suppressing Communism, restricting civil liberties, ruling by decree. The result was to open the gates to reaction. Fascism triumphed. I repeat again: the defense of the legality of the Communist Party in any country is the first line of defense against fascism in that country. Whatever the validity of my guesses on Justice Jackson I am strongly convinced that I'm correct in my previous point, his presidential ambitions. I think Mr. Jackson has his eyes on such worthies as Jim Farley, Mr. Tydings, and Mr. Byrnes and the conservative wing of the Democratic Party. There, for him, is the road to success.

Mr. Douglas estimates the situation differently. He eyes the ADA and the CIO grouping within the Democratic Party. This calls for a fine show of liberalism together with the most ruthless attitude towards Communists and fellow travelers. If in the process of establishing this position, civil liberties get a kick in the teeth—*tant pis* for civil liberties. If Paris was worth a Mass, the White House is worth a few paragraphs of the Bill of Rights. It may be thought I'm doing Mr. Douglas an injustice. It has been rumored in Washington that Mr. Douglas did not sit because he was a friend of Panuch, and therefore might be considered biased. This rumor I reject. It would imply that Mr. Douglas is stupid, and *that* would certainly be an injustice. The basic point at issue was not whether Panuch had told the truth or not. Assume that he had told the truth; the basic point at issue still remained—had the government any right to prosecute statements made without defining the crime and establishing procedures to safeguard the constitutional rights of the citizen? Panuch was irrelevant; the question applies to anyone.

No, it is my opinion that Mr. Douglas knew exactly what he was doing. Had he sat on the case and voted with Mr. Vinson and the conservative group his liberalism would have suffered. Had he voted with the liberal group, he would have seemed "soft" towards Communists, the unforgivable crime in the ADA calendar. By abstaining he was sitting pretty. Not so prettily, I sit in jail. Since then, with the appointment of Justices Clark and Minton on the Court, Mr. Douglas has voted consistently liberal. He can now be a liberal to his heart's content since he will be consistently outvoted. This is the ultimate rule of a liberal, the classic position: loyal opposition without responsibility. I trust, however, that if the time should come, politically, that people will remember his actions and contrast them to Black and Rutledge's. At the time his vote would have counted, Mr. Douglas ran away.

I have repeatedly spoken of Mr. Black and Mr. Rutledge. They were magnificent. As I said, their fight has been a basic experience in my life. Here at the peak of American society was the same fierce devotion to freedom, to decency, to democracy that I had found in the stockyards of Chicago and the waterfront of San Francisco. From the Negro Packinghouse unionists and the Puerto Rican strikers to the Supreme Court Justices, the unity of progressive concepts was unbroken, a sturdy red thread in the fabric of our society. In this continuity, this pervasive democracy, lies the strength of our country, lies my optimism for the future.

Ours is a great nation. Few major powers have such basically progressive history. Our birth was a revolution, one of the truly liberating revolutions in history, which ushered in the modern era. In more than one sense, the French Revolution, the Russian Revolution, the Chinese Revolution have followed the trail we blazed, broadening into a great highway for all mankind. Our history has been less the chronicle of a few leaders than the expression of our people. We have taken from every land individuals, customs, ideas and welded a composite person, the American, with a hard core of idealism, a strong practical sense, an impatience with authoritarianism and the status quo. Until the Soviets, no one in the world matched us in our self-confidence before Nature. We came as masters of our environment, from the pioneer in the forest to the atomic scientist in the laboratory. It is one of our great glories. We are, as a people, generous, self-reliant, and progressive. Never, never, in these dark days of reaction must we lose faith in our fellow countrymen. Never, never, must we forget one simple historical fact: always, in our history, when the chips were down and issues clear, when reaction and progress stood face to face, reaction has been beaten. Beaten by Washington, beaten by Lincoln, beaten by Franklin Delano Roosevelt. And by Jefferson, Jackson, T. R. and Woodrow Wilson. I do not believe we will fail now.

Yet there is no room for complacency. Rutledge and Black fought a valiant fight; but I am in jail. There is darkness as well as light in our country. Reaction has been constantly beaten; it has always made a comeback. Our history as a nation is a proud one, yet we have quite a few blots on it, two of them major. I refer to the extermination of the American Indian and the institution of slavery. The first is irreversible history, we can't do anything about it except not to forget. The second, however, still bears bitter fruit.

Jim Crow is our national shame. Of all the seamy streaks in our society, none is so evil and none so dangerous as our racism. It poisons the life of the country at every turn. Southern Dixiecrats wield a power in politics out of all proportion to the people they represent. With few exceptions, they wield their power for evil. Culturally, ethically, artistically, Jim Crow poisons our roots. It reinforces all the worst prejudices in our land: anti-Semitism, chauvinism against national minorities, intolerance of all kinds. Abroad, it flavors American actions with an unmistakable taint of white supremacy. The people that say and think "nigger," "kike," "wop" are bound to think and say "frog," "chink," and "gook." We must cleanse America of this poison. It will not be easy, but it is in no way impossible. Nor difficult, either, once we have retired the Rankins and the McCarthys and exposed their manipulators and masters, the big business interests in the United States.

Today, the face of reaction is seen more and more clearly. McCarthy has become a symbol. As one who has felt the lash of reaction on his hide, I must emphasize again and again that McCarthy is not the main danger at the present time. McCarthy did not start the current witch hunt. He didn't develop Budenz. He did not give impetus to hysteria. McCarthy is riding a monster he did not create; a monster bred in the last place in America that should be a stable of reaction—the White House. Mr. Truman started the witch hunt and my case is the classic example of what depths of chicanery and hypocrisy were reached.

The Truman administration must bear the primary responsibility for undermining civil liberties in our country. They started it, and by their actions have made themselves vulnerable. The administration uncaged the jungle beasts that now stalk them. McCarthy turns his claws on Mr. Truman, but who sharpened his claws? Who fed him red meat? The government shaped the Hewitts and the Budenzes. McCarthy uses these perjurers and the administration is defenseless.

I offer my own case as evidence—a case so bitterly fought for two years. After the rehearing it was finished. I entered jail.

Nine

I entered jail for the second time in March 1949, this time for keeps. The struggle was not wholly over; it shifted to obtaining a pardon, a parole, or a reduction of sentence.

My sentence was one to three years. Most people, I find, fasten on the one year and talk of it as such. I did myself. Nothing could be more erroneous. The operative figure is the three years. My sentence was a three-year sentence as given in federal courts. What my sentence meant was that I had to serve a minimum of one year before being eligible for parole. But since federal prisoners are eligible for parole after serving one-third of their sentence, I was in exactly the same position as a man with a straight three-year sentence.

Three full years is a stiff sentence. A very stiff sentence. Involuntary manslaughter, for example is five years. Ex-Congressmen May and Thomas, who were crooks, got a year and a half. Three years is a tough sentence, and Charles Ford, the trial attorney, was confident that Justice

Keech would reduce sentence. Ford's confidence rested not only on the history of the appeals, but also on a very important factor: my wife was seriously ill.

This development was new. One morning in January 1949 I saw Edith get up, walk two steps and then crumple to the floor in a startled moan. It was frightening. I jumped up, picked her up, and put her in bed as she shivered in a terrible panic. "I can't walk," she said. "I can't walk!" She couldn't. The nervous control of her muscles had failed. I quieted her with words about fatigue and psychological pressures, but I was deadly worried. Our family doctor came and examined her. He told her cheerfully to rest and not worry. Outside the sick room, however, it was a different story. He told me bluntly the worst: all the symptoms pointed to multiple sclerosis.

Multiple sclerosis is a disease that attacks nerve centers. Control is lost over various parts of the body: eyes, legs, arms. Not much is known about the disease. Often it is fatal. Sometimes the victim is permanently paralyzed. A few permanently recover. The disease is unpredictable— characterized by doctors call "remissions." This seems to be a fancy word for relapse. The patient seems to be getting better and then bang, a setback. It is a terrible disease and its effects are serious. The general health is undermined. My wife went down to a weight of ninety-odd pounds. The psychological pressures are also serious. We tried to keep her from knowing the truth. After a few weeks she could move a few steps, on my arm, and we took her to be examined by Dr. Foster Kennedy, one of the foremost neurologists in America. He examined her thoroughly and told me privately she was a very sick woman.

At about this time my mother was also ill, with a spinal ailment that necessitated an operation. I was entering jail, therefore, leaving behind a hard-hit defenseless family with two small children, one five and one two years old, and two ill adults. Friends helped all they could with money and time, but clearly the situation was precarious.

Armed with affidavits from various doctors, Ford petitioned for a reduction of sentence. He had other powerful arguments. Of the original eleven counts, nine had been invalidated by the Court of Appeals. The last two counts were so questionable as to result in a split Supreme Court. Rarely has a man been sent to jail on more dubious legal grounds; rarely was a family so needful and worthy of help. Furthermore on September 1, 1948, Congress amended the False Claim Statute, reducing the penalty from ten years to five.

I was taken from jail to come before Judge Keech. Several other inmates were in my batch, including the old sex offender I mentioned in an earlier chapter. Justice Keech, looking at me with eyes cold, hating and merciless, denied the motion. He went out of his way to emphasize why. There was no reason, he said, to change his mind. The sheer effrontery of his remarks was breathtaking. Here was a man, a jurist if you please, who had ruled all eleven counts valid. He had been proven wrong, as wrong as he could possibly be, nearly 100 percent wrong. One would think that professionally he might have a little humility—or at least keep his mouth shut. But not this "honorable" specimen of Southern racist. The fact that my family was in tough shape was for him, I am sure, a source of grim satisfaction. It served me right. It would teach me that my fighting throughout the appeals, my tours, my speeches, my flaying of the government, the FBI, the prosecutor and the judge were all well known to him, intensifying his anger and his vindictiveness. Justice Keech was showing his mettle. This self-ordained prig saw no reason to change his mind.

I stood and eyed at him, trying to give him a message with my eyes: "You stink, Your Honor." I could say nothing. He would love to add six months for contempt. Never in my life have I felt such complete, utter contempt for anyone as I felt for Judge Keech. Never, I think, have I been more justified. What a contemptible, self-righteous, sanctimonious, vindictive mannikin! What a sick mind, what a putrid heart, what an evil soul! What a fit representative of his class; that warmongering, blood-thirsty rapacious bunch of cutthroats that call themselves our betters.

I stood there thinking again of another judge like Keech. A hanging judge. Judge Thayer who legally murdered Sacco and Vanzetti. I thought of these two judges, of their sanctimonious righteousness as they defend a system riddled with venal corruption. I remembered Vanzetti's proud boast to the court:

> Sacco has never dreamt to steal, never to assassinate. He and I have never brought a morsel of bread to our mouths, from childhood, to today, which has not been gained by the sweat of our brow.
> Never...
> ...this man called thief and assassin and doomed, Sacco ...
> Sacco's crime will live in the hearts of the people and in their gratitude when Katzmann's bones and yours will be dispersed by time; when your name, his name, your laws, institutions, and your false God are but a dim remembering of a cursed past in which man was wolf to the man...

Wolf was Judge Thayer and wolf is Judge Keech. Thayer got his victims electrocuted; Keech had the desire but not the power. Could he have done so, I'm sure he would have been very happy.

After Keech came the parole board. From here on out I had no hope of consideration by the government, but I felt that we should force them to go on record every step of the way, to strip them of their pious stutterings of impartiality, to expose the black rottenness and hatred in their hearts.

Alone of all federal jails, Washington inmates have one privilege. They can ask the parole board to ask the trial judge for a reduction of the *minimum* sentence. This makes the convict eligible for parole earlier. Thus if my minimum was cut from one year to six months, I'd have a much better chance. As a matter of routine, therefore, I asked the prison authorities to request the parole board to exercise this power. The request was in May. And a few weeks later, one of the federal officials, Mr. Clammer, was visiting jail and passed me on a stairway. He stopped and said: "By the way, Carl, we have turned down your request." There was nothing to say and I said it. Unknown to me, in the meantime Professor Einstein had written a letter to President Truman asking for a pardon. He got a reply from the Department of Justice saying I had not exhausted my legal resources such as asking for a reduction of minimum sentence. This reply was sent *after Clammer had told me I had been turned down*. It was a further example of the cheap tactics of the authorities.

I was at Danbury when the government reply was sent to Mr. Einstein. Technically, I was never eligible for the step on parole outlined above. In view of the answer to Einstein, however, I asked Rosenberg to press the request which I had made before leaving. This was in early August. Rosenberg was told that an opinion of the Attorney General would be needed on the point. Nearly two months later, in late September, Rosenberg was informed that I could ask for a reduction of sentence, but the question was becoming academic since I was coming up before the parole board in December. They suggested the matter be dropped. The judgment came five months after my original request.

I went before the parole board in December. The board had letters from Professor Einstein, General Donovan, Professor Mason and others. The board had affidavits from doctors concerning Edith. She was of course still ill, with ups and downs, and has remained ill to this day. The board had my war record. They had the records of the appeals including the four-to-four decision of the Supreme Court. They had the name of my parole adviser—an Episcopal minister of a neighboring church. They had my clean prison record.

There was no word from the parole board for almost three months. Of a group of eighty Danbury inmates who went up before the board with me, most of them got an answer within four or five weeks. I was the very last one to be notified. The decision: parole denied. It is a simple sober fact that, irrespective of crime, other inmates received greater consideration from the board. I could quote literally a hundred instances; I limit myself to two. A banker who had taken nearly a million dollars, a famous case in its day, had also received a sentence of three years. He was paroled one month after serving his minimum sentence. J. Parnell Thomas, sentenced from six to eighteen months, got parole on his eighth month in jail and, later, a complete pardon from Truman.

The parole denial was not unexpected. A petition campaign for a presidential pardon was initiated. Again we had little hope. Again we wished to have it on record. Most important, it was a way of bringing to the attention of prominent, non-left Americans what was going on in our country.

The Defense Committee was limited in resources, and therefore limited itself to obtaining signatures from leaders in various walks of life. The response was good. At this time Jennings Perry wrote another column, this time in the *Daily Compass*. He wrote in part:

> this reminded me to write to President Truman asking him to pardon Carl Marzani. I hope my petition reaches the President while he is at Key West under the blue skies, where not even a little hill obstructs his horizon and a man *feels* physical freedom like a reprieve.
>
> Marzani is in Danbury Jail in Connecticut, 1300 miles north, and his sick wife and two kids are in New York City where winter grudges spring. I have never been in jail, but I know Carl Marzani ...
>
> Carl Marzani in my eyes is as good and decent a citizen as I am or as President Truman is.... I have sent off my petition because as one patriotic citizen, as one taxpaying capitalist, I am certain Carl Marzani has never harmed or intended harm to me or any other in our pretty land; because this is the time of the year when any proper man with two kids should be out looking for a house with a white fence.

The Defense Committee finally had a petition signed by over one thousand prominent Americans, including three Nobel prizewinners: Professor Einstein, Professor Shapley, and Thomas Mann. General Donovan, my wartime boss, signed. There were 118 college professors, including 32 from my alma mater, Williams College. There were eight professors from Harvard University, including Mason, Hocking, Jones, Sorokin, and Coolidge. There was Alexander Meiklejohn, former president of Amherst College; Professors Commager, Brewster, and Lynd of Columbia. Others were Professors Emerson of Yale, Rice of Wisconsin, Weymouth of Stanford. These men and women are in the very front rank of American education. There were also 37 clergy and 57 lawyers. There were writers such as Norman Mailer, Louis Untermeyer, Millen Brad, and James Gow; also playwright Garson Kanin, actress Hilda Vaughn, artist Raphael Soyer, and architect Gregory Ain.

The petition was sent to the president. He never even saw it. I received notification from, the authorities:

> We have received a memorandum from Mr. Daniel M. Lyons, Pardon Attorney, containing the following: "Please advise Marzani that in view of the entire record relating to his case, the conclusion has been reached that his petition for clemency does not merit submission to the President; that the application has been filed and that no further action thereon is contemplated."

Examined closely this is a fantastic statement. These few lines are pregnant with meaning—none of it is honest or honorable. The Pardon Attorney (i.e. the Department of Justice) is filing the petition and forgetting about it. It says to 1,000 prominent Americans, "Sign, and be damned to you." A two-bit bureaucrat in the department takes it upon himself to decide whether or not he'll let the president receive a petition, specifically, and under the law, correctly, intended for the president.

But there is more to this communication than arrogance. Notice the choice of words. The petition, he says, does not "merit" submission to the President. Why not? Is it that the persons who signed it do not "merit" attention? Nobel prizewinners, professors, artists, lawyers, clergymen, are all these people so much riff-raff to be contemptuously dismissed? Are you a fit judge, Mr. Bureaucrat? Or is the lack of "merit" due to the content of the petition? It asks help for a family in distress, an ill woman, two small children—is there no "merit" in this? Where shall we go for "merit"? Shall we go to those Nazi criminals released wholesale by the American military government on "retroactive good time" years before their sentences were served? Should I have been guilty of mass murder, genocide, racism, Nazism in order to "merit" consideration? Is this what we have come to in America since FDR died?

The reason (if such a word can be applied to such thinking) for the lack of "merit" according to our bureaucrat is found in the previous phrase, "in view of the entire record relating to his case." Those words unwittingly reveal the position of this gentry. For what "entire record" is he talking about? Is he referring to my work during the war, the unsparing effort, the endless hours, the unstinting drive? Or is it the record of Hewitt, psychopath perjurer, or of Drew the police spy and agent provocateur? Is the "entire record" the phrasing of the indictment, all its incendiary verbiage of stirring up racial hatreds and taking over the Army and the Navy? Or is it the packing of a jury with Negroes, the antics of the prosecutor, the venom of the judge? Or are you referring to the record of nine unconstitutional counts of the indictment? Or is it perhaps the record of the divided Supreme Court? Or the record of Justices Black and Rutledge blasting the government's impudence and tyranny? Is it all this, Mr. Bureaucrat, that you mean by the "entire record"? No, this is not what you mean. What you mean by the "entire record" is that I fought back, inch by inch, appeal by appeal. That because of my fight, court after court found against the government until it stood exposed. What you mean is that I, poor and comparatively helpless, didn't fold up under your attack. That I dared approach and persuade men like Arthur Garfield Hays and Osmond K. Fraenkel. That I dared raise money from other poor people, by dimes, by quarters, and half-dollars, to fight your rotten Department of "Justice" to the last hard-gotten cent. Each one of these coins created political havoc against the administration. This is what you mean; this is what you hate.

The word "entire" means you know and resent the films made for the Wallace campaign, the speeches for Wallace, the support of the Progressive Party. The word "entire" means you know and resent every single meeting, every single pamphlet, every single leaflet that exposed your vicious finagling. You resent the fact that I did not knuckle under; that across the length and breadth of the nation I pilloried Kelley, Clark Keech—exposed their hypocrisy, showed them up in all their filth before the final judges, the people of our land. This is what you hated. That I fought. That I should have the impudence to fight the federal government; that I should have the nerve to strip it, expose it, tell the people the why of all this filth—how Washington has been delivered into the hands of hucksters; literally, how the policies of FDR have been subverted. This is what you mean by the "entire record" ... the record of my fight. Pray, what did you expect? Did you think I would kiss the jackboot that tramples under my freedom and my family? Who do you think you are dealing with, anyway?

The reader may well say at this point, well, what did *you* expect? I expected nothing else from this scum after I saw what they did during the trial, how political and class hatred dominated the prosecution. But the point is that the government has maintained throughout that there was no political issue involved in my case, that it was just plain, ordinary, common crime. The point is that in criminal cases parole and pardons are predicated on such things as the family needs of the inmate, his ability to get a job, the kind of people who will vouch for him. Parole and pardons are *not* predicated upon how much suffering the government can inflict, how much revenge the government can obtain. By all the rules of parole, by all the spirit and intent behind those rules, my applications for parole or for pardon warranted the highest consideration, not the contemptuous rejection of a low-level bureaucrat.

This is why the rejection is revealing. The government is saying: "We hate you and we fear you. We hate your politics, your ideas, your convictions. We will make you pay for them, make your family pay for them. And to keep you quiet we'll keep you out of circulation as long as we can." I say, Okay. I say this is class politics, class justice, class vengeance. This rejection is the final step, stripping for keeps, *on the record*, the government's hypocritical pretense of "criminal" prosecution. In the process of this class-fostered prosecution, the government has subverted its own laws, transgressed its own rules. It has mocked its own ideals. It has shown the will to go to all necessary extremes to defend its class interest. It will smash democracy to "save it." In its own quaint language, it will "aggress for peace." No other course the government could have taken would have been so instructive to me as to what makes the government tick, what makes the world go around. As I've said, Okay.

There is one final touch to the case, the perfect ending. It is truly the cream of the jest. The reader is aware that I've tried to prove the government's prosecution was political, that the sentencing was political and that the action was shoddy and full of chicanery. The Supreme Court hearing and the events on parole have been given in detail because they support my arguments in the most objective and authoritative manner. I hope the reader is convinced. In fact, I hope the reader is good and angry. If so, this final detail is superfluous—but interesting. It clinches the argument.

There took place in Washington in February 1950 a case identical with mine—identical as to the facts; identical as to the law. A government official, James K. Glynn, was indicted on eight counts of false statements to the government, made in order to get a job. The job was well paid and he had misrepresented his educational qualifications. On February 21 he pleaded *nolo contendere* and was sentenced by Judge Holtzoff, who has the reputation of a very stern judge. Here is Judge Holtzoff's decision:

> this was a case in which there should have been no prosecution, as a matter of justice. True the defendant made certain false statements. That was very reprehensible, ethically and morally. But if we are going to send to jail all who tell falsehoods, I think we had better go ahead and build some new jails.

The Court is of the opinion that this prosecution should not have been instituted. *The false statements were not made under oath* [my italics] ... it is a very inadvisable thing to prosecute all who tell a lie...

The Court is not going to impose a prison sentence and place the defendant on probation, because the government does not feel that the defendant's record should be marred in this manner. The Court is going to impose a small fine.

The fine was small indeed. It was $25—that's right, twenty-five dollars for an offense that I got three years for! The case was identical except for one difference: there was no Communism in the background of the Glynn case. This is the final proof, if any were needed, of what really motivated the "Honorable" Keech, who in many ways, represents the epitome of the government's villainy.

Keech sticks in my throat. To the routine class hatred of the Tom Clarks, the Kelleys, the Perelmans, His Honor added the personal hatred of the Southern racist. He hated me, directly, with all the considerable fury of his mean soul, the prissy mind, the atrophied heart. He hated me for my admitted ability; he hated me for my unrepentant attitude. My very confidence undermined the structure of his beliefs, the very foundations of his existence. I was subversive, indeed!

There was more to it. To Judge Keech, I was not only a social arsonist, a criminal destroyer of "law and order," but I was also a traitor to my "class," the college-bred managerial strata of the population. I had used my education to "subvert" the society that had suckled me. This is the kind of resentment to which Perelman had given lengthy expression before the Supreme Court. This attitude, I'm sure, was also Keech's and it fueled one basic emotion: fear. Fear was the drive behind Keech's venom and hatred. Whether he knows it or not, His Honor was panicky. The seemingly solid ground he walked on was only a thin, precarious crust over quaking social changes—possibly, implacable social upheavals.

One can hardly blame His Honor. His world was reeling. There I was, under his closest scrutiny, and he could not understand me. An immigrant, favored by fortune, a product of the educational system of the United States, recipient of the finest college and university training available in the capitalist world—and what had happened? I'd come out a radical, a Communist if you please! This was contrary to all expectations. How could such an enormity take place?

I'm sure that Keech must have realized that he couldn't blame Joseph Stalin. Moscow had not been my training ground. A liberal Catholic school in childhood, an American grammar school, an American high school, an American college, an English university—these were my training centers. American history was the blueprint of my development, American teachers the channels. And what of my indoctrination? Why this:

> I pledge allegiance to the flag of the United States and to the Republic for which it stands; one nation, indivisible, with liberty and justice for all.

And this:

> We, the people of the United States, in order to form a more perfect Union, establish justice, insure domestic tranquillity, provide for the common defense, promote the general welfare and secure the blessings of Liberty to ourselves and our Posterity, do ordain and establish this Constitution for the United States of America.

And this:

> Four score and seven years ago our fathers brought forth upon this continent a new nation, conceived in liberty and dedicated to the proposition that all men are created equal.

On and on. Page after page, volume after volume—the great testament of American democracy. Through it all, reverberating in the vault of my mind, is the soul-stirring trumpet call of America—the assertion of the brotherhood of man! Listen, Mr. Keech:

> America, America.
> And crown thy good, with brotherhood.
> From sea to shining sea!

Listen:

> Oh say does the star-spangled banner yet wave,
> O'er the land of the free
> And the home of the brave.

Brotherhood, Mr. Keech: white and black, red and yellow; Catholic, Protestant, Jew; the ignorant and the cultured, the healthy and the lame; worker, farmer, teacher. The native and the foreign-born—Czech and double-check American. Brotherhood, Mr. Keech! Dreadful, isn't it?

If out of such American education can come radicals like myself, and they certainly can, then Judge Keech has reason to be frightened. If without benefit of the Kremlin, I can learn about the class struggle from James Madison, and I can, Mr. Keech has reason to tremble. When my educational background was put into the record at the trial, I could almost see the little wheels in his brain, madly whirring, computing the inevitable result: Shut the schools down! For a start, change them. Drive out the liberals, the thinkers, the free spirits. Stop democracy; turn the clock back!

Does all this seem literary hyperbole, dear reader? Look around you at the schools in your community, your state, your nation. Look at the high schools and the colleges and the universities. Teachers' oaths in city after city, firings at every level. Out of such purges, fascism flourishes. To Hitler, democracy was a breeding ground for socialism, for Communism. This is also the theme song of the McCarthys and the Peglers: that the New Deal is socialism, that the TVA is Communism. I say it's a lie. The future of democratic development in America will, if peaceful, find its own path, the path of the TVAs, social security, free medicine and education.

The danger in America today does *not* come from Communism; it comes from native fascism and it is a tragedy that the man from Missouri, FDR's vice-president, has been maneuvered into such undemocratic policies. This is the significance of my case. It is a tale of government chicanery, government illegality, government vindictiveness. It is in many ways a ghastly tale of petty men; it is also a warning tale of dangerous men. Men like Keech are doubly to blame because judges should be the best defenders of our liberties. That is what they are trained to do. While a Rutledge or a Black magnificently upholds the finest tradition of the judiciary, judges like Keech demean it and besmirch it. I say to Judge Keech: You are the real subversive, not I. You is undermining American democracy, not I. You fear ideas, fear the ferment which is stirring peoples everywhere, the changes in an awakening world population. You fearfully wish to stop them and it is out of fear that you strike out so blindly, so fiercely, so bestially. As I fight you, and such as you, I know that I am defending our best democratic traditions; I know proudly that I do love my country, am suffering for its better future. I, Mr. Keech, am the patriot today.

I say to you, democracy will not lose. I say you will fail. The world *is* changing. Who's going to hold it back, the ineffable Tom Clark? The music-hall McArthur? The unspeakable McCarthy? Be fearful, Mr. Keech, your quivering nostrils do not deceive you. You smell defeat ahead. May I remind you, most honorable Judge, of another fine American song, *John Brown's Body*. Remember it? "He is trampling out the vintage where the grapes of wrath are stored." Remember? Go ahead and fertilize the grapes my honorable, fearful, cultured racist, go ahead. You are doing fine. But rest assured, those grapes will mature, they will be harvested. Rest assured, you will drink the vintage. Until then, comfort yourself with the daily headlines. In GI lingo, sweat it out.

Index